A Larger Circuit

AN ODYSSEY IN MINISTRY

WILLIAM H. JACOBS

BALBOA.
PRESS

A DIVISION OF HAY HOUSE

Balboa Press books may be ordered through booksellers or by contacting:

Balboa Press
A Division of Hay House
1663 Liberty Drive
Bloomington, IN 47403
www.balboapress.com
1 (877) 407-4847

Print information available on the last page.

ISBN: 978-1-5043-5592-6 (sc)
ISBN: 978-1-5043-5593-3 (hc)
ISBN: 978-1-5043-5591-9 (e)

Library of Congress Control Number: 2016906173

Balboa Press rev. date: 04/26/2016

FOREWORD

I began this effort to tell the story of our ministry in order that our grandchildren might know something of our lives before they came along. All of them arrived on the scene after my retirement from the Air Force Chaplaincy. Most of them remember us only later after we had retired from serving Methodist churches and were living at Canyon Lake, Texas. Because of distances most of them have heard only bits and pieces of our (Pat and myself) ministry challenges throughout the world. This is an effort to share with them the exciting and sometimes difficult experiences of those earlier years.

I believe it is important to highlight the great blessings we have received during these years and also to lift up the names of some of those who God placed in our lives who provided guidance and support along the way. As we recollect these experiences it is easy to see that many folks we met along the pathway gave us the necessary assistance and mentored us in such a way that our ministry became possible and fruitful. We are grateful for each and every one of them and their friendship as well as their help. Without them, the story would be different and our experiences would have been dearth of the richness we enjoyed. When I recall, not only professors and pastors, but also parishioners and neighbors, it is with warm feelings of God's grace administered to us through so many along the way. So, this is as much their story, as it is ours. I have used the term 'ours' in most places because my ministry became 'our' ministry after I met the love of my life, Pat. She has been the stabilizing and encouraging power throughout these years. Although I begin with my arrival at undergraduate college, I will digress from time to time to pick up the threads of life that led to current events.

CHAPTER ONE

In 1948 the only telephone in McMurry Hall at Central College was a pay phone in the lobby downstairs. (This is now Central Methodist University in Fayette, Missouri, which is pretty much in the center of the state.) McMurry was a men's dormitory, as all were single sex dorms in those days. The very term 'pay phone' has a quaint sound to it in our digital era. There was another phone in the dean of men's apartment but that was for his personal use only. Later they did install a phone in the main desk office, but it was available only when a student assistant was there a couple of hours each afternoon and useful only for local calls. The significance of this becomes clear when I tell you my dorm room was 419, which means it was on the fourth floor of the building. And there were no elevators in that building! (Nor in any other building on campus at that time!) Of course, there were no private phones in student rooms nor had the cell phone made its debut in that ancient time!

If anyone tried to reach a student by telephone they would call the pay phone in hopes that someone passing by might answer it. Then the trick was to get them to yell for the person being sought or take a message and deliver it to you! Obviously, no loud call would reach me on the fourth floor and it would be unlikely for anyone to choose to climb the stairs to tell me I had a call on the phone in the lobby! It never happened. But I often thought that if it did happen, while the considerate messenger was on the way, someone else would have either hung up the phone thinking it had been left off the hook, or hung it up so they could use it. It would be equally unusual for someone to have paper and pencil as he walked by the phone, even if he were of a mind to answer in the first place. Sometimes someone would answer, take down a message and pin it on the bulletin board. There it might languish among the notices from students seeking rides to St. Louis or Kansas City on an upcoming weekend or holiday.

Few students had automobiles in those days. Those that had autos most likely were veterans who had returned to attend college on the GI bill and probably were married as well. In fact, the rules of the college were that students who lived on campus had to show their need to possess an auto because of work related activity. There were some students who resided at home in the community or nearby and, of course, drove their autos to the campus.

Married students, residing on campus in the 'Eagle Village' housing or in the community were exempt from this restriction. I rented a room for two years in one of these on-campus units from my older brother Gene and his wife Katie after he came to college on the GI bill during my sophomore and junior years. These units were Quonset huts built by the government during World War II on campus near the football field. (On my last visit I discovered these had been torn down and a soccer field installed in their location.) There was a two-bedroom unit in each half of the hut. The apartment included a bathroom and a utility room, as well as a kitchenette, dinette and living space all open to one another before the 'open' living area was popular! The government had built them to house students who were there in what was called the Navy V-12 program. From 1943 to 1946 the United States Navy had many of these programs at universities across the country to train officers. When the war ended and the program closed out, the colleges were given the opportunity to purchase the units on their campuses at minimum cost. Someone told me the Central units were bought for a dollar a piece! They initially became housing for married veterans on the GI bill at Central. The monthly rent was $25 plus utilities. It was one of these units - 7A - that Gene rented and I sublet a bedroom during the school years of 49-50 and 50-51. Gene dropped out of college at that point to go into an auto body repair shop business with our Dad. I returned to McMurry Hall (on the second floor this time) with a roommate for my final semester. I finished school in January 1952 and returned for commencement exercises in June of that year.

Other notices placed on the bulletin board involved opportunities for temporary employment in the small community. These ranged from manual labor (for instance, bucking hay bales in the fall of the year on a nearby farm) to typing for a professor or a student who lacked the skill and the necessary equipment to produce a decent term paper. The latter became a good source of income for me, as did the former effort on farms. The farm work was hard and dirty, which meant that many students shunned it. Working my way through school meant that I was not choosy about this effort but all too happy to earn some extra money. Some farmers paid a dollar an hour for the 'hay bucking' trek. In the case of typing, the going rate to produce a document for a prof was 35 cents an hour. One could do better by typing term papers at a dollar a page, guaranteed error free. With good typing skills this became lucrative for me.

I also signed on to work in the dining facility, however as a freshman I was placed on the waiting list for this job and that meant mostly 'on call' when some one was ill or gone for a weekend. The pay for dining room work was not in cash, but was factored into your meal plan. For each meal you worked, you were credited with a meal in the following term. Work a meal and earn a meal. This work was also hard until you became senior enough to work the serving line. The other tasks involved scraping plates, running the cart from the rear of the dining area to the kitchen at the other end of the huge room and operating the 'clipper', the commercial dish washing apparatus. The latter was the most arduous and least desirable. As a substitute, I would sometimes work one job or another, depending on whom I was standing in for. As a result I gained experience in all of the various facets of the operation.

During the year I was on the fourth floor, I learned always to check the bulletin board as I passed through the entrance lobby. Let me digress for the rest of this chapter to relate how I came to live on the fourth floor. No one in my family had gone to college before I did. When World War II ended, my Dad was transferred back from Flint, Michigan where he was involved in the assembly line of the General Sherman tank, to St. Louis, the Fisher Body plant, to assist in getting the production of civilian automobiles (Chevrolet) started once again. We lived in the St Louis suburb of Maplewood from October 1945 until the summer of 1947. I was enrolled in Maplewood-Richmond Heights High School. During this time I thought I wanted to be an engineer of some type, probably architectural, though I confess I didn't really know much about what that meant.

A good buddy of mine from football (which was my sport both in the ninth grade in Flint, Michigan and again at MRH in Maplewood) and I decided one day to skip school since there were no tests scheduled and only a half day of classes so that teachers could attend a workshop in the afternoon. For some lame-brained reason, we made a plan to 'hitch-hike' over 100 miles away to Columbia, Missouri to check out the campus at the University of Missouri, including the school of engineering. Not the smartest day plan for two high school sophomores! Obviously, we thought it would be easy to get a ride there and back and be home at a normal time! Actually, we got a total of two rides, separated by a lot of walking, to arrive there before 11 in the morning. Quickly, we realized that we didn't have time to fool around on campus if we were to get back to St.

Louis and home at a normal afternoon timing. So, taking a couple of pictures of the historic columns from an early building now gone, and a fast run to the engineering department location initially where we discovered we couldn't see the dean without an appointment, we headed back to the 'riding the thumb' transportation system. We were lucky enough to catch a ride with a university student heading to St. Louis who dropped us right at the high school campus. Home on time, but without much to show for our journey other than having made it, we frequently laughed about our adventure and how it might have turned out, had we not been living under a lucky star. (Our term at the time.)

This goal of becoming an engineer was encouraged by several of my high school teachers and counselors. I was relatively intelligent and, with application, could do well in most all my courses. That's not to say that all my grades showed that ability. I often slacked off on homework, once I felt I understood the principle that was being advanced. (I fear some of my progeny inherited that tendency along with my intellect!) I wrote to the university and acquired information on the requirements for entry. During this time, I was somewhat oblivious to the possibility that the cost of attending college might preclude my doing so! I had no knowledge of scholarship possibilities, nor did any of my high school counselors suggest or encourage my application for such. My parents had not made any plans for any of the nine of us to attend college. (I am the seventh down the line in this large family.)

I played on the football team during my two years at Maplewood Richmond Heights High School. I started out trying to play fullback. However, I just wasn't fast enough or big enough for that position and I wound up playing guard. I enjoyed football. The coach insisted that all football players go out for track. Again, I wasn't fast enough to sprint, but I had great endurance and, although I set no records, I could hold my own at the 880 yard and at the mile distances. One afternoon, coming off the track after workouts, I was approached by a young man (I guessed he was in his twenties) and asked if I had ever thought of modeling. I looked at him askance. No. I had not. He told me he was looking for young men with good bodies to model for his art class at Washington University across town. No. No. No. I wasn't interested in modeling anywhere! He may have been really an artist, but I didn't like the prospect of standing around or sitting down nude while someone drew my picture, since that's what he indicated he had in mind!

Later, in the year after our hitchhiking adventure, I was drawn to a public speaking contest that was held by the Methodist Churches around the nation. (Now the United Methodist Church, but then, following the unification in 1939 of the Methodist Episcopal denominations (both north and south and Protestant it became known only as the Methodist Church until its union with the Evangelical United Brethren Church in 1958 when it became United). The contests were sponsored by the Methodist Youth Fellowship (MYF) groups at each local congregation and then at a sub-district, district and, eventually conference wide and national levels. I was fifteen years of age and active in the local MYF. In the local contest, I was chosen as the winner. This led me to be involved in the sub-district competition and there I placed second. But both first and second place contestants were involved in the district event a couple of weeks later.

I was encouraged by family members and my pastor Alfred Watkins to use the same talk I had given already. With a little more polish, they kept assuring me, I would likely win the district event and move on to the conference competition. On the Saturday night prior to the Sunday evening presentations, I looked over my manuscript very carefully and retired early so that a good night's rest would be my starting point. To this day, I'm not sure what awakened me in the night. Perhaps it was the 'trolley' that ran a half block from our house all through the night. I think the conductor was required to ding his bell as he approached and crossed Bredell Avenue to warn anyone on or near the tracks. However, this happened every night and I can't recall it ever awakening me in the night. I have a different explanation for what awoke me. In any event, I arose and went directly to my little desk and the ancient portable Smith-Corona typewriter. As I look back on it, I didn't really think much about what I was doing. Over the course of about 30 minutes, however, my fingers guided the keys to complete an entirely new manuscript. When I finished the last sentence, I crawled back into bed and slept peacefully the rest of the night.

I didn't say anything on Sunday morning about the new manuscript. In fact, I had not told anyone about it at all. Sunday School and Worship services with the family and then Sunday dinner at home were on their usual schedule. When we left for the church (the district competition was held at our church, Immanuel Methodist) I placed in my suit coat inner pockets the two manuscripts, one in each breast pocket. To be honest, I had not decided whether to go with my previous talk or risk the one I'd created in the night. There were five contestants, two from our sub-district, two from another sub-district and only one from the remaining sub-district. By the draw of numbers from a bowl, I was to be the fourth speaker.

When my turn arrived, I got up from the chair and walked to the pulpit. At that moment my hand reached into the appropriate pocket and withdrew the new talk. I spread it on the pulpit and began my presentation. Considering that it was new to me the night before, it went very smoothly throughout. I had chosen to speak on Jesus' challenge found in the last chapter of Matthew, in which he commands his disciples to go into all the world and preach the gospel. My previous talk had focused on the experience of the Good Samaritan and the need for all of us to look out for the strangers who needed help. Now I finished with the challenge that Jesus had given his followers and my last sentence was, "I hear that challenge and I will go into the world to spread the gospel." And with that, I took my seat.

I'd like to tell you that I won the competition and went on from there. But, the fact is, I didn't even get second place! That ended my involvement in the MYF speaking endeavor. After the

7

announcement of the winners, I had to listen to one of my siblings tell me I had made a big mistake in changing my talk at the last minute. I just nodded my understanding of what she was saying. My pastor, on the other hand, was more interested in my sincerity involved in the conclusion. Was I serious about preaching the gospel? I nodded that I was and felt that I was called to this task. He had a very brief prayer with me in the midst of the folks enjoying the reception in the hall downstairs and said, 'we'll talk some more about this later'.

The following week, the Reverend Alfred Watkins gave me a phone call. He had been the pastor at the Immanuel Church since before World War II when we lived in St. Louis and attended that church. After we returned to St. Louis (now living in a suburb) we resumed attendance at the church. He wanted to discuss with me further my interest in 'preaching the gospel', which he interpreted as entering the ministry of the church. He told me a little of what was involved in attending college and then seminary and the process of becoming a pastor in the Methodist denomination. Alfred was a native of Virginia and had a soft accent from that area. I listened carefully but didn't commit myself to anything at that point. However, that summer I attended the Methodist Youth Camp at Arcadia, Missouri. (Epworth Among the Hills was located in the foothills of the Ozarks about 100 miles Southwest of St. Louis.) We were given an opportunity to write our intentions for Christ on a 3x5 card, pray about it and then thrust it into the fire as a personal promise to God. I made a commitment at the campfire the final night of the weeklong event to become a minister. It was a very moving ritual that hundreds of youth have entered into through the years, both at Methodist youth camps and numerous others as well, I imagine.

When I returned from camp that summer, Alfred Watkins asked me if I would accompany him to Dixon, Missouri in the Ozarks where he was conducting a weeklong 'revival'. My task would be to help lead the singing in the evening services. I'd had no formal voice training at that time, but had a strong singing voice and knew all the old Gospel Hymns. (When we traveled as a family through the years, we always went by automobile. Too many of us to buy tickets for sure. And we always carried some old hymn books - covers long worn off of them - and would sing frequently as we traveled along.) As the time drew closer to the trip to Dixon, Missouri, Alfred asked me if I would consider being the 'youth speaker' on youth night on Wednesday of the revival. He encouraged me to use the talk I'd used in the speaking event when I declared my intention to preach the gospel. As I look back on it, this was a bit of bravado on my part, as a fifteen year old, to agree! But I did. Alfred taught me a great deal about prayer long before I became his associate after undergraduate school. But that's a story a long way down the list from now. I remember his visiting our home when I was a child and gathering us all in a circle in the living room, he had us join hands. My Dad was a part of the group, but my mother was in the hospital with the birth of my youngest brother Charles who began life with illness. Alfred prayed for my Mom and for Charles.

On our way to Dixon, Missouri that summer, Alfred stopped in the middle of nowhere to pick up a hitchhiker. I don't know why he did it, but I later did the same thing often enough. (The world has changed and I don't believe I would pick up strangers on the highway any longer.) It turned out that in the course of conversation this young man was without work and without money and was hitching a ride to Springfield, Missouri where he'd been promised work by an uncle. When it came time for us to turn off of the main highway to go into Dixon, he had to resume his hitchhiking. But, before he could get out of the car, Alfred put his arm around my back and onto the young man's shoulder and offered a prayer for the young man and his success in getting work. He asked him if he was a Christian and when the young man indicated he had never made a profession of faith in Christ, Alfred led him to do that and offered another prayer for his future growth in Christ. As the young man got out of the car, Alfred handed him some bills. I didn't know how much he was giving him and didn't ask. I knew he would never repay it since he didn't even know where Alfred was from. That stayed with me for many years as I entered ministry and for some years served in a poverty area of St. Louis myself and often gave money to strangers.

That fall, it was back to school, football, MYF, and all that went with being a high school junior. Meanwhile, my parents were discussing and planning on moving from Maplewood to the farm forty miles Southwest of St. Louis near Lonedell, Missouri. My Dad had inherited a small amount of money when his father, Wolf Jacobs, died in New Orleans, in 1938. With this he had bought this 168 acre farm with intentions to retire to it someday. Prior to the war, there was no electricity nor indoor plumbing and so moving there had not been a realistic option.

CHAPTER TWO

Once more I must digress to discuss the aborted effort in 1940 to move to the farm. One older sister (Dorothy) was married and the other two oldest sisters (Mary Elizabeth and Edith May) were out of high school and working but living at home. A family of tenants that had been living in the farmhouse left when the father (Elwood Shrum) went back to work for the state highway department. My folks decided to begin the transition to the farm that year. (The war interrupted this possibility and the effort was not resumed until 1946-47.) My mother and we six youngest children moved to the farm. The two older ones (Dave, Jr. and Evelyn) were in high school and rode a bus to St. Clair, Missouri ten miles away. The next three in age (Gene - three years plus older than myself, and myself and Norman - three years younger than myself) attended the one room school known as Hickory Flat elementary. The latter was about three miles away from our farm by road, however, walking it could be accomplished in somewhere between a little over a mile and a little less than two by cutting through the woods, a neighbor's field and then to the school. Which shortcut we took usually depended upon which field the neighbor's bull was in that day! Charles was the youngest and he remained home with Mom all day.

My Dad came out every weekend and my Mother went into town during the week - usually on Wednesday- with the large cans of cream for the creamery. She stayed overnight and returned the next morning.

There was no electricity and no indoor plumbing at that time. We had a number of milk cows, hogs, a flock of sheep and some beef cattle as well that needed to be cared for. We also had a team of horses that were used for pulling plows, discs, harrows, etc. We children took care of all the chores each day under my Mother's supervision. The two 'live at home' older sisters took care of the housekeeping with my Dad in town. We also had a Farmall tractor that was used for the more difficult plowing and hauling things about. My Dad had a 1938 Chevrolet he drove in town and back and forth to the farm. We also had a 1933 Chevrolet pickup truck that my Mother drove back and forth to the feed store or the creamery. Although I got to drive the tractor some, and on rare occasions with my older brother, even the pickup truck, mostly I walked! Sometimes we would ride the horses, but we had no saddles, so it was strictly bare back - with a gunny-sack thrown over the horse to keep us from sweating!

This was not an ideal arrangement, of course, but I think my folks figured it would work until my Dad could see his way to retire to the farm or drive back and forth to his job in the city. There were thirteen of us in the Hickory Flat elementary school, with one teacher. Gene, Norman and myself constituted three of the thirteen! Education took place for all eight grades in the one room. Well, not really. Like many country schools, they taught every other grade each year. This worked out okay for Gene. He was to be in the eighth grade and this was even class year. For Norman, the second grade was okay as well. In my case I should have been in the fifth grade, however they weren't teaching fifth that year, so I moved into the sixth grade group. I think there were three of us! Had the arrangement continued, I suppose I would have completed all my schooling even younger than eventually occurred.

A number of vivid memories remain from those few months in the rural setting of America! Of course, the walk down the path behind the house to the outhouse (which we used to refer to as 'Aunt Tilly' - I have no idea why) to take care of necessary biological needs remains strong. The Sears catalog (or was it Montgomery Ward - we had both) and the requirement to tear off a few pages and 'soften' them by wrinkling them prior to use remains with me. We boys rarely made the trip unless we had to sit on the rough open seat to take care of business. Otherwise, we mostly wandered to the back fence and unbuttoned or unzipped and did what we needed to do. And, if we were down by the barn or in the woods, any tree worked - even to the use of softened leaves for that kind of emergency. We surely wouldn't make the trek back to the house for such things. I don't think my sister Evelyn was so inclined and I know she hated the spiders that inhabited the outhouse. My Mother probably did as well, but never mentioned it.

The old farmhouse was a large two story wooden building. We three older boys, Dave, Gene, and myself, slept in one of the upstairs bedrooms. Evelyn had another of those to herself. The two younger boys, Norman and Charles slept downstairs next to my Mother and Dad's room. Remember, I said no electricity in those days! After sundown, kerosene lamps or lanterns provided what light we had. The latter were used when going outside - to Aunt Tilly or the barn - even early mornings for milking. Lamps were used inside downstairs, but when we boys went up to bed - it was with a lantern. The room we slept in was a very large space and included a large double bed that Dave and Gene occupied and a 'daybed', which was my place to sleep. A door from the room led into a closet that had been created beneath the slanted roof all along that side of the room. The door was at one end of the closet, which was dark, of course. To complicate the matter at the far end of the closet from where the door was located was an old dresser with mirror that I suppose had been put there for storage. This meant that when you entered the closet and looked to the left you were seeing the mirror at the other end of the closet, approximately 12 feet away. You can guess the rest. Your own reflection in the darkened room that showed in the mirror was eerie at best and downright scary for a nine year old. Entering the closet with the kerosene lantern didn't help. In fact, it intensified the scariness of the reflections.

None of this was helped by the frequent refrain of my older brother, Dave, that it was believed that 'ole man Dickinson' (previous owner of the farm) had hanged himself in that very closet. I have no idea if this was true or not, but Dave could make it sound true! Now you know why I begged to stay up as long as possible and not be required to ascend to the haunted room by myself. Many an evening, I worked incessantly to keep my eyelids from closing until either Gene or Dave - or both - were ready to make the lantern lit trip to our bedroom!

Many other memories were made during these few months living on the farm. I helped Gene run the hand cranked separator which divided the whole milk between the cream that went into ten gallon milk cans to be taken to the creamery and the skim milk. Most of the milking was accomplished by Dave and Evelyn, and occasionally Gene. No electricity so no milking machines! I tried my hand at it, so to speak, but was not really successful. (I got my chance years later when we moved to the farm.) The skim milk had a blue hue to it and was taken in 'slop' buckets to the hog pen and fed to the hogs. (I think it is the same thing as the 'percent' milk many of us pay extra to purchase at the store these days!)

We played in the hayloft. The barn had been built many years before and although the roof likely had been replaced with its current corrugated metal sheets, the interior was still made up of huge logs laid crisscross 'Lincoln log' style to create the two haylofts and the corncrib. The haylofts were divided by a drive through area and the corncrib was carved out of one end of one of the lofts. The hay wagon was pulled through the middle (either by the tractor or the team of horses) and the hay was thrown by pitchfork up into the lofts. As needed, it was retrieved the same way. It was a fun place to play, climbing up high on the logs and jumping into the soft hay. There was the occasional black snake to deal with in the barn, but they were harmless and probably more frightened of us than we them.

Just a few yards from the barn was a huge old oak tree. We built a tree house in that old tree. I suspect Dave did the engineering, Gene did the holding things for nails and I was given the task of getting some more pieces of wood. There were always pieces of lumber somewhere in the barn lot, left over from whatever project had been the latest event. The tree was huge. I was small so my recollection of its size may be wrong, but I couldn't reach around its trunk. There were three levels to the tree house when it was finished. Great fun could be had playing there. It was still a neat play area years later when we moved to the farm. Alas, the old tree was hit by lightning sometime since then and is gone.

The farm was about a mile from the highway and the gravel road showed on the maps appeared to go all the way past the farm and several miles to Catawissa, Missouri. I believe it does today, but in those days, there were no houses past ours, and the county only maintained it somewhat as far as our gate. Later, when we lived on the farm, it had been extended to the end of our property to service a fire observation tower that had been erected. Today, it is paved blacktop. What this meant in those days was no one came down that road unless they were coming to visit us. Imagine then the surprise when several old cars (even by 1940 standards) came driving down the road and up the drive toward our house. It was mid morning as I remember the event. Anticipation of visitors was exciting for my siblings and myself. Not so with my mother. She took one look at the vehicles and the poorly dressed folks who began to dismount and made a decision. I heard her say, 'those are gypsies and they have no business here'. There was a 410 gauge shotgun that hung over the front door on a rack. My mother (all five feet tall) stood on a chair

15

and retrieved the gun. She went to the door telling us to remain behind her. I think my brother Dave stood right next to her as she pointed the gun at the folks in the road and called to them - "You have no business here so just get back in your cars and move on!"

I don't know what their feelings were at seeing this tribe of kids standing behind this short, plump woman as she threatened them with the old weapon. I'm not sure she knew how to use it, however, it is likely she did. I doubt that she would have fired at them, but then maybe she would have. In any event, they quickly re-mounted their vehicles and drove away. We never saw anything of them again. Dave later learned from some of the kids at school that a band of gypsies were traversing around and often stealing whatever wasn't nailed down if no one was around. In some cases it was reported they would just squat and stay for days or weeks in an unoccupied farmhouse.

The cream separator I mentioned earlier was located in the fruit cellar because the cream was then stored there until it could be taken to the creamery. (The fruit cellar was at the end of the house, dug down into the ground and covered with additional dirt. A large water cistern fed by gutters all around the house provided the water. This was right next to the fruit cellar.) Remember, we had no electricity so coolness was not available except when a chunk of ice was bought at the feed store two miles away and brought home for the icebox. Just as there was neither air conditioning nor refrigeration, there was no central heat. On a cold morning, we dressed as rapidly as possible and hurried down to the kitchen where there would be a fire in the wood cook stove. Standing by the wall just behind it, was a place to get warm. One turned around periodically to warm the other side!

Sometime between Thanksgiving and Christmas, I think the arrangement wore out for my Mom (and maybe my Dad as well). My Dad found a couple willing to move to the farm as tenants and we moved back to the city. The permanent move to the farm had to await the end of the war, electricity and indoor plumbing and my Dad's willingness to drive forty miles each way to work everyday. I resumed being a fifth grader! (And later that year the Hickory Flat elementary school, bereft of students, was consolidated with the Sycamore elementary school a few miles away and closed its doors. The building was later purchased and converted into living quarters and remains such today.)

The summer before that when I was about eight years old, Gene introduced me to cigarettes. We had looked around the house and basement until we found six empty soda bottles worth two cents each for deposit. We made our way down to McElhenny's convenience store on the corner across from the playground and Roe School. With the twelve cents we received for redeeming the bottles, we bought a pack of Marvel cigarettes (eleven cents!) and a pack of Sen-Sen (breath mints were a penny - came in a little paper packet). Retreating to the bushes in the playground, Gene showed me how to light a cigarette. Three puffs and numerous coughs later, I gave it up. I never smoked cigarettes the rest of my life! After Gene had finished his 'smoke', we headed home, chewing and sucking on the Sen-sens for all we were worth.

We walked in the back door and there was Mom at the sink, facing away from our entrance. She spoke immediately, "You boys come here and let me smell your breath!" Now, what kid thought that Sen-sens on your breath would fool a mother, must have been light on brain-power! Inhaling as we opened our mouths, in hopes that would pull all tobacco smell within, we lined up for her inspection. "You boys have been smoking! Go to your rooms and I'll deal with you later." What extra-sensory abilities she had were beyond us. Only years later did we discover that a neighbor had seen us in the bushes lighting up and had called our Mother and given us away! Although I tried a pipe a few times in college, thinking it looked distinguished for a philosopher to do so, I gave it up as too much trouble and too messy! By the way, my Mother never told us we would be punished by Dad when he got home. She took care of whatever needed to be meted out. Usually she sent us to our room, or to the bathroom, where we might wait in anticipating miseries for sometime before she came to carry out the task. I suppose it would be child abuse today, but we often were paddled with the large wooden hairbrush she kept in the bathroom. I believe I held the record for the time it got broken while I was being paddled for something I surely deserved. Her technique was to lay us across the toilet lid and paddle us with a couple of quick strokes. One of the reasons for this posture, I early decided was because when my Mother sat down, she had no lap! Her belly occupied the space where a little one might be held to paddle. However, she had plenty of lap when she wanted to pull us up close and give us a hug or read a story!

The house in Saint Louis we lived in when I was a boy had been built and modified by our Father. I think it began as a four-room cottage! Rooms were added, as were children. Eventually there was a second floor with four small bedrooms tucked under the roof, dormer style. A sunroom on the first floor later was enclosed and for a time was my bedroom. A porch across the front of the house was later enclosed as a large sunlit room. The house was raised and a basement was installed beneath it. A garage was built in the basement and the driveway circled the house and wound up at this garage. (Ground level entrance to the garage/basement allowed for many things that would not have been possible otherwise. For instance, we often had brooders with chicks in them. My Dad actually brought a young heifer home from the farm to calve in our basement! He was worried that she would have a problem for her first calf and the tenant on the farm was not dependable enough to take care of her! City ordinances either were not as strict concerning live stock or not enforced. Probably the former because we had several neighbors with chickens.) The lot on which this house was located was in the middle of a block! It didn't face a street, but faced the city playground (park) that occupied the other half of this large double block. If you can imagine it, there were houses on three sides of our half of the double block, including my grandmother Moise's house that faced Kraft Avenue and was directly behind our house. I believe my mother's father, Grandfather Eugene Moise owned the entire block at some point and sold off parts for the bungalows that stretched around the three sides of the house on Mitchell Avenue, Kraft Avenue and Glades Avenue. My father owned a strip down the side of the Moise house that included having our mailbox and address as 1915 Kraft Avenue, although as I indicated, the house actually faced the park the opposite direction.

The four bedrooms upstairs were allocated to the older girls and boys. At one point, Mary Elizabeth and Edith May were in one bedroom and Dot and Evelyn were directly across the hall in the other bedroom. These rooms had normal ceilings. The bedrooms at both ends of the hall were under dormers and had slanted ceilings. Dave had one of these to himself and Gene and I occupied the other one after I outgrew the sunroom downstairs (or probably because younger ones came along and were moved into it.) Dave had a fierce territorial desire to protect his space from the rest of us! And with his ingenuity, frequently had the room booby-trapped with some device to surprise the intruder and to let him know his space had been invaded. When my Dad's Uncle John Stapleton (younger than my Dad) stayed with us - as he did from time to time when he was unemployed - this was his room (he was single).

John Stapleton frequently played tricks on the rest of us when he was staying with us. On a dark night, he might slip outside and attach a wire or string to a screen and make weird noises to frighten us (when our folks weren't home, of course.) His trickery got him into deep difficulty on one occasion. He installed (with great difficulty) a strong twine cord considerable distance from the boys' bedroom at one end of the hall through eyelets and down through the attic and into the bedroom at the other end of the hall. By attaching this cord to the bottom of the spring on the daybed, he planned to wait until we got to bed and then jerk the string making the bed jump and thereby scare us considerably. His only problem came when he was under the bed attaching the string and he heard someone coming. He thought it best to just be very quiet until whoever it was had left. He couldn't figure out who might be home that time of the day but it became apparent when he could see my Mother's feet and legs entering the room. Now he was afraid he would frighten her and decided the best course was to be even quieter! This might have worked fine had it not been for the fact that one of us (either Gene or myself) had failed to make our bed that morning and it was the one he was hiding beneath! When my Mother leaned on the mattress to retrieve the covers, she nearly crushed him below the bed. He dared not cry out for fear the fright would be even greater. We only knew the story when he told it on himself several days later, after he had played the scary trick with his long cord.

The size of the lot allowed for a large garden and eventually a clay tennis court on the garage side of the house. At some point, my Dad acquired lights from the salvage yard at Fisher Body where he worked, so the court was lit for playing at night. He surrounded it with high chicken wire to keep the tennis balls from leaving the property. In order to enjoy the court activity more, he built a shower in the basement, directly over a drain. With a curtain around it, wood slats over the drain, and solar heated hot water, it became a valuable accessory in a house with nine children and only one bathroom! We boys, especially, took most of our showers in the basement. (The solar heated water, way before its time, was a creation of my Father. He mounted a large galvanized tank - also acquired from salvage - outside the South wall to provide the hot water. There was an auxiliary gas hot water heater that could be used to heat water for the shower, or for the bathroom upstairs. Most of the water upstairs was heated during the cold season from the coal fired furnace in the basement that included coils to heat the water and maintain hot water for the house through the hot water tank in the basement.)

The size of the property and its location next to the park and a block from the elementary school made it an ideal place to raise nine children! With a large family, there was always someone to play with. In fact, most kids in the neighborhood enjoyed playing at our house as well. With the playground right over the fence, there were swing sets, seesaws, circle swings, sandboxes, and slides. In the summer, the swimming pool was less than a football field away. It had no deep end, but was great for just learning to swim. There was a ball diamond and in the summer the usual city recreation department teams - softball, soccer, etc. Some of these teams travelled to other city parks for competition. I played on a 'junior' dodgeball team during that time and I remember one of the best trips to another city park for a game was on the north side of town. Next door to the park was a place that made the waffle cones for the 'drumstick' ice cream treats. Any that were broken were put in a barrel outside the back door. It was great fun to go over there and get several of them to eat. I'm sure the health department would make that illegal and impossible today!

Gene and I often played together because of our nearness in age. Actually, several years ago, I realized that I was more distant in age from the one older than myself (Gene was 3 years plus May to February older than I) and the one just younger than myself (Norman was 3 years plus December to May younger than I). One of the biggest fiascos occurred when I was about nine years of age. It began with Gene and I tossing a small rubber ball back and forth down the hallway that led from our parent's bedroom past the bathroom and into what we called the 'music room'. (The old piano was located in that room, hence its name.) As we moved further apart in the hallway, the tosses were a little longer and hence required a little more force. Finally, Gene was all the way back in our parent's bedroom and I was all the way into the music room, standing in front of the French door that led from the music room into the enclosed front porch. Now, the tosses really required force to get the distance, and of course, as boys we began to increase the force to make the catch more difficult! My hardest throw was caught and returned with a great heave. I just stepped aside in order not to be hit by this missile! The result was broken glass and paddled backsides for both of us!

Christmas was always a special time. Not only did we attend whatever religious services were held at church, we had our own celebrations with lots of carol singing. Mary Elizabeth, who could play the piano quite well, (she later served as a church organist) would provide the music and the rest of us would gather around the piano and sing. This happened with gospel singing as a family sometimes as well as holiday time. My Dad was usually the instigator of these events since he loved to sing and loved having the family together. (This wasn't always met with great approval - as in the evening services in St. Clair UMC many years later when he volunteered us all and later insisted on the family sitting in the choir and providing the special music one Sunday evening. Both my wife Pat and my sister Evelyn were 'great with child' and really didn't want to be in front of everyone, but he insisted until it was embarrassing not to join in!)

On Christmas mornings, all were up and dressed and had breakfast before we were allowed into the living room to see the tree and the presents. The older ones were allowed to stay up and decorate the tree and those who were younger were surprised by it the next day as though it had magically appeared in the night (probably brought in a sleigh!) After breakfast on Christmas morning, we would all line up by age with the youngest at the front of the line. On signal we were allowed to parade into the living room to see the magical display. (The tree was located in the corner of the room on the mountain that was part of the 4x8 train board display.) One of the older children (which meant one of the three oldest sisters) would be the 'Santa Claus' and find the presents under the tree and call out the name of each one, working to provide equity in the number of gifts to each one. For the most part, as I was growing up, it was one 'major gift' for each one, plus many smaller gifts that consisted of needed clothing items! After 1938, when my Dad acquired a 8 mm movie camera, all of this was carefully documented! These visual remembrances are still greatly appreciated.

One of the best examples of the movie renditions occurred when brother Norman got his Christmas surprise! All the older children had either made at school or managed to buy some gift for each of our parents. Norman was too young to do either, but he had gotten an orange (as had we all) at the Church Christmas program/party. He determined to wrap that up as a gift for Dad. He got some green tissue paper and gathered it in a wad at the top of the orange and tied a ribbon around it and with someone's help, marked it for Daddy from Norman. You can imagine his surprise when the gifts were being doled out and his name was called and he was handed what surely looked like the orange he had wrapped for Daddy! Looking confused, he was reassured that the tag had his name on it. He carefully worked his way through the ribbon and opened the package, only to discover it now contained an ordinary potato! He somehow knew it was a prank, but was still looking confused as everyone laughed!

During the years prior to World War II, our family routine was quite simple. During the school year, we came home from school, did whatever homework was involved in the day's requirement, any chores that might be assigned and were washed up and ready for dinner when Dad arrived home from work. He would go change out of his 'work' clothes (which by the time I was old enough to notice was suit and tie as a foreman or superintendent) and then to the bathroom to wash up for supper. We were expected to be at the table by then, with the exception of any of the older girls who were helping put supper on. Our dining table was large enough for all of us to sit around it. In fact, it was not unusual, especially on the weekends, for additional folks to be around the table. This might be my mother's mother (Grandma Moise, my maternal grandmother who was widowed and lived next door) or my Dad's Uncle John (Stapleton - my dad's uncle was several years younger than my dad). In addition, there might be friends of one of us who had been invited to have a meal with us. (Always checked out with Mom in advance.) In the years just prior to the war, my older sisters were dating and so sometimes it was a young man of their acquaintance who was there.

My Dad always sat at the 'head' of the table, my mother in the place to his right and my oldest sister in the place at his left. (He was left-handed and so the head of the table didn't restrict his left handed eating! And when I say it was the head of the table, I mean it was the HEAD of the table.) The meat platter always was set in front of my Dad. After grace was said (assigned by my Dad and given by one of the children) he began the serving by helping himself to a piece of meat and then passing it to the one on his left. It would proceed around the table and arrive back at his spot with a last piece of meat remaining on the platter for my Dad. Of course, part of the time, the youngest was in a high chair between where my Dad and my Mom sat.

Evelyn, the youngest of the four girls, sat at the end of the table closest to the kitchen door. For that reason, I can remember her often being asked to retrieve something from the kitchen, perhaps ketchup or additional bread. Over the years, I can remember on more than one occasion someone giving her an additional errand. "Evelyn, while you're up, would you bring more milk." Or, "Evelyn, I need another napkin while you're up." Later, I told that story to our children, and they adopted the technique. They would request from whomever had gotten up, "Evelyn, while you're up …"

(Oh yes. Ketchup. My favorite condiment when I was growing up. I could eat anything if I could put ketchup on it. On one occasion, I was lacing my piece of liver rather heavily with ketchup and my Dad cautioned me, "Hey, that's not gravy! We have to buy ketchup." I still like ketchup and often make the comment that French fried potatoes are an excuse to eat ketchup.)

The meal was eaten in relative quiet, although my Dad might have something to say about his day. Children always took their cue from him in terms of speaking at the table during the meal. He would ask us, one by one, starting with the oldest, how our day had been. As the meal began to wind down, he would often give us 'questions' to test our day. He was great at asking spelling questions or arithmetic questions, always scaled toward the age of the one expected to answer. For a man with only a sixth grade education, he had a considerable acquaintance with both spelling and arithmetic!

No one left the table early without requesting being excused for some reason or other. When Dad was finished and ready for us all to be excused, he would announce that the table needed to be cleaned up and the dishes washed and put away. The older ones took care of this when I was small, but as they moved on the chores fell to each age group in their turn. My Mother supervised the putting away of the left over food (nothing was ever thrown away!) and different ones took turns washing and/or drying the dishes. Was this always harmonious? Of course not. We were kids. Occasionally a discussion would take place as to whose turn it was to do what. And, once in a while, someone would try to escape his or her chore by heading for the bathroom as a necessary activity and then try to wait out the chore time! Of course, my Mother was on top of all these tricks and they rarely succeeded! My Dad would retire to the living room with the newspaper. (He always took an evening paper - The St. Louis Star Times - because he said he didn't want to come home to a morning paper that had yesterday's news in it! And he thought the Post-Dispatch was much too liberal.)

On Saturday evening the meal was often hot dogs and beans. We boys, especially, liked that meal. One of the humorous things that I recall was one Saturday evening when we were having that menu and Dave, Jr. (the oldest boy but the fourth in age) had gotten a second hot dog from the platter. He said to my Dad, "Daddy, can you toss me another bun?" We were all taken back when he did exactly that! He tossed him another bun, clear across the table. As I recall, my mother's only comment was, "Dave?"

Sunday dinner always followed Sunday School and Church. Again, when the family got home, my Dad would attack the Sunday edition of the Post-Dispatch (the Star Times didn't publish a Sunday edition) while my Mom and the older children - meaning mostly the three oldest girls - put dinner on the table. If all nine children were at home, which was true for the most part as I was growing up, and there were guests as well, then the table would be groaning by the time all was arranged. We children never were consigned to a different table. My Dad and Mom thought we should all eat together.

I mentioned that Gene and I were close and played together a lot. We also got in trouble together a lot! One of the earliest times I remember in which this occurred was at church. Somehow, every Sunday we all got ready at once to go to Sunday School even though we had only one bathroom. The bathroom was not for putting on make up, however, girls did that in their bedroom in front of a vanity mirror. My mother went to Sunday School along with the children, at least when she was not giving birth to one of us! (In later years, she taught an adult women's class. She always referred to them as her girls. I remarked that 'girl' was the only noun with a past tense!) My Dad never went to Sunday School. He had a deep and abiding faith in Jesus Christ, but he was not expressive about things except with family and with co-workers and then only about work. He would drive us to church and then return home to get ready to come to worship. He preferred to sit in the back of the church but not on the back pew. In back, in case he had to take one of the children out for correction or comfort, but not in the back pew because people often would brush against the pew as they made their way to the outer aisle! Our task as children was to get from the Sunday School downstairs to the sanctuary and 'reserve' his pew by sitting in it. We would even spread out along it if necessary! By the time I can remember, most of the oldest sang in the choir, so the task of reservation was left to we younger ones.

My Dad always sat on the end near the center aisle where it was most convenient to get up if he needed to take one of us out of the worship service. As I've said, he was left-handed and so it suited him to be on the left end of the set of pews that were to the right of the center aisle. I don't remember whether or not there was a nursery during worship, but I'm pretty sure none of us were ever in it if there was. We sat together, filling up that pew even when some of the older ones were in the choir. We were expected to be attentive to what was going on in the service, however, on occasion, we might take the pencil from the rack in front of us and write on the Sunday bulletin! If we were far enough down the row, we might get away with playing tic-tac-toe with whoever was next to us, or even 'hangman'. I learned how to fold a paper airplane out of a church bulletin from watching an older brother do it in church service. As long as we were not disruptive, our parents tended to overlook those behaviors.

On one Sunday, Gene and I were sitting right next to each other. (We would have been seven and ten years of age.) Obviously, we were not paying much attention to the sermon! As one or the other of us swung our legs back and forth, we discovered it made the pew 'rock' ever so slightly. With an elbow or two between us, we finally got our swinging in a rhythm where the pew really rocked. This didn't last very long before Dad, sitting at the other end of where we were realized what was happening. A stern look from him and we stopped our behavior. Nothing more was said about the incident. When we got home, and dinner was being prepared, he instructed us to each get one of the straight chairs from the dining room and bring them to the living room. We were asked to line them up next to each other and sit on them. Then he said, "Now. You boys can swing your legs back and forth until dinner is on the table." We began tentatively, but were encouraged to swing more physically. Each time we slowed down, he would look up from his paper and nod at us to continue somewhat more rapidly. This continued for about thirty minutes while dinner was being put on the table. Then we were invited to return our chairs to the dining room and have Sunday dinner. Not another word was ever said about the incident, but we didn't swing our legs in church after that!

With the large number of siblings in the family, we were never without playmates! Sometimes neighborhood kids came to play with us, knowing they would be accepted as part of the group. We could organize our own ball game, frequently playing what was called 'rounds and others'. It allowed for each one to play at his/her own age level and talent ability. There were always special allowances for the younger ones playing, such as the pitcher standing closer and lobbing the ball more easily. I know there were times when the youngest was allowed on base through deliberate errors! My Dad was a great playmate in these games when he was available on a Saturday. We also played cops and robbers or cowboys and Indians. Our history indicates that none of us became violent because of these endeavors! We not only used guns carved out of whatever was available (rarely a purchased toy gun, not because of principle but lack of funds!). We created 'rubber' guns used to fire large rubber bands cut from old inner tubes. Dave, the oldest, was ingenious in his efforts in this regard. He managed to make 'automatic' weapons that fired several rubber bands without 'reloading'. On occasion, my Dad would participate in these activities, usually sneaking up on someone who least expected it! Cruelty or meanness was never a part of these 'play' activities!

We traveled quite a bit as a family when I was growing up. As a family, we made a trip to the Wisconsin Dells. I remember the Indian (Native American now, I suppose) dances that were put on at night. We made a trip to Niagara Falls. I never did find out why my Mother thought it was important to have a honeymoon trip to Niagara Falls when she had been married for many years and already had a raft of children! We made a trip to Portland, Oregon in the summer of 1934. My Mother's only sister and family lived there. In the course of this journey we visited Yellowstone Park. I have a vague recollection of the bear that stood up at the side of the car and peered in at us. Poor thing was probably more scared of this car full of people than we were of him. I don't remember directly, but as in many cases heard the story so many times that I think I remember it - my persistent question of the day, 'will we stay in one of those cabinets again tonight?' Of course, motels were non-existent. Cabins were the order of the day. You paid a certain amount regardless of the number in the family and we always had bedding along with us and would eat both dinner and breakfast in the 'cabinet'. Lunch was mostly picnic style along the way. The year of the trip to Portland is easy to remember, since my mother always said she found my brother Norman in the mountains on that trip and he was born in December of 1934!

I remember that my Dad built a small shelf like bench behind the front seat and some of the younger ones sat on it. (No seat belts in those days.) The older ones got the rest of the back seat. The oldest always got the front seat between our parents. On some of these trips, I was the youngest and got passed from one to another! Singing old hymns and well-known popular music was most of the entertainment, although as I got older I participated with the others in typical 'highway' games. (No video games nor DVD players and in fact, I can't remember that we had a radio in those early trips.) Each one would choose a 'make of auto' as their choice and would count each one of that manufacturer that came down the road. We also played "I'm going to Portland (or somewhere) and I'm taking - fill in the blank with a word starting with the next letter of the alphabet". The next person would have to repeat all those that had been chosen and add another with the next letter of the alphabet. This game might be restricted to the words chosen having to be an animal, or a vegetable, or some other category. Another game involved working through the alphabet by finding the letters on the signboards along the highway. Whoever got through the entire alphabet first was declared the winner. (We passed on most of these games to our children in our many travels.) Sometimes, my Dad would hold spelling tests or arithmetic tests along the way. He would ask the question to each one in turn, working to make the question appropriate for that one's age. As I already mentioned we did this around the table at home following dinner often.

During the time when the next tenants lived on the farm, the old house burned to the ground. As best I can remember hearing the stories, the tenant family had gone to town (St. Clair, ten miles away) to go to the movies. They had left a chicken brooder in one of the downstairs rooms with small chicks in it. This was before running water or electricity at the farm. It was kept warm by a kerosene heater and may have been left on too high a setting. The result was that the chicks got too warm, caught fire and that began a fire that burned the house to the foundation and the nearby tool shed and chicken house were destroyed. I remember after the fire seeing the large (24 inch diameter) sawmill type blade from the huge table saw that was used for cutting logs. It had been hanging on a wall in the toolshed and had taken so much heat that it was curved from the fire.

The following spring, my Dad built a new house on the same location, using some of the left over stones from the original house as part of the foundation. The new house was one story and consisted of a duplex arrangement with four rooms on each side, double entry doors on the front and doors at each end. One of these units was for the tenants to live in and the other was for us as a family when we came on weekends and other occasions. This house still stands on the same spot (now on a concrete slab). It was later remodeled into a single three-bedroom unit, bathroom and utility room added and still later a large enclosed porch wrapped around the rear quarter. I lived in this house my senior year of high school when my parents (summer of 1947) made the move from the city. By then, a well had been drilled at the corner of the house, a two car garage built at that corner to include the well house and, of course, electricity and running water made available. With a septic tank installed, the house had all the modern conveniences. The cistern at the end of the house was retained, as was the fruit cellar adjacent to it. I think neither of them is in use today. The well remains as the source of water for the house there and four others built by and for three married sisters and one married brother around the circle. All of that belongs in another story about what I call this 'ordinary family'.

CHAPTER THREE

World War II disrupted our family life just as it did most Americans. I remember vividly coming out of the Maplewood Theater on a Sunday afternoon and hearing the newsboys shouting, "Extra, Extra, Read all about it. Japs bomb Pearl Harbor!" It was a rare day when we were allowed to go to the movies and then mostly on a Saturday. Evidently there was a movie playing locally that was appropriate for us to attend and would only be in the theater from Sunday through midweek, hence our unusual attendance on a Sunday. When I heard the newsboy's shout, I didn't have the slightest idea where Pearl Harbor was and I'm sure I did not know what a 'Jap' was either. But it all sounded very ominous to a ten year old. By the time we got home, my Dad was listening to the radio for the latest reports.

Within a matter of weeks my Dad was transferred by General Motors (where he had been employed since the 1920's, first by Fisher Body and then General Motors as they absorbed Fisher Body) to Flint, Michigan to assist in opening a tank plant. He was living there by the end of the year. The factory was in Grand Blanc outside of Flint. By 1 March, we had moved to Flint as a family. The married sister, Dot, of course stayed in St. Louis. Mary Elizabeth and Edith May (the oldest and next to oldest) were both employed and moved to an apartment together in St. Louis. The rest of us moved to Michigan. I believe this was my first trip on a railroad train. The family always travelled by automobile everywhere we went. It was a twelve-hour trip and we had reserved recliner seats in the club car for the journey. We left very early in the morning and arrived in the early evening. We took meals in the dining car. I was pretty impressed. Dad met us in Detroit and drove us back to Flint about sixty miles away in a blinding snowstorm. We stayed at the Durant Hotel - another first - until we had a place to live. My Dad, who disliked the notion of renting, had rented a house for us to live in. Within the next year, when he determined the war wasn't going to be over as quickly as he thought, he sold the house in St. Louis and bought a house in Flint. We lived in it until the end of the war when he sold it as we moved back to the St. Louis area.

The following year, my oldest brother Dave dropped out of high school during his last year. (He always claimed it was Dicken's "Tale of Two Cities" that did him in! Many years later, his children persuaded him to test and get his GED certificate!) He became employed at the tank plant considered 'essential wartime industry'. However, after a period of exemption from military service, he refused any further deferment and joined the military service. He really wanted to be in the tank corps since he knew the General Sherman tank being built there quite well. However, he was sent to Selfridge Field in the Air Corps and later went through a series of training installations on the East Coast and became a radar man (when the word was hardly known). He eventually served throughout the South Pacific, including the Philippines and finally Japan at the end of the war.

After my oldest sister, Mary Elizabeth and Bill Morgan were married in Saint Louis; Edith May moved to Flint as well and lived at home, working at the tank plant throughout the rest of the war. The rest of us settled into the wintry weather of Michigan! My

Dad always said Flint had two seasons, winter and the fourth of July! It wasn't that bad, of course. (At the end of the war when my Dad had orders to move back to Saint Louis, he took an old pair of shoes to work and offered them to anyone who wanted them, with the accompanying statement that he wouldn't need shoes back in Missouri! He wore a pair of 'Halloween' bare feet over his actual shoes so it looked like he was without footwear.)

Gene and I got ourselves into trouble one Sunday evening while we were living in Flint. I think one of the younger brothers, probably Charlie the youngest, was ill enough that we were excused from attending evening services. We were to stay home and take care of Charlie and Norman (a couple of years older than Charlie and over three years younger than myself.) After a while, we had rounded up enough coins to purchase a popsicle that we could split between us. (five cents in those days) We would buy it at the drugstore a block away. Gene wanted me to do the shopping. I didn't want to go in the dark all the way to the drug store - about a block away. But I didn't want him to go and leave me there either. Since Norman and Charlie were both sound asleep, we made the ill-fated decision to go together!

This was a bad choice, of course. Little did we know what was transpiring at the church several miles across town! Somehow, in the wintry evening, the boiler system of the church heating system blew up and set the church on fire! (I know. Holy Smoke!) The result was that services were cancelled and our parents headed home early. As Gene and I rounded the corner toward the house we could see the back of the family automobile protruding from behind the hedge that marked the property line! The smart thing would have been to finish the popsicles! Instead, we threw away our half eaten treats and proceeded to the house where our Dad was awaiting us on the front porch! Gene stepped up on the porch and Dad took his right hand in his own right hand and applied his leather belt to the other end! I stood until he was finished and let Gene go into the house and then stepped up and took the same punishment! Good lesson!

Because Dad was a night superintendent at the plant throughout the war, he chose to use his daytimes for study and intellectual advancement, working his way through algebra to calculus and then drafting through engineering drawing - all through the International Correspondence Courses. Since everyone else, except my Mother was off with daytime activities, the solitary time allowed him great study time. I only learned many years later that he had taken courses in 'Foremanship' from the LaSalle Institute in Chicago by correspondence in his early years at Fisher Body. Although he had dropped out of school as a sixth grader, he spent most of his life studying and learning and had a great aptitude for self-improvement. He and Mom were great readers and passed that interest on to most of us.

He set up a drafting table in their bedroom and used it for most of his study activity. The family pet at the time (Dinky, a cross between a Irish Setter and a Curly Retriever) was trained by my Dad to carry things up and down the steps. So, when the mail came, my mother would give it to Dinky to take upstairs. My Dad then might send some of it back to her. On one occasion, he came downstairs to read the morning paper (a change from earlier days when he thought the morning paper had old news in it. Now working nights, the morning paper had the latest news!) He looked up and noted Dinky standing on the stairs and looking down at him. The dog clearly had something in his mouth, but it was not obvious as to what it might be. Dad told the dog to drop whatever he had in his mouth. The dog did as he was told and my Dad's upper plate of false teeth came bouncing down the carpeted stairs! They had bothered him that morning and he had left them on the bedside table. Dinky did his retrieving quite well. Of course, my Dad accused the dog of trying to bite him with his own teeth!

During the time we lived in Flint, Michigan there was a race riot in Detroit. It began evidently when a black soldier asked a white girl to dance with him at some recreation place on Belle Isle near Detroit. As a result of this a fight broke out and soon, the entire place was in a major scrap among the races. Although Flint was 60 miles away, there was considerable tension as to whether this might spread there. (Given social media and the television of today, the situation might have been worse.) I was attending Emerson Junior High School at the time. (Seventh through Ninth grades were taught there, immediately adjacent to Flint Northern High School that included tenth through twelfth grades.) After my Dad had decided to purchase a house, we moved several blocks from where we had been living. This meant that I was no longer in the Emerson district but should have been going to Longfellow Junior High School that was much closer. However, because I had older siblings who had been at Emerson and were now at Flint Northern, I was allowed to attend Emerson. I rode my bicycle to and from school every day (something over two or three miles away). Whereas Longfellow was an almost all white student body (because of where people lived) Emerson had a major mix of races. I didn't find any problem with that until the Belle Isle riot. The racial tension spread far beyond Detroit.

On this particular day, I was going out the East entrance in order to go home with a buddy after school to work on a project. Normally, I went out the West entrance toward where we lived. I had moved my bike to the racks out the East entrance during a class break so I could ride with my friend to his house. Just as we were going out the door, a disturbance occurred. According to later testimony, it happened because a girl (colored in those days? Now African American) grabbed the hat from a friend, a white boy, as a joke. Someone, misunderstanding the playfulness, pushed her and took the hat back. She hollered and pushed him. Then a general pushing and shoving began. I was just trying to get out the door and away from the melee. My friend and I made it outside to the bike racks where I discovered my right trouser was cut and bloody. I never knew who slashed me, but I still bare the scar on my right knee. At the height of the fracas, the principal came out and shouted for the students to stop! The chair he stood on was jostled and he fell to the floor. About that time, the coach came out of the gym and just began grabbing students at random and shoving them against the wall, hollering all the time to 'stop this shit'! Order was restored long before police arrived.

The following two weeks were marked by patrol cars around the campus each day and uniformed police in and out of the hallways. Nothing more ever came of the incident. But I have the old scar on the outside of my right knee to remember the incident!

CHAPTER FOUR

I had two brushes with the law as a youngster! Both were somewhat unusual and resulted in no record on my part. The first happened when we lived in Maplewood after World War II. One evening when Aunt Estelle (my dad's sister) and her husband Harry were visiting with us. A knock at the door brought me to answer it since the adults were in conversation. It was a uniformed policeman from the city of Maplewood. He asked me if I was Bill Jacobs and I acknowledged that I was. He then said, "Well, you'll have to come with me down to the station for some questioning concerning theft."

I looked shocked, I'm sure. Before I could answer, my Mother came to the door and inquired about his visit. When he told her that I would have to come with him to the station for questioning, she informed him that it would not happen unless she or my Dad came along. He agreed this was fine. My Mother, knowing that my Dad would prefer not to go, told him she would be right with us. By the time we got to the station, the desk sergeant informed the officer and us, that we need not be there after all.

The boy across the street, about a year younger than myself, had been brought in on charges of pilfering things from a next-door neighbor's house. Among the things he'd taken were some 'war' bonds (which he would not be able to cash) and some other checks (which he would not be able to cash.) He had been 'hired' by the neighbors to watch the house and water their plants in their absence. That's when he took these things, all of which they recovered from him. Under questioning, he told them I was with him when this happened. So they came looking for me. By the time we got to the station, he admitted that he was by himself and I didn't know nor have anything to do with the theft! (We were neighborhood friends only, since I was in public school and he was in a private church school.) When we returned home my Mother insisted the officer come in the house and explain the situation to my Dad, but more importantly to my rather proper aunt and uncle so they would know that I was not a criminal!

The other occasion did not involve police at all and I never told my parents about the situation until years later. The summer before we moved to the farm (1946) I applied for and was accepted for a job at Scruggs, Vandervoort and Barney (one of St. Louis' oldest department stores.) A friend had told me they often hired students in the summer time and at Christmas to assist with the 'package' chores. In those days, if you purchased something at the store (true I believe of other stores in the city at the time) and did not want to 'carry' it yourself, they would deliver it to your house, usually the following day.

The procedure was for the package to be kept in the department where you purchased it until a 'package' boy came around with a large box on wheels (most were 4 foot by 6 or 7 foot by about 4 feet high) and picked it up and took it to the delivery department. On occasion, it would go first to the giftwrap section and then to delivery. This was the task for which I was employed. I would spend my day from an hour before the store opened until an hour after it closed, pushing the cart around and picking up packages and delivering them to the basement delivery department. After I had been there a few days, the package department superintendent decided to keep me primarily running errands for him. This meant making an emergency visit to some department because they had a package that needed to get to delivery before the vans left that same day. Also, I picked up most of the giftwrap packages and delivered them either to the basement delivery department, or in some cases, back to the department where they had been sold. This was in case they were to be picked up by the customer who was shopping elsewhere in the store. For this job, I was paid $21.00 per week. This was paid in an envelope on Friday each week (although we worked on Saturday as well. Stores were not open on Sundays in those days.) The envelope would include a small paper slip indicating it was for me for the week previous. It would also include the cash payment for my salary. After taxes, it was $18.99! There would be a ten dollar bill, a five dollar bill, three ones, and ninety-nine cents in change! On Mondays, an additional dollar in cash was given to each one by our supervisor for dinner since the store didn't close until 9:00 p.m.

About halfway through the summer, I was notified by my supervisor to report to the personnel section. When I arrived I was asked to wait in the outer office. After about thirty minutes, the personnel director came out and told me it wouldn't be necessary for me to be there after all. I could return to my supervisor's office and resume work. I did as I was told and asked my 'boss' what this had been all about. It seems as though one of the other package boys had been stealing hosiery packages from the ladies lingerie department. When he was caught with several of these packages in his locker, he was taken in for questioning. He told them that all the boys did it. When asked whom he meant by all the boys, he gave my name to them along with a couple of others. By the time, they had rounded up those who had been named (I was the last among them) he had confessed that he was the only one doing this! I continued my work throughout the rest of the summer. Often I would get a call through a 'floorwalker' in a department to go immediately to my supervisor's office. There I'd be given one or more rolls of gift ribbon to take to the giftwrap department or perhaps directly to one of the wrap stations in another department. In each case, I would deliver the ribbon and return with the empty spool that it was replacing. The ribbon stock was kept in my supervisor's office under lock and key!

I bought my first suit while working at the department store. I think I paid $18.00 for it, on sale. The coat fit perfectly and the trousers were altered to fit me and had what were known as 'pegged' legs, with the bottom at a 15 inch size! I think it was what the so-called zoot-suiters were wearing at the time and I was pretty proud of it.

My decision to pursue the ministry of Christ for my future led me to re-think the possibility of attending the University of Missouri. Instead, I was encouraged to think about attending Central College in Fayette, Missouri. (As indicated earlier, Central has morphed from its original name to Central Methodist College and in more recent years it has become Central Methodist University. Although its main campus is still in the small Howard County seat town of Fayette, in recent years it has developed a number of extended campus programs throughout the state as well as an on-line presence.)

Central was the only Methodist church related college in Missouri at that time and had between 800 and 1000 students, most of whom either lived on campus or commuted from nearby communities.

After my high school graduation, I went to work with my older brothers Dave and Gene at the St. Clair Cement Block Company. This was a business that Dave and brother-in-law Bill Morgan had founded that year. Bill was operating a company in St. Louis (Null and Morgan Coal and Materials) that had been his father's company. It was a small business and Bill did most of the work himself with some day labor assisting. The plan for the block plant was to make concrete blocks for the area, fifty miles Southwest of St. Louis. When, and if the company became successful (It did not for several reasons) then Bill would move his efforts there as well. Concrete blocks were just beginning to be used extensively in construction. In fact, all the four houses on the farm (other than my folks' house) were built from blocks made at that plant, though some were later given brick facades. My arrangement with Dave was that he would give me transportation to and from work, buy my lunch and deposit $20 per week in the bank for me. Since I had no transportation otherwise to find work, this was fine. I would arise in the morning bright and early (well, early) and milk the cows, slop the pigs, feed the chickens and leave for work with Dave about 7. When I returned in the evening, usually somewhat after 5 but occasionally much later if we had deliveries to make as well, I repeated the morning chores. (I had been doing these chores ever since we moved to the farm that summer of 1947. Each morning, I was awakened when my Dad left to drive to St. Louis to work and began my chores. Chores and breakfast finished, I would walk the 3/4 mile from our house to the highway to catch the bus for high school in St. Clair. In the evening, the process was reversed.) It was this $340 I had with me the day I enrolled in college. True to his word, Dave had put $20 in the bank for me each of the 17 weeks I worked and then withdrew the cash for me at the end of the summer.

By the time I had made the decision to seek admission at Central, I was in the midst of my senior year in high school. This was in 1947-48 and many colleges were stretching to house the increased enrollments that the GI bill brought about after the war. Central was no exception. Its enrollment had swelled considerably and dormitory space was limited. Freshmen were required to live on campus. Some upper classmen rented rooms in the community; some from college professors whose homes were large and had extra space. All women were required to live on campus unless living at home. Since I was a 'late' enrollee I was consigned to a dormitory open bay area in the basement of McMurry Hall (the primary men's dorm on campus, although Wills Hall - an ancient wooden structure - did contain space for about 30 athletic scholarship males). I was told there would be 12 of us in the area in the basement. There was a bathroom with showers down the hall from the area where our beds and wall locker closets would be located.

When I arrived on Labor Day 1948 to begin my college experience, it was this open bay dorm situation that I expected. My Dad had the day off from work and so he and my mother drove me to the college from the farm where we lived during my senior year of high school. (Three years in large city high schools were capped by my senior year in a school with a senior class of 28! I had so many high school credits from carrying extensive numbers of classes that I needed only three credits to complete my requirements in St. Clair High School. I took speech, art, and typing, two study halls and gym class! I would expect folks to think the speech class was good for someone planning on going into the ministry and I'm sure that is true. But the typing class was the real benefit - it allowed me to type for professors and term papers for fellow students and earn some extra money while in college!) I had all my worldly possessions in a borrowed suitcase and a pressboard laundry case.

The latter were ubiquitous in those days. No Laundromats existed as yet. So, it was normal to 'mail' your laundry home in one of these cases. They had a metal frame on the lid where you inserted a 4 by 6 card with your mailing information, including return address. When the laundry was finished at home, it was placed back in the case, the card was turned over to reveal the return mailing instructions and you received it back in a couple of days. All in all, it took close to a week to send the laundry home and get it returned. This meant you had to have extra clothing to wear while some was always in the mail. The post office actually had a special laundry rate in those days. I utilized this system for only a few weeks before I discovered a woman in Fayette who would do all the laundry I could put in a laundry bag for one dollar! She washed, dried, and ironed everything, including dress shirts! It ended the anxiety of whether or not the clean underwear would return in time or if one might have to rinse out some and hang it on a line temporarily stretched across the room.

Now, back to my arrival in Fayette on Labor Day 1948. You would have to have known my Father for this paragraph to make much sense to you. We arrived in Fayette and followed the signs on the edge of the campus to the administration building. My parents remained in the automobile while I walked up the steps and across the walk to the main entrance. An upper class student was there to welcome newcomers and encouraged me to go on into the Admissions Office and the Bursar on the first floor. I was seventeen years of age. This was a new experience - the first time I had been on this campus. When I went down the hallway where the admission sign protruded, I walked up to the open service window. There I met Miss Martha Ricketts. When I told her my name, she looked on her list and checked me off. She handed me a packet that gave me information about my class schedule, and more importantly, about the orientation sessions and testing that would occupy my next couple of days. With that, she sent me down the hall to the window marked Bursar. (I don't think I knew that word prior to that day!) There the young man (Eugene Potter) took my name and looked on his list. He informed me there was a possibility of a room assignment change if I was interested.

I asked what that meant in terms of cost! I had been awarded a scholarship of $125 per semester because my grades were adequate and I was enrolling as a pre-theological student. This would be subtracted from the semester charge and that would leave me a balance of $295 to pay for room, board, tuition and books. They had indicated they were going to take off an additional $50 from this amount for my willingness to live in the open bay arrangement. Now, the bursar informed me, there had been a cancellation of a student who had reserved a single room on the fourth floor. If I chose to take that room, I would lose the additional $50 discount, but they would not charge me the additional $50 that normally was added for a single room accommodation. If you are following the arithmetic involved, you know that I had to pay $295. This I paid with cash that I was carrying with me that day.

43

I agreed to take the single room versus living in the basement open bay. I would forego the discount but not have to pay the premium for a single room. The only drawback, I was informed by the bursar was that the room was 419 on the fourth floor of McMurry. Again, there was a restroom with showers down the hall (the same on all floors of McMurry). So I forked over $295 of my cash and received the slip that would authorize me to pick up the key to 419 from the front desk office at McMurry. I went back to the car and told my folks what I'd done and they agreed it was probably the right thing to do. (Some upperclassmen who were returning but had registered late and some cancellations resulted in the basement open bay unnecessary!) I directed my Dad to drive to the other end of the campus where the men's dorm was located. I went in the front entrance and found the men's dean at the desk who welcomed me, looked at my admissions slip and gave me the key to 419. I went back to the car and retrieved my borrowed suitcase and laundry case and took them up the steps (no elevator) to my room. I emptied the borrowed suitcase and returned it to the car where I kissed my Mom goodbye and told my Dad to be careful driving home and waved to them as they drove away. I was off on a college career! My room and board were paid up till the end of the semester in January and I had $45 in my pocket to spend as I chose. All I had to remember was that by January, I needed another $295! That's why I was living four floors up from the only public telephone in the building! Remember, that's where I started this story.

Every College and University has homecoming events. Central was no exception. Of course, the schedule involves a football game and a homecoming dance. (The years I was at Central were great in the latter regard because the 'big band' era was trying to recapture audiences. As a result my years at Central saw big bands coming for our homecoming dances: Hal McIntyre, Gene Krupa, Tony Pastor and similar national names appeared at our small college.) The homecoming event always kicked off with a parade around the town square (the county courthouse). My freshman year, I was invited, encouraged, coerced to lead the parade. I agreed to do so. Then I found out the rest of the story! I was to wear a nightshirt, a top hat and carry a bathroom plunger as my baton! (I fear there are pictures to affirm this ridiculous appearance of mine!) It was the only year I participated in the homecoming parade. The later years, I was playing football and getting ready for a homecoming game.

CHAPTER FIVE

L et me add some significance to the telephone being four floors down from my room. In mid-December, 1948, just before time for Christmas vacation from school, I found a note on the bulletin board by the front desk for me to call Dr. Clinton B. Galatas. It took me a moment to remember just who this might be and then only recalled the name because his daughter, Ellen, was also a freshman and I had met her at various Orientation programs. He was the district superintendent for the Methodist Church, Fayette District and had his office in the education wing of the on-campus Methodist Church, Linn Memorial. The note had no date on it and I couldn't remember when I'd checked the bulletin board so I wasn't sure how long since he had tried to call me. I wasn't exactly sure why he wanted to reach me either.

I went to the pay phone and put in my nickel and dialed his number at the office on campus. When Dr. Galatas answered, I identified myself and asked what I might do for him. I thought he'd probably heard about my typing for some of the professors and maybe wanted to hire me for that purpose. Instead he began by asking me, "Aren't you going to be a preacher?"

I tried not to stammer in my surprise, but responded, "Yes, I plan to someday."

"Well," he continued, "have you thought about serving a student charge while in school here?" (Charge is the general term assigned to positions to which Methodist pastors are assigned. Perhaps it dates to Charles Wesley's hymn, "A Charge to Keep I Have.")

After a moment of hesitation, I said, "Well, I hadn't really thought about it since I'm only a freshman."

"Have you gotten yourself a license to preach?"

The Methodist system has a program in which laymen may become pastors of churches through a licensing system. It requires a study course, an interview at the local church level that may lead to recommendation to the district committee on ministry. If that latter examines the credentials and the candidate passes the interview at the district level, he or she may be licensed as a local pastor and assigned to serve a church or churches. There are some restrictions on what such a local pastor is authorized to do and this has varied through the years depending on the General Conference of the Methodist Church and its approvals that are published each four years in the book known as "The Methodist Discipline".

I told Dr. Galatas that I had read the books of the course of study and taken the exam over these books, but I'd not been interviewed by my local church or district, so was not yet licensed. After he determined that my church membership was in the St. Clair Methodist Church, he informed me that I could become an 'associate' member of the Linn Memorial Methodist Church on campus; they could interview me and recommend me to the Fayette District committee on ministry who could interview me and authorize my license to be issued. I listened carefully and responded that I guess I ought to look into that. His reply was "come over to my office this afternoon and let's talk about it."

When I visited the District Office that afternoon, Dr. Galatas had all the paperwork laid out for me to request from my home church associate membership in the Linn Memorial Church and a letter for me to sign requesting the local church interview me pursuant to recommending me to the District Committee on Ministry that would be meeting right after the New Year! He told me, "I like to get you preacher boys when you are new here because then I can get at least three years of work out of you serving the rural churches we have in this district."

I acknowledged all that and told him I'd talk with my parents and my home pastor about it over Christmas vacation. He agreed that would be a good idea and said he would look for a meeting between us when the Christmas break was ended. "By the way," he added, "I have a circuit of three little country churches that you'd be just right for. The student who has been serving them is finishing school this semester so I need someone by the first of February." (I didn't know it at the time, but the student pastor he was referring to was Ray Blanchard. Ray was a veteran, now finishing his degree and planning to go on to Perkins School of Theology at SMU in Dallas in the spring term. He was dating Ellen Galatas at the time and they later married!) I told Dr. Galatas that I wasn't sure, even with my licensing that I knew how to be a pastor as yet. His reply, which has stuck with me in the years since was, "You go out there and love those folks and they'll teach you what you have to know." He was right!

My conversation with my parents included the fact that I had not earned enough money to pay the $295 I needed for the second semester. I had been offered one of the full-time positions in the dining facility for the second semester because there were vacancies occurring as some seniors either graduated mid-term or opted out of working their last semester. If I took an appointment to serve these three little churches, I would be unable to accept this position, since I'd be gone every Sunday and possibly the entire weekend. I had counted on the number of meals I had worked part time so far plus this full time assignment; along with what I was earning by typing for professors and producing term papers for other students to cover my costs for the second semester. I calculated that I would be approximately $100 short of my goal. On the other hand, the three churches known as the Triplett Circuit (named for the one church in a small town) would pay me $100 per month collectively. Complicating the matter was the fact that I would have to acquire some means of transportation. My folks agreed to loan me the $100 I needed to pay for my second semester's room, board, tuition and books.

I returned from Christmas vacation with a letter authorizing me to become an associate member of the Linn Memorial Methodist Church, signed by the pastor in St. Clair, Missouri. I also had a check for $100 from my folks to help finish my second semester's costs. As for transportation, I wasn't sure what I could do as yet. When I visited with Dr. Galatas, he accepted the letter and said he would transmit it to Dr. Melvin Koch, pastor of the church on campus who had agreed to call a special committee meeting to interview me. After that, there would be a meeting of the local charge conference to recommend me; the district committee would interview me and, with approval, my license would be issued by Dr. Galatas. In fact, these things occurred and my license was issued to me in February of 1949. I was a seventeen-year old licensed local pastor in the Methodist Church, with an assignment as pastor-in-charge of the Triplett Circuit!

Actually, I went with Ray Blanchard on the second Sunday in January and met the folks from the three churches and began preaching the following week. My transportation needs were to be met temporarily by riding with another student pastor, Howard Hardeman. Howard, now a senior at Central, served two churches just beyond where my churches were located. Although he often spent the weekend visiting his churches, he would temporarily only go on Sundays, picking me up at the dormitory and dropping me at a gas station in Brunswick, Missouri. There a church member would pick me up and take me to the church where I was preaching that morning. After the ladies of the church had fed me Sunday dinner, (the ladies at the three churches ran a roster and took care of me the entire three years for Sunday dinner) someone would take me to the church at which I was to preach that evening and then back to Brunswick to be picked up by Howard in the evening. We would ride back to campus together. Howard was a veteran on the GI bill, unmarried and living just off campus in a private home where he rented a room. This would work for the remainder of the semester and by the first of June I would find my own transportation. Howard turned out to be a valuable mentor during these long drives back and forth on Sunday morning and evening. I think I gave him a dollar toward gas each week. Brunswick was about 40 miles from Fayette. A dollar doesn't sound like much, but you need to know that gasoline was in the low twenties per gallon and occasionally as low as 16.9 during the frequent gas wars that stations entered into.

While home on spring break, I managed to purchase an old 1933 Chevrolet from a brother-in-law for $50. I drove that old car for three years and sold it for $50. It was the best investment in an automobile that I ever made! It was a four-door sedan and, although not much to look at, was mechanically sound. I put a lot of miles on it in the following three years. After my brother Gene came to college (driving a 1941 Chevy that had been my folks) we managed to keep our cars running without outside assistance. He knew a lot more about mechanical things than I did, but I was always good for 'grunt' and 'go get parts' help. I never experienced a breakdown on the road with that old vehicle. I can't say the same about other cars I've owned!

The only problem I had with the old car was of my own making! One evening, Bill, 'Zeke' Winters (who was my roommate when I moved back into McMurry Hall for my final semester before completion of my degree) and I had been down to 'small' Paul's to get a 'brain sandwich' and then return to study at the dorm. As we drove up Church Street that runs along the West side of the campus,

Zeke remarked that the sidewalk was as wide as my car tread. I could probably drive right up the sidewalk. The curb along this street is not perpendicular to the street, but a sloping curbing. So without further thinking, I drove up the curb at the next crosswalk area and proceeded to drive up the sidewalk to the circle drive entrance to the dorm parking area. I knew I couldn't make the sharp turn through the two columns at the entrance to the circle, so I cut across the grass intending to just jump the curb into the circle drive. Unfortunately, I miscalculated how deep this curbing was and I came down hard on the other side of the curb. Quickly I realized that I had lost steering control! I stopped immediately since I was not going very fast anyway. I got out to inspect my problem with Zeke's help. We isolated the problem as the connecting rod that held the two front wheels in sync with each other as having come loose at one end. The rod had dropped down, and left me with steering only one front wheel and the other just skidding. Zeke crawled under one side while I was under the other side. We discovered that the rod was held to its connection on the wheel with a cotter pin. This had sheered off when I dropped over the high curb. I was pretty sure I had some nails in the back seat in a bag from a job I had been working on that week and quickly acquired one, intending to insert it where the cotter pin had been and bend it over.

About that time, while I was under the car, a flashlight appeared with its bright beam focusing on me. It was 'Pop' Thurmond, the college night watchman. He asked, "What're you boys doing?"

Thinking as quickly as possible, I replied, "Pop. I'm in trouble. The cotter pin broke on the tie rod to the steering. I'm lucky we weren't killed when it caused me to jump the curb and run up into the circle."

"Well, can you fix it?" he asked.

"Yes, I've got an old nail that I think will hold it till I can get to the shop tomorrow."

"Well," he stated, "Let me hold the light there where you can see what you are doing." And he held his flashlight beam under the car until I got the nail inserted and bent over. When I was finished and back in the driver's seat, he said, "Now you boys be careful. Broken old cars can be dangerous."

We agreed with him and drove around the back of the dorm to my parking place, laughing all the way.

By the end of the second semester, I had gotten into a routine with my churches, often going on Friday night or Saturday and returning on Sunday night. In addition, I repaid my parents the $100 I borrowed to cover my second semester tuition. In the next chapter, I want to share some of my experiences in serving the Triplett circuit of the Methodist Church. I believe I learned more from these patient parishioners about ministry than I did later on in my graduate seminary education experiences. Much of what I learned in those graduate courses made sense because of the mentoring I had received from faithful Christians in the churches of the Triplett Circuit.

CHAPTER SIX

I n the summer of 2013, my wife Pat and I made a trip to Missouri and among our goals were to visit these three churches. I didn't have a map nor did I have the slightest notion of exactly where these churches were located. When we arrived in Brunswick, Missouri, I instinctively turned on a country road (now paved though all were gravel in my college days) that I thought led to Zion Church. Indeed in a matter of some fifteen miles, we found the church. A family of the church membership was holding their family reunion in the church hall and so the building was open! When I was the pastor there, we began a program called the Lord's Acre Sale each year. (These programs developed in many rural churches. Members were encouraged to set aside an acre of their farm in which the produce would be given to the Lord's work. In the case of the Zion Church, many of the members chose to raise a calf, hog, or some sheep that would be designated as their contribution to the sale that was held at the end of the harvest season. Zion was the only one of my three churches who entered into such a program.) We raised enough money that in the last year as I was leaving, the church had a basement constructed beneath it and central heat installed. Since that time an addition of a church hall with kitchen was constructed. We were able to visit folks (none of them from my era - nor did they remember any of them - though some family names sounded familiar to them from the community) and take pictures within and outside the church.

We left there to head toward Triplett. I knew how to get there from my map, but had no idea where Prairie Chapel was located, nor did we find it that day. (I recalled Dr. Galatas' words to me concerning this church. He said it was "a church where the living keep it dead and the dead keep it alive." He referred to the fact that there was a very small nucleus of folks who attended and supported the church, but there was a cemetery that attracted many folks back each Memorial Day and the contributions that day kept the church going. I suspect this is true of many rural churches to this day.)

We arrived in Triplett with the disturbing realization that it looked very different from my remembrances. We were told there was no Methodist church there, only one of the Christian denomination (Disciples of Christ.) Both existed when I was serving there. We had services on the first and third Sundays at the Methodist Church and the Christian Church had a pastor visit, preaching on the second and fourth Sundays. I was there on all fifth Sundays as well. (There are four each year, one per quarter.) We drove around the little community and were saddened by what we saw. Many of the streets were overgrown, gravel where there had been blacktop, potholes aplenty and abandoned houses on nearly every street. Some of the yards appeared as though the wilderness was about to retake them. It was a sad visit.

I have so many rich memories from those days of ministry that it is difficult to choose which ones to share in this story of my odyssey. Some may be inspirational, as they were for me, and others are just humorous and illustrate my innocence and ignorance! From the time I was seventeen years old until I was past twenty, I was the pastor of the Triplett Circuit of The Methodist Church, in rural Chariton County, Missouri. During that time I received $1200 per year from the three churches together. It came in sporadic amounts. Some times I would receive a small amount each time I visited the particular church, usually in cash from the treasurer. Often, it was 'past due' when received. When harvest time came, the churches would always 'catch up'. On several occasions during this three-year period I was called upon to conduct funeral services for church members. In most cases, I would be given some stipend, usually in a thank you card. For the most part, it was $10 each time. It was not much, but it often was very welcome at a needed time.

The folks who were members of these three churches taught me far more than I taught them in the three years I served there. They were an invaluable part of my ministerial education. As I indicated previously, much of what I learned later in seminary was integrated into the valuable training these wonderful folks shared with me. Some of this took place in the churches themselves, but mostly I learned from them during the visits in their homes. Each week I was entertained in someone's home for Sunday dinner. Often, I spent the entire weekend staying with one or two of the families, enjoying their fellowship and Christian care and concern.

Some of what I learned was not theological but was human and often humorous. I noted on one of the first Sundays at old Zion Church that one of the men stood up during the hymns but never opened the book nor sang. I asked him later if he didn't like the hymns we were singing? He told me that wasn't the problem. His statement was, "Preacher. I was cut out to be a singer, but I wasn't sewed up right, so I don't throw everyone else off by singing!"

I conducted my first funeral while serving the Triplett circuit. I arrived one Sunday morning (early in my assignment while I was still riding with Howard) at the church in Triplett. There was only one automobile parked in front of the church and Cecil Sanders and his wife Violet were sitting on the front steps of the church building. (The Sander's daughter was a classmate at CMU.) Howard let me out and traveled on his way. I asked Cecil where everyone was this morning? It was unusual for there not to be a fairly large number of cars. Cecil asked if I had not gotten the call from the funeral home. I was taken aback by this comment. "What funeral home call?" He said, "About Bill Koch's grandson?" (You will recall what I told you about living on the fourth floor and the phone calls that were occasionally answered and notes left on the bulletin board. My failure was to check it regularly!)

"What about Bill Koch's grandson?" I asked. "Oh, the baby was stillborn and they are all out at the homestead awaiting us to come for you to conduct a service."

We got into Cecil's car while he was telling me this news. I had only attended one funeral in my life up until this point. It was when my maternal Grandmother (Moise) had died while we lived in Michigan in 1943. My Dad drove us all night from Flint, Michigan to St. Louis, Missouri so that we could be there for the service. I was twelve years of age and I slept through the entire service. Now, I was being asked to conduct a service for a stillborn baby!

One of the things I had received shortly after Christmas of this freshman year was a note from the Women's group at the Methodist Church in St. Clair with a check for $50 enclosed to help me with my need for books. Since my class books were covered by tuition at Central (mostly checked out from the school and returned at the end of a semester), I decided to use the money to buy books that might assist in my ministry. I ordered these from the Methodist Publishing House. I still have some of them and they are all inscribed in the frontispiece with the words, 'bought with money from the St. Clair WSCS' (Women's Society of Christian Service - now usually called the United Methodist Women.) Among the titles I chose to purchase was my own copy of the Methodist Discipline (from General Conference 1948) and the Methodist Book of Worship. I carried these two in my old briefcase wherever I went for years.

I opened the recently acquired Methodist Book of Worship as we drove out in the country to the Koch homestead. Imagine my relief when I found in the index the notation, 'service for the infant dead'. I had time to read through a couple of times and we arrived at the farm. There were more cars there than we usually had at the church on a Sunday morning. We gathered in a crowd in the family living room where there was a tiny casket that held the body of the stillborn child. The crowd overflowed onto the porch. When the room became quiet, I read, word for word, the service for the infant dead from the Book of Worship. I improvised a brief prayer at the point that the service indicated a pastoral prayer would be offered. When the service was over I received a great number of comments about how it was the nicest, most meaningful service for an infant they had ever attended. I was saved by the Book of Worship!

A couple of years later I had another experience with a funeral that nearly became a disaster. Usually I would be notified by the funeral home, but occasionally I would get a phone call directly from the family when they desired my services. In this latter case, I was now residing in Eagle Village with my brother Gene and Katie (his wife) in the extra bedroom I rented from them. Now I was not dependent upon some kind person answering a pay phone and taking a message and posting it where I might find it on the bulletin board. Instead, I installed a telephone in the apartment. It was there for all our usage, of course, but I paid the basic fee each month since I felt it was there primarily for my needs, both as a pastor and as a single student on campus! When they rarely made a long distance call, they would always reimburse me as soon as the bill arrived.

In this case the phone call for the funeral came from the funeral home in Brunswick, Missouri, which was the nearest town to the Triplett Circuit churches. The phone systems in rural areas were not all that great in those days and long distance sometimes complicated the matter. I answered the call myself, so it was not because of any confusion in transcribing the message. I heard clearly that there had been a death in the Adams family and my understanding was that it was Uncle Robbie who had died. The time of the service and the date were clear. It was to be at the home. Listening to the crackly message from the funeral director, I repeated it to him and got his acknowledgement. The schedule called for 10:30 a.m. on a Saturday.

That was always desirable from a student standpoint because it didn't interfere with class attendance. I told him I would be there in plenty of time.

On the following Saturday I left in plenty of time to arrive in Brunswick, Missouri well ahead of the 10:30 schedule and parked in front of the Funeral Home. I was surprised that there were no other autos there as yet but thought it was because I was somewhat early. However, when I tried the front door, it was locked. Furthermore, so was the side door. I got back in my car and drove a couple of blocks to the business district only to discover that most stores also were closed. Finally, I found the drug store open and went in and asked the young lady if she knew about the funeral. She replied that she did. It turns out that the service was not at the 'home', meaning funeral home to me, but at the 'home' meaning where they lived out in the country! Now, my timing was tight, so I quickly got in my car and headed for their home in the country. Fortunately, I'd been there before and knew where I was going. As I pulled into the front yard, where there were many automobiles parked, I looked up at the house. There on the front porch was Uncle Robbie. I thought it was Uncle Robbie whose service I was there to conduct! Now, I discovered the phone call from the funeral director was only trying to define the family and that the funeral actually was for Aunt Rosie! Quickly retreating to my automobile as though to retrieve some additional book, I opened my notebook in which I had my meditation all typed out and hurriedly changed all the 'he's' to 'she's' and the 'hims' to 'hers' and the 'Robbies' to 'Rosies'. The rest of the day was somewhat anticlimactic compared to my arrival discovery!

I might add to my 'funeralizing' experiences the service I held at the Prairie Chapel Church in which the service was at the church and the burial was in a family cemetery out in the middle of a field. The rains had been heavy and the dirt roads were muddy. From the church we made our way to the family farm. There the casket was transferred to a wagon pulled by a tractor. A family member drove the tractor and the funeral director and I walked on each side of the narrow wagon stabilizing the casket so that it would not slide forward or backward or sideways! The funeral director had come prepared with heavy overshoes. I finished the day with my shoes caked with mud, my socks soaked with mud and the cuffs on my trousers in bad need of cleaning!

The church at Triplett had a parsonage right next door to the church, however it had been a long time since there was a resident pastor living there. Mostly the circuit had been served by a series of retirees or more recently student pastors from Central Methodist University. While I served the circuit, the parsonage was rented out for fifteen dollars a month to a family. On the other side of the church was the home of Mrs. McCausland. She was in her 80's or maybe 90's. I stayed often with her when I was in the community overnight. She had an old reed pump organ in the living room and she loved to play it and sing with me! Her favorite was "Amazing Grace". The first time I was there and we sang together, she told me the story of how she sat on her grandfather's lap when she was about eight years old and heard him sing the old hymn. Then she remembered having reached up to his chin and pulled his head around and asked him, "Grandpa, when were you blind and now you can see?" And he explained to her about being blind to salvation and eternal life until his eyes were opened and he accepted Jesus Christ as his savior. She had asked him if she could do that and he agreed she could. Right there in her grandfather's lap she accepted Christ and he offered a prayer for her. She'd been a faithful Christian ever since then.

It was difficult for her to pump the old organ with both feet, sitting on the bench and see the music and the keys all at once, because of her bifocal spectacles. So most of the time, she would stand on one foot, pump the organ with the other foot and we would sing together! She was a great inspiration to a young pastor.

CHAPTER SEVEN

I conducted only one wedding during the three years I was serving the Triplett Circuit. This was the wedding of a schoolteacher (early 40's and never married) and a bachelor farmer in the area. According to the older members of the Prairie Chapel Church, it was the first and only wedding that had ever been conducted in the church building. The claim was bolstered by an ancient, stained register book that was part of the membership files kept by the local church treasurer that listed births, baptisms, church member accessions, deaths and other events in the life of the church. Even the amounts received for maintenance of the cemetery at the annual Memorial Day services were recorded, but no weddings. Evidently, folks who married from the church did so at home or in the local judge's chambers. (When the wedding was being planned that I conducted, one of the older men said to me, "no wonder we're a dying church, nobody ever got married here!") It was a gala occasion when Catherine and Harold exchanged vows in the one-room church before a goodly crowd. I've thought about the matter since. I was not old enough to be married without parental consent at the time, nor could I own an automobile in my own name in Missouri at that time. Here I was solemnizing the vows of a couple, each of who were twice my age!

If the reader knows anything about Methodist church organization and administration, then you know that it is a connectional denomination. This results in a hierarchy of administration and financial considerations. Conferences, Districts, and local boards are all related to one another. The funding of this administration as well as various mission causes beyond the local church is covered by what is known as the apportionment system. There is a formula established within the system that eventually results in the local church being assigned their 'fair' share of the overhead and the outreach causes of the denomination. To simplify the matter, it is based in the ratio of the local church membership and budget related to the total of all churches within the annual conference (which is not only an annual meeting but refers also to the structure of the organization.)

Each local church has its own administrative board; the name of this has changed through the years from Board of Stewards to Administrative Board, to various other titles. It was Board of Stewards when I was serving the Triplett Circuit. Each of the individual churches on the circuit had their own Board of Stewards. In the case of the Triplett Circuit, I discovered early on that very little cash was put in the offering plates in worship each Sunday. Instead, the members of the Board of Stewards divided up the names of the member/families and took responsibility to 'collect' their contributions from them in an orderly, but not necessarily regular fashion.

For instance, it was obvious that many farmers had little cash until harvest time or the sale of livestock. The stewards would collect contributions at that time and turn them over to the treasurer who would then disburse funds as necessary.

I mentioned earlier that I often was paid in an erratic way and most frequently with cash. It had become the custom of the Triplett Circuit (and I suspect many other rural churches of that time) to give their share of conference apportionments and district apportionments (the latter including funds that were used to pay the district superintendent and district office expenses) when the district superintendent visited for the church 'quarterly conference'. The development of the quarterly conference system within Methodism is another topic that needs to be explained elsewhere. Its existence and function are of interest to my story here. There was a time when rural churches were served by local pastors, mostly uneducated beyond the licensing procedure. Then once each quarter the superintendent (presiding elder in the old Southern church) would visit, conduct the business of the church (or charge as it was called) preach and celebrate the sacrament. At various times it was permissible for the local pastor to celebrate the sacrament, but at other times it was deemed that only an 'ordained' pastor could do so. Much of this evolved during the days of the circuit-riding pastors. During my days on the Triplett Circuit, I was authorized to celebrate the sacrament in the local parish to which I was appointed and did so at least once per month in each local church.

Much has changed in America since the early days of circuit riding pastors. For one thing, automobiles make it possible for pastors to travel greater distances. This evolution has continued down to our own time in which the geographical size of conferences and districts has been enlarged since modern transportation and communication makes it possible to economically serve many more churches during the same length of time. In addition, many of the rural churches have closed as our society has become more urban and changes have allowed folks to travel greater distances to attend worship services. This evolution was beginning to take effect during the late 1940's when I began my ministry on the Triplett Circuit. As a result, the new superintendent (when Dr. Galatas retired) announced that he would only come twice a year to each parish rather than four times a year. He would come to conduct a 'charge' conference at the beginning of the fiscal year in order for them to adopt their budget and accept their apportionments for the coming year. He would return for a 'fourth quarterly' conference toward the end of the year for final reports and election of officers for the ensuing year. These would not necessarily be on Sundays either, but would occur on whatever schedule he established.

The initial reaction on the part of some of my parishioners was to state that if he was only coming twice a year then he should be paid only for coming twice, not the full amount. It took some serious discussion on my part to convince them that the amount he was paid was an annual amount in the apportionment system no matter how many times he actually visited the churches. So when he came, they somewhat begrudgingly gave him the 'half' then due. The annual conference sessions in Methodism were held in the fall, around the first of October. This allowed for harvest to be completed and therefore rural members of the conference could attend and there were funds available to complete the payment of the apportionments for the year. (Our urbanized society has resulted in Methodist conferences being held in late May or early June now. School is out and it is an easier time for pastors to move to new locations.)

The first year that the new superintendent had implemented coming only twice a year instead of quarterly, two of the churches on the Triplett Circuit had not raised enough money to pay out the apportionments. When I approached the two treasurers and indicated that we should really send it in even though the superintendent had already made his second and last visit for the year; the response I received was that they just had not collected enough money yet. Crops had not done well. Hog prices and cattle prices were down. I was determined that I would not go to conference without the apportionments paid. I informed the two treasurers that I would pay the apportionments myself (the total for the two was about the equivalent of my income for the two months from the three churches - $200) rather than have the churches listed as behind in apportionments. I didn't receive much encouragement from either one of them. When I arrived in Chillicothe, Missouri for the conference sessions on the first Sunday afternoon in October, I went to the conference treasurer's desk in the entry hallway and informed him that I had the remainder of the apportionment funds for the two churches. He received the cash from me and gave me a receipt for the full amount. As the afternoon session of clergy ended (held separately from the lay session on that first day only), I was met by the treasurer from one of the churches. He asked me how much I had paid on behalf of the churches. When I told him the amount, he opened his wallet and gave me a full reimbursement with the comment, "our preacher ain't gonna pay our responsibilities." I never knew whether they had collected the funds or if he had advanced it. It was the only time throughout the years of my ministry that I almost paid the church apportionment myself.

Of course, in later years, for most of the charges I served, the treasurer would send in a check once a month to cover the apportionment cost. In the case of the last charge I held, they voted each year to pay our apportionments in advance early in the calendar year (the conference had changed its fiscal year to match the calendar) and then to offer to help out poor churches in the district that might not be able to pay their share.

I noted one Sunday at Zion church several visitors whom I'd not met before. After the service, I introduced myself to them and discovered that they were members of a now-defunct Congregational country church several miles away from Zion's location. The older of the men, John, seemed to be the leader of the group. I got his name and location of his farm and offered to come visit them. He 'allowed' as how that would be fine. The following week I drove to their farm. His wife told me he was out in the field bringing in some hay. I asked if it would be all right if I walked out there and said 'howdy'. She said that would be fine.

I took off my coat and tie and left them in my old Chevy and wandered out to where I could see him working by himself. He was 'forking' hay up onto a hay frame wagon hooked up to the tractor. I noted an extra hayfork on the wagon and after saying hello, picked up the fork and began to assist in the process of getting the hay onto the wagon. Other than howdy, he didn't say anything to me, nor did I interrupt the important labor task by talking. When we had gotten all the hay up from where it had been mowed and left in windrows, I climbed up on the back of the tractor and rode with him back to the barn where I assisted in getting the hay into the loft. We hadn't exchanged more than a dozen words up till then. He invited me to come in for a glass of cold tea and we proceeded into the kitchen. We talked a while together and then I asked if I could offer a prayer. He and his wife quickly agreed and we prayed together, giving thanks for the harvest and the good weather.

The next Sunday I arrived at Zion church to discover the place was full of people. When I finished my sermon that Sunday and gave an invitation (as I always did) for those who wanted to dedicate their lives to Christ, or re-dedicate themselves or join the church, John stood up and moved forward. When he did so, all these strangers I had not known stood up and came forward with him. I received 38 new members that day! This was the entire remaining membership of the discontinued congregation several miles away. The leader of the group, with whom I had met, was a descendant of the founders of that little church. When he decided they ought to give up on the old church ever coming back, he announced his intention to become a member of Zion Methodist Church on the following Sunday and they all followed him. This remarkable event was written up by my District Superintendent and later published in the "Christian Advocate", a national Methodist monthly magazine! The membership of Zion Church was increased by about 30% on that day alone. Over the years, I discovered that words were not as important as being with someone.

Gus Martin was the custodian at Zion Church during my tenure, and probably for many years prior to that. He worked as a 'hired' hand at a farm that belonged to church members. He lived there on the farm in a little house behind the family home. He was eighty years old when I first met him. He would come to the church early on Sunday morning and check to see all was in order and then return Sunday afternoon to sweep up and see that all was neat and orderly for the week. I mentioned the church was raised and a basement was installed the last year I was there. A central heating system was installed at that time as well. Prior to that, the church consisted of the one main sanctuary space and a small room on each side of the entry foyer at the back of the room. (Of course, this was the front of the church building from outside.) One of these small rooms was used as a children's classroom during Sunday School and a bit of a nursery during church services. No one presided over a nursery, but anyone who had small children could retreat there with them during the worship hour. The other small room was the custodial storeroom, coal storage bin and catchall for anything else not suitable to be in the sanctuary.

During the winter months, Gus would arrive early enough to 'fire up' the large potbelly stove in the middle of the building, right in the middle of the center aisle! It was coal fired in those days. On a really cold day, it would take the chill off the building at best! It was not unusual for some of the folks to get up from one side and move to the other side just before the sermon in order to 'warm' up both sides! Unfortunately, this preacher didn't have that luxury. The stove put out enough heat that I would feel warm on my face and freezing elsewhere! And, of course, I couldn't just turn my back on the congregation. In the middle of every sermon I ever preached there in the cold wintry times, Gus needed to stoke the furnace! I tried varying the order of worship to see if I could escape his work during the sermon, but it was of no use! He would get up from his pew, go back to the little room and loudly fill the shovel with coal. He would proceed to come back to the stove in the middle of the church, open the door of the stove with an edge of the shovel and then rear back and shovel the load of coal into the furnace. With this, he would use the shovel to slam the door shut and with a grunt or two, return the shovel to the storage area and return to his pew, sitting down with a deep sigh. To get this picture fully in mind, you must remember when he was rearing back to shovel the coal into the stove he was directly opposite and about 20 feet away from where I was standing trying to preach!

I never knew much about his education level. He didn't talk much about that, however, he would show up on a Sunday morning and want to know if I had read some obscure story in the newspaper. Of course, I had not. Certainly not on a Sunday morning when I was either driving to the church, or if staying with a family, visiting with them over breakfast. He would quote these stories to me verbatim! I was told by some of the church members that Gus had a good heart, but a weak mind! He certainly had a good memory! But, I never was able to change his pattern of tending the stove. I'm fairly certain that at some point he had been told that the stove would probably need stoking about halfway through the service, maybe during the sermon. He fulfilled that responsibility without fail!

My service to the Triplett Circuit ended when I completed my undergraduate career at Central Methodist University in January 1952. I had planned to remain and serve the churches until Conference time or when I left to attend seminary in the fall of that year. But another phone call changed much of my plans at this time. I mentioned that my brother Gene had left college at the end of his second year to enter into a business arrangement with our Dad. Since I was not a GI, I was not eligible to rent the Eagle Village apartment on my own. This meant moving to the dormitory. So when he and Katie and their newborn daughter Cindy left to move back to the farm near St. Clair, I moved into a room in McMurry Hall.

In order to be eligible to live in the dorm for the summer, I needed to be enrolled as a student. I signed up for eight hours of biology, including the laboratory time. I found a roommate and took up residence on the second floor of McMurry Hall. My lectures were Monday and Wednesday mornings and my laboratory times were the same days two hours each of those afternoons. I needed to round out the schedule to nine hours so I signed up for a one-hour piano lesson from Professor Opal Hayes, head of the piano department. (I had taken accordion lessons for a couple of years on a little twelve bass accordion before the war. When we moved to Michigan, I didn't find an accordion teacher but signed up for piano lessons with a private teacher. That lasted only a year when I found that my love for football exceeded my willingness to practice piano!) This summer schedule meant that by Wednesday evening, I was finished with attendance requirements. Many weeks, I would leave on Thursday and go stay with church members on the Triplett Circuit until Sunday evening when I returned to the campus. These summer school hours meant that I only needed 7 hours in the fall term to complete my degree requirements. (Had I gone to summer school the year before I could have graduated that summer. However, my parents were making a trip to California and Oregon and I wanted to go along and so I did not go to summer school that year.) But, I had been playing football for the last two years and had to carry a minimum of 12 hours to be eligible for varsity sports. (One of my fellow team members thought it unique that a 'preacher' played on the football team, hitting as hard as anyone else. He decided to call me little Jesus! It was a bit of embarrassment during a game when he would let out a chilling yell, 'go get 'em little Jesus!') So the fall term became an easy ride. I took Minor Sports for Men, Philosophical Approach to Modern Civilization, Play Production, a Voice lesson and Vocal Conducting. Again, these courses had their class times scheduled so that they were all morning classes and ended by noon on Friday. Except during the football season, this allowed me to drive to the churches and spend the weekend. During football, I made the trip on Saturday morning or evening depending upon whether our game was Friday night or Saturday. (As an aside, my voice professor would admonish me each week that I was using my voice to shout too much, either at football games or when preaching, he wasn't sure which! I assure you it was the former. I've not been much of a 'shouting preacher'.)

I became active in little theater while I was at Central. I had never been in any kind of dramatic production until my senior year of high school in St. Clair. The senior class always put on a play for a couple of nights during the fall semester. As I remember it was a spoof on mystery stories called "The Shop at Sly Corner." I played the part of an Army major in the play. I borrowed a uniform from a local man, Skip Reed, who had served in the Army in World War II. It was a set of the old 'pinks and greens'. (By the way, I bought my first driver's license from Skip. He ran a gas station/repair shop on the edge of St. Clair. There were no tests in those days. I merely brought my birth certificate proving I was sixteen years of age and gave him fifty cents. He got to keep half of that for issuing the license and sent the rest to the state of Missouri.) As I remember, the funds raised by play tickets went toward covering costs of the senior prom (which was held in the school gym and therefore was not an expensive enterprise anyway.)

When I arrived at Central the initial placement tests that all freshmen had to take placed me beyond having to take freshman English, traditional grammar and composition. Instead, I was put in an advanced creative writing class. I enjoyed this greatly and, in addition, the professor was involved in little theater at the college. As a result I wound up playing in nine different productions before I graduated. This included a couple of Shakespeare plays as well as several others and one evening of one act plays in which I was able to direct as well as play a role. One of the Shakespeare plays was "The Merchant of Venice" which was presented 'in the round' in the Eyrie, the student union building. My brother Gene was also in this production. I played the part of the romantic young man Bassanio and Gene was the merchant - Shylock, the money lending Jew. He grew an authentic beard. The entire production was done in modern dress. Gene won the acting award for the year for his portrayal. The drama professor later tried to convince me that I should attend the Pasadena Playhouse and continue with an acting career. She had a recommendation for me all written up and had discussed this with a friend of hers who was on the staff in California. I appreciated her compliment, but insisted my calling was to the ministry. I suspect this experience of involvement in little theater assisted me in my preaching later on. Preaching is not acting, but presenting a sermon in a stirring fashion is far better than reading it with boring tedium! I was also involved in little theater in a couple of communities during my Air Force career.

Many of my professors at Central had a deep influence on me. Among those most involved with my academic career would be the professors in the department of philosophy and religion, since this was where most of my course time was spent. Dr. C. Eugene Hix, the department head, was the most influential of these. I took every course he taught from Introduction to Philosophy in my sophomore year to Philosophical Approach to Modern Civilization in my last semester. In addition, he was advisor to Phi Rho Kappa, the philosophy fraternity in which I became involved. This small locally organized group was limited to 12 members! Someone had to graduate or drop out before another could be considered eligible! I was invited to become a part of it the second half of my sophomore year. I took Logic during that semester and was invited a year later to teach that class on several occasions when Dr. Hix had to be away from the campus.

A somewhat humorous event in my last semester at Central occurred while I was taking the course on Philosophical Approach to Modern Civilization (the only course in the department I had not completed). I played a bit of a prank with Dr, Hix. His Philosophy course tests usually consisted of a question or two or three on the chalkboard concerning the topic or philosopher that the class had been discussing and reading. His instructions were to write what you know about those questions. Small blue essay booklets were the destinations of your words. The stack of them would be on the corner of his desk and you were free to use as many as your mind and time would justify. It was not unusual for a student to fill up two or three of these during the hour-long class period. Yes, he did read them all, because you would get them back with marks and comments throughout and a grade on the front of the first such booklet.

On this particular occasion, after I viewed the questions on the board, I placed the textbook on the floor in front of my desk, quietly and carefully removed my shoe and sock on one foot, which I placed on the textbook. Then I began to write. Remember, this was my final semester and the last course in the department for me to take. After a few moments, Dr. Hix looked up at me and called my name, "Mr. Jacobs?" Although he called me Bill around campus and at philosophy club meetings, students in most classes were addressed in this more formal way in class. (I never even considered calling any of my professors by their first name!) I replied to his query, "Yes, Dr. Hix?" He continued, "What are you doing with your shoe and sock off?" In a straight-faced look and even tone of voice, I said, "It's called Osmosis, sir." "You put that shoe and sock on right now. I don't want to know what your feet think." All in the class laughed, as did he at a later time when recounting the story.

In addition to the class time and the monthly Phi Rho Kappa philosophy club meetings, I often baby-sat his children (as well as the children of Dr. Floyd Patterson, the religion professor). During my years at Central, Dr. Hix built a house overlooking the city park. One street that ran along the West side of the park included private homes and several faculty members bought lots there and had homes built. Dr. Hix had the framework and basic part of the house constructed by a contractor and then set about doing most of the interior work himself. He hired me to assist in a number of those projects, including when he installed a baseboard radiant heating system in the house. In later years, whenever visiting on the campus, I had the opportunity to visit him and his wife Betty. He was well into his nineties when I last visited and his vision was dimmer and his mind was diminished in its sharpness. Betty wasn't sure she was able to help him understand who I was. We continued correspondence with her for several years after that until her death.

He had a deep and abiding influence on my thinking processes and my evaluation of issues and people.

I mentioned that Dr. Floyd Patterson was the religion professor. The only class I had with Dr. Patterson was my freshman religion class. He was advisor to the Kappa Chi organization of students who were declared as pre-theological in their career choices. In the middle of my Junior year, he was recalled to active duty as an Air Force chaplain during the Korean War. Later, when I was on active duty I had several opportunities to visit with Chaplain, Colonel, Floyd Patterson. He was a good professor and an outstanding chaplain.

It would be difficult for me to choose other individual professors and coaches who made an impression on me while at Central. The list would include nearly the entire staff. Many from classes in which I was enrolled were important in this regard. Some were involved in extracurricular activities or athletics in which I participated. (I skipped football at first because I thought it was for those on athletic scholarship and beyond my abilities and time constraints, especially after I began serving the little churches. However, when my brother Gene came and played football, I re-ignited my interest and went out and played on the same team with him. He then left Central, but I continued with football.)

Now, living back in the dorm during my final semester, the telephone in the lobby of McMurry Hall came into play in my life once again. I found the message on the board when I came back from football practice one afternoon. My boyhood pastor, Alfred Watkins had called and wanted me to call him. He even suggested I call collect! Nice! I placed the call and reached him at home that evening. His first question was to ask me, "Where are you going to seminary next year?" His assumption was that I would graduate in June 1952. I had applied already at Duke, Emory, and Boston seminaries, all Methodist institutions and had received tentative approval from all three, pending receipt of my transcript from Central. In each case I had written the dean and indicated that I was working my way through school, was licensed to preach and had been serving a circuit of rural churches for three years and hoped to continue this possibility in seminary. One had not responded and the other two had indicated they made no promises of employment until the student was actually present and enrolled. I shared this information with Alfred and also the information that I would complete my studies by the end of January and then return for commencement exercises in June.

Alfred asked me if I had considered attending Eden Theological Seminary in Webster Groves, a suburb of St. Louis. Eden, in those days, was a seminary of the Evangelical and Reformed denomination. (It is now affiliated with the United Church of Christ resulting from the merger of the E&R denomination and the Congregational Christian denomination.) I knew about it only because of its location. I had an Aunt and Uncle who lived in Webster not far from the campus and it was right across the street from Webster College (a girls school in those days but now coed Webster University) where some of my Maplewood classmates were in attendance. I didn't know much about the school otherwise, however Alfred proceeded to tell me about the institution. Fully accredited, acceptable to the Methodist conference for Methodist pastoral students because they offered a course in Methodist history, doctrine and polity that had been approved by the Methodist University Senate, and the alma mater of the Niebuhr brothers, Reinhold and Richard. I knew both the Niebuhr names from having read some of their books.

The rest of Alfred's message to me was he needed an assistant pastor where he was now serving at Lafayette Park Methodist Church in south St. Louis and I could have this position if I wanted it and attend Eden. I was surprised by all of this and asked if he could write me all the details and I would get right back to him. Within the week, I had received a lengthy letter from Alfred. I would be paid a sum of $300 per month while I was full time after arriving the end of January and then at half time at $150 per month when I began school in the fall of 1952. In addition, this would put me in ministerial service in the St. Louis Annual Conference where I would have easy access to the Conference Board of Ministry in the process of my ordination. It all seemed too good to be true! That very night I wrote him back and accepted his offer. Thus, instead of remaining as pastor of the Triplett Circuit until conference time or fall of 1952, I was moving to St. Louis immediately after the end of the semester in late January. I returned to the campus in early June for commencement exercises and discovered that I was awarded the T. Cecil Swackhammer award for most potential in ministry. In addition to my name in the graduation program and a certificate, it included $50 prize money. It was unexpected and a nice surprise. I suspected at the time that Dr. Hix was the source of my nomination for this award. He certainly was the source of my nomination for an honorary Doctor of Divinity degree from Central in 1973. To my knowledge, I am the only military chaplain ever so honored by Central Methodist University.

CHAPTER EIGHT

O n advice from Alfred Watkins, I checked on the downtown YMCA as a place to begin my residence in St. Louis. It was not too far from the church and would be a safe and clean place to rent, plus I'd have the advantage of the "Y" pool and other facilities. It sounded like a really good idea and so I began my time in St. Louis living there. My rent was by the week, so I was in good shape financially to be able to do that. No contract, no lease, no advance payment, etc. My room was on about the fourth or fifth floor, I've actually forgotten. I slept very little that first night. I blamed it on the excitement of being in a new place, new bed, and new employment. The next night I didn't sleep any better and I became aware then of the impediment to my sleep. All night long - and I mean all night long - I could hear the clanging of the trolley cars and other traffic going by on the street right beneath my window. You may think that on an upper floor I would not hear them, but I did. My years of living on or near the campus in a small, quiet town did not prepare me for the noise of the city.

My sister Dot (Dorothy) and her husband Bud (Raymond Timpone) lived in Maplewood, not all that far from where we first lived in St. Louis or when we returned after the war and lived in Maplewood. She offered for me to bring my laundry out to her house since she had an automatic washer and dryer in the basement of her apartment (really a four-family arrangement). When I came the first time and told her of my predicament with the noise downtown, she said she thought she had a neighbor who rented out a room. When I expressed interest, she called the neighbor and that very afternoon I went a half block from Dot's to check out the room. It was only $25 per month. It was a nice room on the second floor of the home, and although the bathroom was across the hall, they had another on the first floor that they would use so I wouldn't need to worry about not having access when I needed the bathroom. Since I was paying a little more in my weekly rental at the "Y", I agreed immediately to take it.

I lived there for the next several months, while working as an assistant at Lafayette Park Methodist Church in south St. Louis. It was farther for me to drive to the church than from the "Y" but it was quiet, cheaper, and just a half block from my sister and brother-in-law's house on the same street. This worked out to be an ideal arrangement from February till September. In September, I began my studies at Eden Theological Seminary and took a room in the dorm there. The rooms were set up with a living/study area in the middle and a bedroom on each side. I didn't know anyone there at the time so I took whomever they assigned in the other bedroom as my roommate. This led to some interesting experiences.

My roommate in this first semester was a strange fellow. Older, he had been a salesman of some sort before answering a call to ministry. He was from an Evangelical and Reformed Congregation just East of St. Louis in Illinois. He was quiet for the most part and I had a difficult time imagining that he could sell anything to anyone! He spent very little time in our living area, which consisted of desks facing each other next to the window and a couple of easy chairs and a small coffee table. Our clothes closets were connected directly to our bedroom areas. As in the case of most dormitories in those days, the bathroom and showers were down the hall. He tended to study in his bedroom, sitting cross-legged on the bed rather than at his desk. One day, I came back to the room between classes to find that he had left a little notebook open on the desk. It wasn't really on his side, but sort of in the middle. I glanced at it before pushing it back to his side of the desk. What I read caused me to look further at the page.

His writings were really weird, to the point of sounding like a cross between science fiction and some guru's proclamation. As I read further, I became concerned about my safety in the same apartment with him. People who became headless, others who were deformed and still others who drank human blood; all were a part of his writings. I hoped he was just trying to make it as a fiction writer but I wasn't sure and keeping with the rest of his weirdness, I did close my door at night after that. Alas, there were no locks on the interior doors, only the one to the hallway. I was greatly saddened a year later when I heard that after he dropped out of school at the end of that quarter, he subsequently had committed suicide. I think it was the first person I had known who did that. In my years after seminary, I came much closer to suicide cases, especially during my chaplaincy service.

During the time I was living a half block from my sister's apartment, I received my first speeding ticket. My old 1933 Chevrolet had been replaced (sold for the same $50 I'd paid for it three years before) with a 1946 Plymouth. I had the money to buy it, however, I wasn't 21 years old as yet and under current Missouri law could not buy anything in my name that required a title! Fortunately, my sister's husband Bud (Raymond Timpone) agreed to put it in both our names. After I became 21 the following May, he was quick to encourage me to take his name off of the title so that he would have no liability! Dot invited me to visit them for dinner occasionally and for lunch now and then. On one of these occasions, I was driving to her house from the church for lunch. My route took me along the parkway that wound its way through Forest Park. It is part of the interstate system now, but in those days was referred to by most as the 'speedway'.

The speed limit on the speedway was minimum 40 and maximum 50 at that time. That was the fastest street in town, since none of the interstate system through the city had been built. As I drove along the speedway, driving too fast, I admit, I suddenly heard a slight buzzing sound and looked out my window to see the floating head of a motorcycle policeman looking back in at me! If he had flashed any lights or run a siren, I had not seen nor heard them. He signaled to me to pull over, which I promptly did. In accordance with usual procedure, he asked to see my driver's license. I readily complied. (There were no requirements in those days to prove you had insurance, although I did.)

He looked at my license, which listed my address as Route 1, Robertsville, Missouri, my parents' address. I carried that address on all my driver's licenses for many years after I was in the military because it was easier than changing addresses every time we moved. Furthermore, I considered myself a Missouri resident, paid my taxes in Missouri, voted (by absentee ballot) in Missouri. He inquired as to where I was going. I told him I was going to my sister's house in Maplewood for lunch. Then, he wanted to know where I was coming from. From the Lafayette Park Methodist Church. He looked at me in doubt. I was dressed in coat and tie as I always was on any day I was at work at the church. And what had I been doing at the church on a weekday morning. I am the associate pastor there. He looked again at my license ascertaining my age, I suspect. Oh, really? He said. Yes. I'm the associate pastor there. I reached in my shirt pocket and took out one of my church business cards to show him. He studied it. Then he said, "Well, you were speeding and I will have to give you a speeding ticket. If your collar were the other way round and you were on a religious mission, I might have excused that." He walked to the rear of my auto, with his foot on the bumper, wrote out the ticket with my license plate number and brought it to me to sign his copy of it for a receipt. Then he told me to slow down. He got on his motorcycle and drove away!

I'd like to say I learned my lesson, but apparently I did not. Later that year, I received another speeding ticket for being seven miles over the 35 mile speed limit on Lindell Blvd. I didn't give any excuse, even though I actually was on my way to the Billy Graham Crusade down at the Kiel Auditorium in St. Louis and slightly late! In the case of the first ticket, I called the American Auto Association office, because with my membership I was assured they would represent me if necessary in such cases. In fact, they would even go to court and pay my fine and bill me accordingly. I chose not to do that but to attend the court myself and pay my own fine. (It turned out to be $35 plus $20 court costs. I was lucky that day to have some cash with me because I discovered they didn't take checks or credit cards.) I had opted to do this because I wondered how the process worked, never having been in court before. Bad decision and bad experience. They made those of us who were representing ourselves wait. First, all the lawyers (including one from AAA) were allowed to enter pleas and pay fines. Then, they went through all the other cases before them including public drunkenness, lewd and immoral behavior, and numerous other degrading kinds of activities. I had been told to report at 9 a.m. I didn't get out until after 2:30 p.m. I never made that mistake again. The second ticket, I let the Auto Club pay my ticket and send me a bill. (All told, with hundreds of thousands of miles of driving in places all over the United States and many parts of the world, I've had only a couple of other tickets through the years.)

I mentioned that I told the officer I was the associate pastor at the church. This was true though unusual. I was prepared when I arrived to work with Alfred Watkins to be an assistant of some sort, since I was not yet ordained, although licensed and pretty well experienced after three years of serving the Triplett Circuit. However, Alfred determined that I was to be called the associate pastor and had my business cards printed accordingly. Lafayette

Park Methodist Church was a large old congregation in the South St. Louis area. With approximately 2000 members, it had a very active program and Alfred folded me into the activities very quickly. When I think back to the schedule I was expected to keep, I realize that it was beyond what most would have anticipated. (This was modified after I began seminary in the fall and my salary was modified as well.)

I was to be the primary staff person working with the religious education program and the youth program. We had a very large Sunday school program with numerous adult classes as well as classes for all the children's age groups. The youth program included Intermediate MYF (Methodist Youth Fellowship for students in the junior high grades), a Senior MYF program (those in high school), and a Young Adult program (singles out of school to include some in college). I mentioned earlier that I had directed the music when I went to Dixon, Missouri with Alfred to conduct a revival. So, part of my task was the music program. Remember, I had taken a course in vocal conducting! So, I had responsibility for five choirs! The adult choir was the most important, singing in both morning services each week. Then, I had a senior high choir, a junior high choir, a children's choir and a cherub choir! The youth choirs sang in most evening services. All the choirs had rehearsal each week, with the adults meeting in the evening and the others in after school hours except for the cherubs. They met in the early afternoon.

Do you think this was enough activity to keep me busy? Well, in addition to this, Alfred expected each of us (himself and me) to make fifty prospect calls per week to look for new members. These were not 'cold call' situations but were visits to folks who had visited the church at one time or other or been involved in the activities there for some reason. In some cases, children in the family were involved in our Sunday School or youth group but the rest of the family were not. Monday morning, the two of us would sit down together and go over the prospect cards (3x5 cards with names, addresses and phone numbers when the latter were available. Many folks did not have phones in their homes and, of course, cell phones did not yet exist.)

We would report to each other about our visits from the week prior, making notes on the cards that were kept in card files alphabetically. Then, Alfred would dole out the cards for the ensuing week. As time progressed, some were folks I'd called on already one or more times. Others were people I had met in the various activities of the church. Some were new names to me completely. I sometimes got additional instructions from Alfred. As in the day he handed me a card with a woman's name on it. The address was 1413 Dolan Place, third floor rear! (Yes, I still remember after all these years.) The card indicated there were three children. No adult male name was there. Alfred said to me, "Go there in the daytime and don't stay too long. She doesn't have a very good reputation!" When I went, I found the house, made my way through the narrow passage between it and the brick house immediately next door, climbed the steps to the third floor rear porch and knocked on the door. She answered and admitted me. The children were there (two were not yet school age) and we had a nice visit. She expressed appreciation for the visit and for the children's Sunday school experiences. We had a prayer and I departed.

Most weeks I made all fifty of the visits assigned to me. Alfred had always made more visits than I had! But, then he didn't have to be concerned about the choirs, youth groups, Sunday school classes needing teachers, etc. He did have the overall responsibility for administration. It laid the groundwork for me to develop the habit of visitation evangelism. This became a strong part of my ministry both in the military and later serving in Wichita Falls and especially, when I was assigned the task of beginning a new church in Flower Mound, Texas in 1983. But, that story will come later.

The schedule at Lafayette Park Methodist church was an arduous one in many ways, especially for a young college graduate whose service on the Triplett Circuit was mostly on weekends. The weekends at Lafayette Park were also busy ones. We had three services every Sunday and a Wednesday night prayer meeting. The Sunday services were at 0830 and 1100 with Sunday School in between at 9:45. In addition we had Sunday evening services at 7:30 which followed the youth group meetings; Intermediate Fellowship at 5 and Senior at 6. The young adult group met following evening services. The Wednesday night service was at 7 and usually over in 40 minutes and was followed by our choir rehearsal for the adults. We tried to keep that rehearsal within an hour or hour and one half at the most, but of course, in preparation for special times like Christmas and Easter we often ran longer than that and had extra rehearsals as well. Alfred and I and one secretary were the only paid staff members other than the janitor.

Most adult choir members were easy to get along with. They were all volunteers and no auditions were held to see if they could sing on key! Most could and those who could not, usually softened their voices! I had one alto who was a trial. She was in her early forties and had never married. She complained every week about the music. The alto part was too high. The alto part was too low. The alto part was boring. The entire song was either too simple or too difficult. I listened and tried to placate her at first, then tried to ignore her. Finally, one evening at rehearsal (when I'd already had a long day) she started her whining. I asked her if she knew music so well, would she please give me the names of some anthems that she thought would be appropriate.

Sure enough, the next week she brought me a list of three anthems. The next morning, I was downtown to the music store where we bought or ordered our music. By the following rehearsal, I had all three anthems in sufficient quantities for the choir and distributed them at the beginning of rehearsal. When we had been through the hymns for the following Sunday and had worked one last time on the anthem to be sung, I introduced the new numbers. Almost immediately, she began to complain about the alto part. I listened for only a minute, and then told her that this was one of the anthems she had suggested. Furthermore, this choir could only have one director. So it had to be either her or me, and since I was being paid to be the director, I guess it was me. She burst into tears and left sobbing. The rest of the rehearsal was difficult.

The next morning I was in Alfred's office before he arrived. I told him the story and confessed that I had lost my cool. He listened quietly and then said, "Well, Bill. I have a hard time loving that girl myself. Don't you worry about it. She'll be back and probably not much of a problem from now on." He was correct. Within two weeks she came back to the choir and rarely offered suggestions after that.

I indicated that we had three services each Sunday, two in the morning plus one in the evening. As a young associate (not yet ordained though licensed and experienced), I expected that I might preach only occasionally. This seemed to be the practice in other large churches. Some of my contemporaries told me they only preached when the senior pastor was on vacation. However, Alfred assigned me the task of preaching in the evening service when I first arrived. Within a few weeks, he assigned me the morning services every other week, alternating with him in that regard as well as in the evening services. Right after Easter of 1952, Alfred went on an extended three-week mission preaching tour in Cuba. While he was gone, I carried all the responsibilities of the church, including preaching in the morning services and the evening service as well as the prayer meeting on Wednesday evening.

When he returned from this trip, on the first Monday morning, he asked me if it would be all right if he preached all the services the following two Sundays, morning and evening. Well, of course, I agreed. After all, he was the senior pastor and for me to have the preaching opportunities I had been enjoying was unique. He laughed and said, "Some of the folks may think I'm not earning my keep around here, even though they enjoy your sermons." This opportunity of preaching to large congregations each week was a remarkable experience for me early in my ministry. (Alfred's emphasis was always on his pastoral role. I suspected that he spent little time in sermon preparation, since I saw him enter the pulpit with some hastily scribbled notes on the back of an envelope. On the other hand, I had developed early a discipline in terms of sermon preparation that often took me from ten to twenty hours of study and work before preaching. An eminent preacher once told me, that he expected to spend an hour of preparation for every minute he preached. I'm not sure I always reached that standard, but it was a goal worthy of the task of proclaiming God's word.)

Alfred Watkins had a strong sense that we should be serving beyond the walls of the church. This included the prospect visits I've mentioned, but also visits to hospitals and nursing homes. Then, on Saturday evening, he made an effort to reach out with neighborhood evangelism! Directly across the street from the church were two institutions that elicited our attention and activity. First, was the funeral home. Although the owner (Laymon Cooper) was a member of the Lafayette Park Baptist Church a block away at the other end of the park, they frequently called upon us when there was a family without a church or pastor known to them. This gave me additional experience in conducting memorial services and funerals, as well as grave services in various cemeteries in the area, including the National Cemetery at Jefferson Barracks.

The other institution across from the Church on the corner of Lafayette and Jefferson Avenue was the Saint Louis House. This was a public hall venue where many activities were scheduled from time to time. The most regular of these were the wrestling matches every Saturday night. (If you are old enough you might remember wrestlers like Wild Bill Longson and the Strangler, both of whom wrestled there regularly. Professional wrestling was a local sport in those days with little or no television presence as yet.) Alfred's way of reaching out to this part of the neighborhood included our presence on the curb opposite the St. Louis House, on Church property making our witness on each Saturday evening. The program included my playing my little twelve bass accordion and singing and encouraging any who gathered around us to sing along. The old Gospel Hymns that many folks knew were our music. Then Alfred would bring a stirring message of salvation. I would hand out pamphlets about salvation with an invitation to attend church. This was always timed for the half hour when folks would be arriving for the evening wrestling matches. I was never certain of the value of our enterprise, but Alfred would remind me that if we touched one person who came to Christ through what we were doing, then the effort was worthwhile.

I haven't enumerated all my tasks as yet. One more task was for me to change the metal letters in the big signboard in front of the church. Each Monday morning I would go out and put in some kind of slogan or motto to uplift those who passed by. We had a little booklet called Snazzy Church Slogans that I used most of the time, but occasionally I would use one that a church member had seen somewhere else or thought up on their own. Then on Thursday, I would remove the slogan and put in sermon titles for the coming Sunday. I used to joke that it wasn't really the job of an associate pastor to do this, but the janitor couldn't spell and the secretary didn't like to be out on the corner because the neighborhood wasn't as nice as once it had been. Truthfully, I was a target both Monday and Thursday mornings for any of the panhandlers wandering through the neighborhood. It took me close to six months to realize that Alfred had been right when he told me not to give away my salary to these folks! We did have an arrangement among the various denominations in the area to refer folks to a settlement house a few blocks East where they could get a meal and occasionally some additional assistance with housing or medical problems.

The first time I turned one away left me feeling bad. I had seen her in the neighborhood before but she hadn't 'hit me up' as yet. I was at the bulletin board putting in the slogan for the week when she came up behind me, somewhat startling me when she spoke. I turned to see her standing directly behind me. She was short, overweight, dirty, (in clothing and odor) and had few teeth. She smiled at me and held up a handful of pencils about the size of those we put in the church pews for people to use in filling out prayer requests or visitor cards. She told me she was just out trying to sell these pencils so she'd have some money for her lunch. The alcohol on her breath nearly bowled me over. She wanted a dollar for each little pencil stub. I finished the bulletin board task, told her I wished her luck and walked back into the church. I felt bad the rest of the day even after I shared with Alfred my concern. He grinned a little and then said, "we've caught her in the sanctuary stealing our pencils to sell! So don't feel badly."

Then there was the tall young man carrying a small child and leading another by his hand. The second one was obviously barely able to walk at his young age. The man explained to me that he had just been laid off at the bakery (there was one a few blocks away) and he wouldn't get his final paycheck until Friday. However, if I could just loan him five dollars so he could get some milk for the children, he'd be by on Friday to repay me. I looked at the children and thought I must help him out. Besides it was not a gift to a panhandler. He was just an ordinary guy who'd been laid off and was only asking for a loan until he could come back on Friday and repay me. I got my wallet out and gave him the only five-dollar bill I had with me.

I suppose you are ahead of me now and know that he didn't come back on Friday and repay me. In fact, I didn't see the man until over two years later. By now (as you'll learn in this odyssey) I had become the pastor of 'old' Trinity Methodist Church in the north side of town. (More about that later as well.) I was in the parsonage located right next to the church and a knock came on the door. I went to the door and there stood my friend from the bakery. He had a small child in his arms and two trailing behind him, those I had seen before. He told me he had just been laid off at the bakery and wouldn't get his final paycheck until Friday. Could I possibly loan him ten dollars until then and he'd come back and repay me.

I thought for a moment and then I invited him into the foyer of this big old house that was the parsonage. I invited him to sit on one of the chairs in the hallway and then told him that I had met him two years before and recounted our previous meeting. He shook his head and got up out of the chair and said, "I didn't know you was the Father here at this church or I wouldn't have come, honestly!" I made him sit back down and I offered a prayer for him and his children. I gave him a card then that would direct him to Grace Hill House, a settlement house nearby where we pastors were coordinating the supply of food, clothing and any financial assistance that was deemed appropriate. He left rather quickly without much of a thank you. I never saw him again. I never saw the five dollars I had given him either! It had taken me several years to come to the conclusion that the best assistance we could give such folks was to get them into a cooperative program in the neighborhood in hopes of helping them and guiding them into some self reliance as well. When I married later that year, my own financial responsibilities assisted me in better judgment about giving away my income too easily.

Lafayette Park Methodist Church, through the generosity of one of its members had a four-lane bowling alley in the basement and a good size gymnasium above it. (The latter had been created out of an original sanctuary when the new one was built.) This made for a good location for youth activities. We had a boy's club while I was there that included bowling and basketball as well as other activities. Several of our laymen assisted in these programs and I coordinated these activities as well.

Churches are not immune from the problems of the world, as I'm sure most of you reading this already know. We had an organist at the church who was recently divorced. She was young and pretty and had a young son to care for. Somehow a rumor got started about one of the men in the church and this young woman. I'm fairly certain there was nothing inappropriate concerning their relationship. He and his wife had taken to assisting the young woman in her financial difficulties following the divorce. Her ex-husband was not active in the church, neither before nor after the divorce. On one occasion, at an official board meeting, one of the older women in the church got up to denounce this woman, referring to her as a hussy who was disrupting the church. I could see no evidence of this in her behavior and, remember, I was the choir director. As the hush began to smother the energy of the meeting, Bill Gordon stood to speak. Bill owned an insurance agency and was very active in the community as well as the church. He was a member of the Board of Trustees (the group in a Methodist church with responsibility for the physical plant and all assets of the congregation). He looked at the accuser and stated slowly and deliberately, "The only person you can call a hussy, is the one you see in the mirror in the morning." The accusing woman bit her lip and sat quietly through the rest of the meeting. I don't think the encounter assisted in her relationship with Bill Gordon, but it did end the gossip that had been muttering about.

I mentioned that I had the responsibility of taking care of the outdoor bulletin board. I did fine most weeks with both the slogan and the sermon titles. There was one slipup. One week, I placed the slogan in large letters at the top of the bulletin board. "The Devil has gone out of style, but not out of business." That was clever, I thought. But, I failed to see the connection between that and the little advertisement I placed at the bottom of the board until it was pointed out to me later in the day. It advertised a forthcoming fund raising event the single young adults were supporting. It read, "Strawberry Festival on Friday Night. All are welcome." I'm not sure what strangers thought about the connection, but I heard many snickering comments from church members!

CHAPTER NINE

My years at Eden Theological Seminary were years of intellectual stimulation and maturity in many ways. Here, as at Central Methodist, my professors had a profound impact on my mind and spirit. Eden was a seminary of the Evangelical and Reformed denomination at that time. It was based on what I would describe as an old, tough German disciplined concept of study. All the professors had that kind of background; many held advanced degrees from schools on the European continent. They believed in a rigorous pattern of lectures, readings, discussion and extensive writing. The surnames of the list pretty much sums it up: Pflug, Schroeder, Schneider, Nolte, Arndt, Mueller, Wehrli, and Biegeleisen, to name just a few. They expected students to complete the equivalent of ninety hours of classwork over the three-year period of study, although the classes were not yet identified by hours so much as being major or minor courses. (These had equivalence to the hours later identified as they changed to become more like other academic institutions.)

My class entering in the fall of 1952 was the first class that did not require proficiency in the German language upon admission or remedial classes in the language prior to graduation. This was due to the fact that a great many E&R churches still held German language worship services at that time. I had taken two years of German at Central so this would not be a problem for me and, in addition, I was told non-E&R students had the language requirement waived. The seminary recognized that they had numerous students of other denominations in attendance and made allowances for this. In fact, in the case of Methodist students (and we numbered about 12 to 15 out of a student body of about 130) they offered classes in Methodist history, polity and doctrine taught by an adjunct professor from the local Methodist clergy. (A minor friction among students was that the courses taught for Methodist students were considered electives and credited toward completion of the degree, whereas E&R students were required to take similar courses concerning their denomination as mandatory non-credit classes.)

In addition to completing the necessary 90 hours of course work, students were required to enter into fieldwork programs each term (they were on a quarter system of terms - three during the regular academic year and then one summer quarter. Most students used the summer quarter to work or take make up courses.) My assignment for fieldwork was the same as my employment in Methodist churches over the three years. Even the period when I worked at Sebago School was counted as fieldwork (more about this later). Graduation also required the writing of a dissertation in the final year of classes, comprehensive examinations over several of the major topics - church history, systematic theology, and Old and New Testament, as well as defending the dissertation before a committee of professors. At the end of this rather rigorous schedule, a student was awarded (not a doctoral or master's degree) another bachelor degree in Divinity. Years later when major seminaries around the nation moved to calling this second degree either a Masters in Divinity or in Sacred Theology - Eden changed to match that program.

CHAPTER TEN

During the Christmas season of 1952, a fellow student at Eden asked me if I was going to continue working at Lafayette Park Methodist Church for another year. I told him that I guessed I would stay there throughout my seminary years if they wanted me to do so. I had no reason to think that I would do anything other than that. My friend said he had just gotten information that a private school in St. Louis was looking for someone to become a part time staff member and that it would be a marvelous opportunity. Sebago School (named for Sebago Lake in Maine where the school had a summer camp) was located in North St. Louis in two old, very large three-story mansions that were side by side.

The school was not an academic institution at all. In fact, students enrolled there did their academic activities elsewhere - in public schools or private schools. Sebago was founded and still directed at that time by Matt and Margaret Werner. Matt held a PhD in psychology and Margaret Steele Werner was the first woman graduate from Washington University Law School in St. Louis. Sebago School was a 'live-in' institution for students who were of normal or above average intelligence but with emotional or relational difficulties. There were usually eight or ten students enrolled at Sebago, half of them male and half of them female. Each of them came from families with considerable financial resources. They were referred there from all around the country by psychiatrists and other mental health professionals. Matt provided counseling and guidance. Margaret did the same. The girls lived in one of the mansions with private rooms on the second floor. The ground floor included an office and the residence of the secretary/girls advisor, Mildred. The boys lived in the second and third floor of the other mansion. Here the second floor included an apartment for Matt and Margaret as well as some boys' rooms. The first floor included Matt's office, living room, and dining room for all and, of course, the kitchen that served the community. The basement of this building also included a laundry facility. The staff included two women who handled all the cleaning chores, did laundry for all, and provided the cooking for all the meals.

The position my friend knew about was for a boys' counselor, recreation director for all the students and tutor for any who needed assistance with their homework. The position included room and board at the school as well as $100 per month stipend. If desired the person in the position would also be given counselor training by Matt Werner.

I initially told my friend that I didn't think I was interested because I was enjoying the work at Lafayette Park with its many opportunities. I was being paid $150 per month at the church now (scaled back because I was in class and only 'working' part time.) The part-time aspect was that I carried all the responsibilities I had been carrying but was only expected to make about 20 prospect calls per week, mostly in the evenings. The lesser salary at the school would be more than compensated for by the room and board, my friend advised. Without expecting this to mean very much, I agreed to an interview with Matt Werner. I was so impressed with Matt and Margaret that I returned to discuss with Alfred Watkins my consideration of this change in my employment. He expressed his desire that I stay on at Lafayette Park, but pointed out that I might have more study time in the other position as my workload at the seminary increased. After he and I had a lengthy prayer time together, I made the decision to contact Matt and ask if I was the kind of person they were looking for. He quickly indicated the answer was yes, and in fact, he'd been thinking they should offer me an extra $20 if I would take the position. (As mentioned earlier, this became my seminary 'fieldwork' during my employment at the school.)

Although I was given a room on the third floor of the boys building, I kept my assigned room at the seminary. The schedule meant I was free after breakfast each day to leave Sebago and go to seminary and not expected to return until after the school day for Sebago students would be over. One day a week, I was free not to come back to the Sebago buildings. This allowed me the freedom of using the room at the campus of the seminary for study or rest or just hanging around, especially on my free day and night. On the weekends, I was free to attend worship services in the morning and then become involved in some recreational activity with the Sebago students the rest of the day. I was invited on numerous occasions to sit in with Matt as he counseled some of the students. Afterwards, he would discuss with me the goals of the counseling session we had experienced and why he had conducted it in the manner he had pursued.

The students ranged in age from an eight-year old girl to a twenty-one year old young woman. Only the latter was through with academic schooling. She dabbled in a course or two at the university, but mostly was there at the school mansions all day long. All the others were in academic pursuits, but none in the same school with the others. The boys would arrive home between 3:30 and 4:00 and my responsibility began then. One of the boys was having difficulty with his algebra class. I had taken algebra both in high school and in college, so with a little study was able to assist him in his work. One of the girls was taking beginning piano lessons and since I had a smattering of piano, I was able to encourage her. The other tutoring was routine, reading a paper that had been written and giving some encouragement or testing one of them on spelling or arithmetic problems.

Recreation consisted of anything from taking a few of them bowling on a Saturday afternoon to just playing catch in the large back yard area. I'll share five of the more non-routine events during these months. Two involve girls and three involve boys. I mentioned that I was tutoring one of the boys, Mark, with his algebra lessons. On this particular occasion, we were in his room, at his desk, working on some of the problems he had been assigned. He continually 'goofed off' instead of paying attention as I tried to explain the principle behind the solution to the problem. Finally, I said, "Mark, when you get serious about studying this stuff, you come knock on my door and I'll come back and help you. Right now, we're wasting your time and mine." I got up and headed for the door to the hallway. Just as I arrived and began to open the door, I was aware of something going past my head, followed by a thump in the wall next to the door. I looked and there was Mark's 'dip' pen from his desk, stuck in the wall a few inches to the right of the door with an obvious ink splat surrounding it.

I turned and looked at Mark who was sitting at his desk doubled up in laughter. Responding with what I thought would be Matt's response; I said softly, "Mark, I love you, too." And I departed to my room where I had some reading of my own to accomplish. About twenty minutes later, there was a soft knock on my door. I called out, "Yes?" Mark's voice came back with a timid tenor, "Hey, Bill the bastard. I'm sorry. I'll pay attention if you'll come help me with this crappy algebra." (His appellation for me was Mr. Bill when he was being formal. His favorite nickname for me when he was feeling closer was the bastard term he used.) I returned with him to his room and we had a successful tutoring session.

One late afternoon, I was in the living room area of the boys building. No one was around nor had any of them indicated a need for tutoring assistance. I casually sat down at the piano and began to play a few songs from the music book that was on the piano. They were easy compositions of a popular nature. Jane, a precocious 15 year old, a piano student came into the room. I asked her if she needed to practice, in which case, she could have the piano and I would listen. She said she didn't want to practice but would just listen to me for a while. I nodded and continued to play. Soon, I became aware that she had moved directly behind me and was deliberately leaning into my shoulder and rubbing back and forth.

I stopped playing and told her that was unacceptable. She smiled and said she thought it would be fun if we made love. I was taken aback. I said to her, no, we're not doing any such thing. Whereupon, she moved right up against me and said if you don't do it, I'll tell Matt you did anyway. Thinking quickly, I stood up and took her hand and said, "Fine, let's go tell him right now. He's in his office and he'll be glad to know this." Jane looked shocked and pulled her hand away and ran off to the kitchen in tears. She never tried rubbing on me again. I informed Matt of the experience the following day when he and I had some time together. He laughed loudly and said, "She tries those kind of things periodically. It's part of her problem! You handled it just right and I doubt she'll ever try that again with you." She did not.

Matt had experienced a heart attack about three months before my coming to work at Sebago School. I was told about this in my first interview and told that it was one of the reasons they felt they needed another man on staff to take some physical pressure away from him. He had provided the recreation direction before this occurred. I learned that he also had provided any 'strong arm' action previously but felt he should not attempt any such thing after his heart attack. The possibility that I might have to apply this technique was explained but I really didn't see how it would ever happen. Then came the night when I heard one of the boy's door open and close at around ten p.m. This was past the bedtime for each of them, although it was recognized that they might remain in their rooms with their light on and be reading later than that. I was already in my pajamas.

I discerned that the door sound had come from across the hallway from Tony's room. I went quietly to his room and discovered he was not in the room. Then I heard the sound coming from the steps and later the front door opening and closing. I went immediately to the front door and looked out. This was February and the ground was covered with snow. Tony was pacing back and forth in front of the building, smoking a cigarette. His parents approved of his smoking, and Matt, Margaret and myself all knew about it; although the rules for it were quite strict. Tony was sixteen years of age and about the same height and weight as myself. I returned to the second floor and tapped on Matt's door. When he came to the door I informed him about the situation. Matt told me that was unacceptable behavior, both Tony being outside at that hour and smoking outside at that hour. My facial expression obviously was a question mark and Matt said to bring him back in. And, I asked, if he refuses? Then bring him in any way you need to.

I took a deep breath and returned to the front door and walked out to the sidewalk. "Tony," I said, "you know you are not supposed to be outside this time of night and your smoking is restricted from what you are doing now. Let's go back in and we'll talk about what's bothering you."

He ignored me and continued his pacing down the sidewalk to the edge of the property, turning and then pacing back toward the other limit of the two buildings' parameters. I fell in along side of him and repeated my request that he go back in with me. Again, I was ignored. I asked him if he wanted to talk to me about whatever was bothering him. He continued his walk. As we got to the edge of the property again, I reached out to touch his arm and encourage him to come with me. His sudden movement took me by surprise. He flipped his cigarette into the street and turned and took a swing at me with his fist doubled up. I reacted by blocking his swing and catching his arm as it came back and in a rapid movement threw his arm up behind his back and thrust him on the ground. Now, without thinking very much about what I was doing, I rolled him on his back and sat astride him with his arm pulled up behind his head and applied pressure in what I called a Chinese neck lock. He resisted momentarily and then cried out, "You're going to break my arm. Stop!"

I replied, "I will break your arm if you don't come back in the house with me right now. Is that clear?"

Tony's body went limp and he whimpered, "I'll come in. Please don't break my arm."

I released my hold on him, took his hand and pulled him to his feet. We headed toward the front door. Only then did I realize how cold it was and that I had come out in my pajamas and barefoot! Tony went directly to his room and I went to my room as well. He never mentioned the event to me again and I never discussed it with him. Matt got my report the next morning and merely said, 'well done'.

Harriett was the 21 year old at Sebago. She had been under psychiatric care for a number of years. In the process, acceptable in those days, were electric shock treatments. Mostly, they have been discredited nowadays, primarily because they were done in such a random fashion that there was no real prediction of the results. Some patients were helped and some became nearly vegetables in the process. Harriett had experienced a large number of these while in the care of a psychiatrist in California. Finally, her wealthy parents had heard about Sebago School and, upon recommendation of her latest psychiatrist, she wound up as a resident in St. Louis. I suspect some would have described her as weird! One of her problems had to do with eating irregularities. Perhaps she was bulimic but this was before the term was much used. She would dabble in her food at mealtime, eating very little. Later, she would slip into the kitchen and help herself to sweets. Somehow she had gotten hold of a box of chocolates at one point. I don't believe they were hers but she ate the entire box. Then she became very constipated. Her solution to this was to make herself a 'cocktail' of milk of magnesia and cascara. I was never sure how she got these items either. But remember she was 21 and not a prisoner! The result of her cocktail was more devastating than her constipation! She lived in the girls' building, so I only knew much of this from the confiding in me by Matt, Margaret, or Mildred.

Obviously, she didn't need much tutoring from me. She never wanted to go on any of the outings we had. Certainly, she was not going bowling with those little kids! Matt called me into his office one afternoon. He informed me that Frankie Laine, the singer, was in town and Harriett had decided she wanted to go see him perform. Matt made it clear that he had promised her nothing, but if I was willing to take her, he would cover all the expenses and there would be an extra $20 for me. The performance was at the Chase Club on top of the Chase Hotel, one of the exclusive places in St. Louis in those days. I had never been in the Chase, hotel or club! And I certainly didn't move in the financial circles that allowed me to take someone to the Chase club to see Frankie Laine! So I readily agreed.

Our vehicles at Sebago were three. We had a Ford Ranch Wagon that was my preferred transportation when taking two or three of the 'kids' to bowl or some other activity. We also had a limousine - four door, three rows of seats. It was a huge DeSoto automobile. Both this and the Ford had magnetic signs to put on the side of them that identified them as from Sebago School. There also was a 42-passenger bus, like a school bus and it said on the side Sebago School. The latter was used primarily for transportation of children to the Saturday Sebago Day Camp. I mentioned that the Werners had a camp on Lake Sebago in Maine. This was a summertime endeavor. In addition, they had this lovely day camp in Warson Woods, a St. Louis suburb. It was not used in the summer, but on Saturdays throughout the school year. They had a Washington University student who was hired to drive the bus on Saturdays, making its way through some rather well-to-do neighborhoods and picking up a bus load of kids for the day camp. Many others arrived there with parents delivering them and picking them up in the late afternoon.

My responsibility on Saturdays was to insure that our eight or ten from the school's regular program did not get into any problems or trouble during daycamp. Most of the time, all of them attended. (They usually arrived there in either the limousine or the Ford, although occasionally one or more of them might ride the bus.) Matt would drive one and Margaret the other or sometimes Mildred would drive one of them. By and large, I rode the bus unless I was needed to drive one of the other vehicles. Matt had me take the test and get a commercial license shortly after I began working there. This covered me if I needed to drive the school bus (which on several occasions I did when the regular driver was not available) and it covered their insurance when I was driving some of the kids in the limousine or the Ford.

Matt decided for my outing with Harriett I should take the limousine to the Chase Club, removing the Sebago School sign for the evening. I shouldn't worry about parking, but use the Chase hotel valet parking. Harriett's eating habits had gotten completely out of control by now and she had been placed in a room in Barnes Hospital where they would endeavor to 'routinize' her eating. It was a closed ward, so she had no access to anything except what they brought her. After a week of this, it was reported to Matt that she was now on a regular eating schedule. When he visited her the next day he decided, while she was using her bathroom, to check her clothing to see if he needed to take any of it for laundry or cleaning service. Imagine his surprise when he found little packets of food in the various dresser drawers, each one wrapped carefully in either toilet tissue or a facial tissue.

The nurses and aides thought they had routinized her eating habits, because they brought her trays and when they returned the food was gone. Meanwhile, she was wrapping the portions and hiding them until she either wanted to eat them or throw them away! They later confessed that they had wondered how she had managed to eat so much and stay so thin!

It was while she was in this hospital stay that I was asked to take her to the Chase club. I would pick her up at the front door where an aide would bring her and after the show return her to the front door and notify the floor nurse they were bringing her back to her room. It was anticipated that this would be a late night but that was not a problem according to them. I dressed in my best suit, white shirt and tie. When I arrived to pick her up she was dressed in a somewhat shabby looking gray business suit, wearing flats instead of heels and draped with her fur stole. Even my meager knowledge of fashion told me this probably was not the right attire for the evening, but off we went to the Chase Club. Matt had given me extra cash to use for the evening. Use it to eat, drink, tip … whatever you need he assured me. I had been at Sebago long enough to know that all these kinds of expenses were billed back to the family of the individual student. That's why I kept receipts when we went bowling, or to a hamburger place with the kids.

During the course of the evening, there was an opportunity to dance. Being a good escort, I invited Harriett to dance. And we danced several numbers. I have to confess that I kept a lookout hoping that no one I knew would be there and see me with Harriett. Aside from her costume, she was skinny and not the best looking girl I'd been with! I needn't have been worried since none of my friends could afford an evening at the Chase Club listening to Frankie Laine!

From the light fare menu, I ordered Hasenpfeffer, a traditional German rabbit stew. I'd read about it before but never tasted it. On somebody else's dollar I thought it was a good time to do so. Actually, it was quite good. It was served with some little crackers that were delicious as well. We also had some other traditional nighttime snack food. Harriett's age was such that she was allowed alcoholic beverages and although I rarely indulged in such, I did order us each a gin and tonic. I nursed mine the rest of the evening. Harriett almost gulped hers down and asked for another. I told her I would order her one more but that would probably be her limit for the evening. I ordered it and it arrived and she never touched it the rest of the evening.

Harriett was a smoker. As we sat listening to the warm up acts before Frankie Laine was to perform, Harriett took her little cigarette case from her purse and extracted a cigarette. Since, I didn't smoke I had nothing to assist her in lighting the cigarette. She asked if perhaps our waiter could bring her some matches. So, I signaled for the waiter to come to the table and asked if he might retrieve some matches for the lady. He graciously agreed to that. About the time I saw him coming back to the table, I turned and looked at Harriett. She had taken out a cigarette lighter and lit her cigarette. I was embarrassed and thanked the waiter profusely for his trouble. I tipped the waiter at a higher percentage that evening than I think I ever had before or since! After the Frankie Laine performance, Harriett announced that she was ready to leave. I would have enjoyed staying a while longer and listening to the music, but my job was to get Harriett back to the hospital. I did this. The next morning I briefed Matt on the experience. He laughed as he accepted the receipts I brought him and handed me an extra $20 bill.

One other encounter while I was at Sebago might be of interest. On one of the Saturdays in which I was keeping an eye on our kids from the school, I discovered one of our boys had a problem. Joel was sixteen. He had developmental problems with a stepmother when he was a young teenager. When I was first there Joel carried a teddy bear about with him. I thought this a bit odd, but when he would have a temper tantrum he would take it out on this stuffed toy, beating it on the ground and banging it on the wall and punching it severely. After I had been there a few weeks, Matt made arrangements for Joel to acquire a dog for a pet. Matt told me this was an effort between himself and a psychiatrist that Joel visited once a week to move him toward relating to something alive that could relate back.

Joel named the dog Smoky. It was a mixed breed, probably some kind of retriever and sheep dog, with lots of shaggy hair, some of which was of a smoky gray color mixed with light brown. Joel was sent to obedience school with Smoky for several lessons to learn how to handle the dog. The dog slept in his room next to his bed on its own pallet. He was given full responsibility to care for Smoky, including feeding him, seeing that he had water in his bowl and taking him for short walks and cleaning up after him in the yard. One of the things that became clear was that Smoky would not allow Joel to mistreat him. He was known to snap at Joel, but I don't think he actually ever bit him. Although Joel on occasion would swing Smoky's chain at the dog, I don't believe he actually ever hit him either. The dog would bare his teeth and Joel would calm down. It was an interesting experiment in helping him relate to another living being. A promotion, if you will, from the teddy bear days.

The day Joel had a problem at the day camp was on a cold, cold Saturday. There was some snow on the ground and the little creek that ran through the area was partially frozen. (Smoky did not accompany Joel to the day camp since there were so many children there.) Joel had been out of sorts from the time we left the school on the bus, so I was more careful than usual keeping an eye on him. Most of the other kids blended in with the day campers with no difficulty. (Harriett stayed at the mansions because she thought the campers were all beneath her age and status!) In the afternoon, I noticed that Joel had taken off his jacket and was swinging it around over his head. Although he was not near any of the other campers at the time, it didn't look like a smart thing for him to do, plus it was cold enough that he ought to be wearing the jacket.

I approached him where he was tossing the jacket about and suggested that with the cold weather, he ought to put his jacket back on in order to keep warm. He walked away from me rapidly, still swinging the jacket. As he approached the little creek that ran through the property, he looked at me and with a cry of glee, tossed the jacket into the creek. I knew where the landscape folks kept their tools, so I went to acquire a rake so I could retrieve the jacket now lying on the thin ice of the creek. I returned just in time to see Joel drag a rock from the nearby garden area and throw it out on the jacket and sink it through the ice into the cold water. He looked at me and said, "There. That fixes my wearing a jacket!"

I replied to Joel, "You are right. That fixes it. Actually who is supposed to be fixed by your jacket being in the icy water and you standing here in the cold?" I managed to fish the jacket out of the creek with the rake and taking Joel by one hand and holding the rake and jacket in the other hand, I returned to the main lodge building where I turned him over to Margaret to get him close to the fireplace and warm him up. I hung the jacket up to dry out. Fortunately, we had several extra sweat jackets at the camp that were to be used when children showed up without adequate clothing in the winter. Joel was soon covered with one of these. His jacket didn't get dry before we got back to the school. And it had to go to the cleaners then to get it put back in shape.

CHAPTER ELEVEN

I t was nearly the middle of May when Matt approached me to discuss with me an opportunity to join their camp staff for the summer at Lake Sebago in Maine. Room and board and a small stipend were offered. It would be an opportunity for me to continue studying with Matt on counseling techniques and also see the camp in action during the summer. Most of our kids at the school would be there, though not all. A couple of them would return to their parents for the summer time. Matt and Margaret had a couple of sons who would be there also as summer counselors. I told him I would think about it for a couple of days and give him my answer. Matt gave me a copy of his soft-bound book, The Ironwood Plan, to study before the summertime camp experience. He told me I could keep it even if I didn't go to camp with them. I valued the approach to child development in this book for many years before lending it to someone (forget who) and never reacquiring it.

I came out of class at the seminary one day that week and went to the room I still maintained in the dormitory. As I entered the living room area, I looked into my bedroom cubicle and could see some huge shoes at the end of trousers, propped up on my bed. I wondered who would be lying on my bed, especially since it was the middle of the day. Then I heard the deep snores coming from the bedroom. I hesitantly approached the bedroom doorway and peered within. Sound asleep, fully clothed in his suit and tie was none other than Dr. L. M. Starkey, superintendent of the Jefferson City District of the Methodist Church. I didn't know whether I should awaken him or let him sleep and go on to the seminary library where I planned to work on some studies anyway. While I was trying to make that decision, he awoke with a start and sat up straight in the bed.

"Oh, my. Bill, I think I fell asleep in your bed. I apologize. I guess I was just too tired to stay awake, but I knew you'd be back in a little while, according to your roommate."

"That's all right, Dr. Starkey. I don't mind. I hope I didn't awaken you when you still needed more nap." I knew Dr. Starkey from various church meetings I had attended while I was assigned to Lafayette Park Methodist Church. He was a tall, almost gaunt looking gentleman. The young pastors that I knew who served in his district used to joke about his long crooked pointer finger, saying, 'look out if Dr. Starkey points that crooked finger at you. It means trouble!' I found him to be a most understanding pastor of pastors in all my relationships with him, the first of which really developed that day.

"Are you going to be a preacher or some kind of school or camp counselor?" he challenged me in his first sentence after sitting up.

"I'm going to be a preacher, Dr. Starkey. Of course, that's why I'm in seminary and on course for ordination."

"Well, then, you need to get back to preaching. I've lost a pastor In my district and you're just the man I need to take his place." Evidently, a semi-retired pastor had been serving this circuit of four churches and had died unexpectedly. "Winfield Circuit is a larger circuit than you had in college, but I think you can handle it."

"When would this begin, Dr. Starkey?" I inquired.

"Why, immediately, of course. They need someone out there next Sunday to preach and conduct worship in three of the four churches. Actually, only two of them have services this Sunday. Old Alexandria Church has services on Saturday evening." He explained to me that the Winfield Circuit included the town church in Winfield, Missouri; an open country church called Asbury Chapel; another church in the little community of Moscow Mills; and the aforementioned Old Alexandria, located on highway 61, about fifteen miles West of Winfield. There was a parsonage in Winfield that would be mine to live in when I was not at the seminary. Winfield had morning services every Sunday morning at 11 a.m. following their Sunday School at 9:30 a.m. First and third Sundays I would be at Asbury Chapel at the 9:30 hour and on second and fourth Sundays I would be at Moscow Mills at the 9:30 hour. Every Saturday night I would have services at Old Alexandria at 7 p.m. Winfield also had a prayer meeting on Wednesday evening at 7 p.m. followed by choir rehearsal. The annual salary, distributed among the churches, was to be $4200 payable monthly. All the utilities were paid at the church and parsonage as well.

We talked for nearly an hour, till I was almost late for an afternoon seminar. After a prayer together, I agreed to accept this appointment and he gave me maps showing where the churches were located and lists of the officers and key individuals in each community and wished me well the following Saturday. He would be in touch with the folks in Winfield and the other churches and let them know I was coming. Later, that afternoon, when I got back to Sebago School, I met with Matt and told him of my decision. He agreed that it might be the best thing for me, although he had hoped I would come for the summer in Maine and back to the school that fall.

The following Saturday I drove to Winfield. The family who lived next door to the parsonage was active in the church. I had been told they would have the keys to the parsonage and the church building next door. I introduced myself and was given a warm welcome, invited to stay for dinner, with their understanding that I would have to leave early to get to Old Alexandria Church for their Saturday night service. I found the Old Alexandria Church with no difficulty and we had a great worship service that evening. The people there also were warm and friendly. One man told me he was glad they had found a 'younger' pastor, because the last couple of men had been semi-retired. "Why," he confided, "this last one could put me to sleep during the prayer and not awaken me till the closing hymn."

My routine developed quickly during the remainder of the school year. I drove to Winfield on Friday evening. I stayed in the parsonage throughout the weekend, conducting services in the various places as scheduled and visiting families in order to get better acquainted. I drove back to the seminary on Sunday evening after services at Winfield. On a few occasions, I stayed over and drove quite early on Monday morning to arrive in time for my first class. Occasionally, I would stop and get breakfast somewhere along the way, often just a donut and coffee. (This was not always a wise decision. One Wednesday, heading toward Winfield to be there for the prayer meeting and choir practice, I stopped at my favorite bakery and bought a jelly donut and a cup of coffee. Biting into the donut, I managed to dribble jelly all down my tie! Fortunately, I had changes of clothing at the parsonage and was able to recover in time for services.) On those Wednesdays, I would leave immediately after my last class and drive to Winfield in order to be there for the Prayer Meeting and then stay and assist with the choir. Whether I drove back that night or waited till Thursday morning depended on how tired I might be.

By the end of the school term, my routine was pretty much set and then I started all over again, because I chose to live permanently in the parsonage for the summer months. This allowed me to get acquainted with most of the folks in the various parishes on the circuit through visitation and involvement in the various activities, including Vacation Bible Schools. I was called on, of course, for some funerals during this period. The most notable was the burial of an elderly woman from the Moscow Mills congregation. Don't let the Moscow appellation fool you. This entire community was from strong German stock!

In the case of the notable service I mentioned, we had the service in the church at Moscow Mills and then went to the little cemetery in the community. When I had concluded the grave service with the committal, I was prepared for us to depart. But her husband turned to me and said, "Put her down!" He was referring to the fact that the casket rested on heavy straps above the ground level and the open grave, surrounded by 'green funeral cloth'. I looked at him with a question on my face. "Put her down," he repeated. I caught the eye of the funeral director standing back of the crowd of folks and signaled my agreement. He quickly came forward with one of his assistants and, enabling the device, lowered the casket until the top of it was at ground level. Now the open grave could be seen all around the sides.

"Put her down!" her husband ordered. The funeral director looked at me again for some signal. I shrugged and pointed downward. The device was enabled once again and the casket was lowered to the bottom of the grave. Then the old fellow turned to me once again, "Where's the shovel?" Again, the funeral director looked to me! Once again, I shrugged and nodded.

A shovel was produced. The funeral cloth was laid back and the widowed husband plunged into the loose dirt and dumped a huge shovelful onto the casket below. Then he turned to his three sons and one by one, they followed his example. With this completed, he turned to me and said, "Now, we've done all we can for mama. We can go." It was a good lesson in responsibility for a young pastor! Until he had completed all he could do for his deceased wife, he had not fulfilled his responsibilities to love and cherish her till death do us part!

CHAPTER TWELVE

When the fall term began, I resumed my routine of driving back and forth between the seminary and Winfield. During the summer, I had met a young lady (Elizabeth - and I honestly can't remember her last name!) who was home for the summer from college. Her father was the superintendent at the locks on the Mississippi River at Winfield. She was the dam keeper's daughter! We went to the movie a couple of times and out to dinner once. When I wanted to chat with her, I avoided the telephone! The system in Winfield was still old fashioned at the time. The phone on the wall in the parsonage kitchen was old fashioned! You cranked the handle on the side of the wooden box and listened until the operator answered. "Central," she would say, and then, "how can I help you?"

The switchboard for the telephone system was in the living room of a house located right along the main street of Winfield. It was literally positioned in a bay window at the front of the house and she could look up and down the main street and see everything that went on in either direction. On one occasion, someone called for me. When they gave her the number for the parsonage, she told them, "Oh, the preacher's not home right now. I saw him go into the drug store. I'll ring there for him." It was a pretty good system in the days before pagers, cell phones, and answering machines! When I wanted to call out, I learned early the parsonage was on a party line, along with everyone else in town. There were eight homes all on this same line. My number was the same as the others except it was a long ring and two shorts! When I cranked the phone at the parsonage, it made a slight tinkling noise on all the other phones on the system. I discovered from listening carefully, that others would often pick up their phones when they heard mine ring, or when they heard that someone was calling out. As a result of this knowledge, I never made personal calls on the phone. In the case of arranging a date, I would call Elizabeth and say quickly, "Meet you at the drug store," and hang up. She went back to college in the fall and I never saw her again!

Annual Conference in 1953 was held in Cape Girardeau, Missouri. I was scheduled to appear before the Conference Board of Ministry for approval of ordination as a deacon and admission to the conference in the 'on trial' status. (This system has not changed much, however it has better terminology now … 'probationary status' sounds better than 'on trial'.) A seminary classmate of mine at the time was from South Korea. He had been a chaplain in the ROK (Republic of Korea) army and was now an exchange student at Eden, although he was a Methodist. His name was Sung Bo Kang, but most of us found it easier to call him Steve or Stevie. He became a good friend, I think, because we were both Methodists in a non-Methodist institution. He liked to tease me and call me his bishop.

He wanted to attend Annual Conference and so I invited him to ride with me to Cape Girardeau for conference. In those days, many lay folk opened their homes to pastors attending conference rather than them staying in motels. In addition, the meetings were held almost exclusively in the church facility. I was given an appointment to meet with the committee on the day that conference would open with worship in the evening. Stevie and I left before dawn in order for me to get to the church for the appointment I had with the Board.

We were making good time and, although I checked my watch periodically, I believed we would make it in time. About an hour prior to when I expected to arrive in Cape, we passed an auto on the other side of the road with the hood up and a man standing there by it looking helpless. I noted the auto but didn't register much more than that. Suddenly, Stevie spoke, "Did you see man with broke car?"

"Yes, I think I saw him. I guess his car is broke." This was long before cell phones, of course.

Then Stevie spoke again. "You Christian?"

"Well, of course, I'm a Christian."

"You know story of good Samaritan?'"

"Yes, I know story of good Samaritan."

"Then, why you no stop to help man?"

There was a breath between the completion of his sentence and my foot on the brake! I was concerned about arriving in time for my appointment. I had not considered stopping to help someone on the way.

We returned to where the car was stopped. After a discussion with the gentleman, he got in the car and we proceeded to the next small town where there was an auto garage. He thanked us profusely and got out, convinced that the man there would be able to get him back to his car and help him fix it or tow it to where he could get it fixed.

Neither Stevie nor I mentioned the incident again. I arrived at the church in Cape Girardeau barely in time to park, run in to the office and find out in which room the Board of Ministry was meeting. Just as I arrived outside the door on the second floor, one of the members of the committee came out and said, "Bill Jacobs. We are ready for you now."

I never forgot the incident. It has caused me often to look to see what help I might render to folks along the road. Obviously, my meeting with the board was successful and I was approved for deacon's orders and election as a probationary member of the annual conference.

I fully expected to remain at the Winfield Circuit for the remainder of my seminary years and perhaps even beyond. It was a good circuit of churches with some fine folks whom I learned to love very quickly. Then just before Christmas of 1953, I received a call from Dr. Herman Luetzow, District Superintendent of the St. Louis district. (When I was on the staff at Lafayette Park with Alfred Watkins, the churches in Saint Louis and Kansas City did a pulpit exchange and Alfred went to preach in the church where Herman was pastor in Kansas City and then Herman reciprocated with preaching at Lafayette Park. This was my first acquaintance with him and so was pleased when I heard he was coming to Saint Louis as the District Superintendent.) He asked if I had heard anything from the bishop's office or from Dr. Starkey. "No, sir, I've not had any conversations with the bishop's office. My only discussions with Dr. Starkey were some time back following my reappointment to the Winfield Circuit at conference time in October."

"Well," Dr. Luetzow continued, "the bishop wants to move you the first of the year into the St. Louis district."

"To where?" I inquired.

Dr. Luetzow hesitated just a moment and then said, "To Old Trinity on the Northside of town. This old church is on its last legs, but the bishop and the City Mission Society want to know what needs to be done there."

"What am I to do? Will I be the associate pastor there?" I really knew very little about the churches in that part of St. Louis.

"Oh, no," said Dr. Luetzow. "You'll be the only pastor there. The church can't afford to pay a full salary but I argued that we couldn't send someone there without adequate salary if we expected him to go and help us make a determination about the church for the future. Old Trinity is a venerable old congregation. Bob Adair was there for 25 years. During that time the second Goodwill Industries in the nation was started by him and occupied much of his time and much of the church's space. (The first Goodwill Industries had been established several years before in Boston, Massachusetts in a Methodist Church.) He left a couple of years ago and we've had a young pastor there part time since. The congregation has dwindled in numbers, the attendance is down, and the church hasn't paid out its apportionments for many years now. What the city mission society wants to do is assist in the salary to the point that you can go there and determine its future."

I reminded Dr. Luetzow that I was a seminarian and had one more year before graduation and full ordination. He said he knew that but Dr. Starkey had told him that he was convinced I was the man. Alfred Watkins had endorsed the idea as well. (He was a member of the City Mission Society that had responsibility for expending funds in mission endeavors within the city.)

"When would this begin for me? At conference time?"

"No, they want you to go there by the first of the year. Dr. Starkey has someone in mind to replace you in Winfield if you accept this appointment." I must confess that I hadn't given much thought to a Methodist pastor having the option of accepting or not accepting an appointment!

"Can I call you back, Dr. Luetzow? I'd like to talk with Alfred Watkins and pray about this at least overnight?"

"Certainly," he said. "Give me a call sometime tomorrow afternoon."

With the City Mission Society support, the salary was to be $400 per month plus the parsonage with all utilities paid. This was actually a raise from what Winfield was paying, plus it was in the city and therefore less driving than I had been doing getting back and forth to Winfield.

The next morning I called Alfred Watkins and met him for lunch at the Pig Stand on Jefferson Avenue. We talked for a while. We went back to his office at Lafayette Park Methodist Church around the corner from the diner. There we had prayer together.

Alfred pointed out that it might seem that I was going backwards from a 4 point church to a single church that was on its last legs, but he didn't think this was the case. In fact, he said, the number of churches you serve doesn't determine the larger circuit of your ministry. After more discussion, I called Dr. Luetzow and agreed that I would move by the first Sunday in January to be the pastor of Trinity Methodist Church, 13th and Tyler, St. Louis, Missouri. I was again given the charge that my task was to serve the church and determine if it should be closed, re-located, consolidated with another congregation; and what to do about the old building and its condition.

CHAPTER THIRTEEN

hristmas in 1953 was on a Friday. During my year at Lafayette Park Methodist Church, I became close friends with many of the members there. One of the families that took me in was Pop and Mom Campbell. Pop was a long distance truck driver and gone much of the time. They had five daughters and that may explain why they were pleased to have a young single preacher come to dinner often! Actually, three of the daughters were married and two were in high school. The oldest daughter lived in Montana with her husband. The second one lived in the St. Louis area. The third daughter, Linda, was married to a Marine who was in Korea during the year I was at Lafayette Park. She lived at home and was active in my choir. The fourth daughter, Dagma, or Daggie as she was called, was finishing high school the year I was at Lafayette Park and the youngest, Nancy Sue (or Suedie as we all called her) was in high school as well. These latter two sang in my choir as well.

Mom Campbell often invited me to the house for dinner or lunch. In fact, on more than one occasion, she would tell me that if I were in the neighborhood and didn't know where to eat, just drop in. I have to confess she was a good cook and I often took advantage of her open invitation! For this reason, on the day after Christmas, Saturday 26 December 1953, I dropped by the Campbell household. My visit was not only for lunch, but because I had brought Christmas gifts to all of the family to show my appreciation for their kindnesses. I got there in the mid-morning, intending to leave from there for Winfield and my last weekend serving that circuit.

Pop Campbell was home for the holidays and Mom Campbell insisted I should stay and have lunch before I drove to Winfield. They were somewhat excited about my new assignment just across town as well and wanted to know all about it.

As I was telling Mom and Pop Campbell about this change in my residence and preaching assignment, a lovely, young blond woman came from the bedroom hallway to the living room. I just stared! Pop Campbell spoke first, "Are you two not on speaking terms?"

Almost as though we had rehearsed it we replied in unison, "We haven't met!"

Pat Fairris and Daggie Campbell had been classmates all through high school and were the best of friends. In spite of this and the frequency of my visits to the Campbell home, I had never met Pat. Furthermore, the year I was the associate pastor at Lafayette Park Methodist Church, Pat was the education secretary at the Lafayette Park Baptist Church! The two churches were located at opposite corners of the several block square park. The Baptist building was on Lafayette and Mississippi and the Methodist building was at Lafayette and Missouri! You can well imagine how often folks confused the two places. (By the time we met and later married, Pat was employed as a private secretary to a vice-president of a large insurance company in St. Louis.)

On one occasion, when I was associate pastor at the Methodist church I came into the sanctuary to find a florist carrying in a number of potted palms and setting them around the chancel area. I inquired as to what he was doing. He told me he was getting things

116

ready for the wedding that evening. I had to inform him that there was no wedding there that evening. "Are you sure?" he asked. "Yes, I'm sure. I'm the associate here and I think I'd know if we had a wedding planned." He retrieved his paperwork from his truck and we discovered he was in the wrong church! More than once I carried mail that had been mis-delivered to the Methodist Church down the block to the Baptist Church. But, in all of those encounters and the numerous visits to the Campbells, I had not met Pat until that day.

During lunch, I was seated right next to her. When her fork misdirected a small olive or pickle off the table to the floor, I casually mentioned that she was sloppy! She still likes to tell how she thought I was a smart aleck to bring it to everyone's attention! Anyway, I was immediately attracted to her! Call it chemistry or hormones, or fate or maybe divine intervention; I knew immediately that I wanted to love this person forever!

In the course of the discussions at lunch and afterward, my schedule was an item of interest. When I discovered that Pat and Daggie had often sung duets, I quickly invited them to come with me to Winfield and sing at the Old Alexandria Church service that evening and at the services at Asbury Chapel and Winfield the next day. As I look back on it, the idea was a bit crazy! Where would they stay? Well, I had the parsonage and they could stay there and I would bunk with a next door neighbor who was a good friend. What would they sing? Anything from the Cokesbury hymnal that they chose. When would we be back? Sunday afternoon, since with the Christmas holidays, I had no services on Sunday night. With Mom Campbell's encouragement, Pat called her mother and soon the plans were made.

Daggie got her stuff together and we went by Pat's house to pick up her things and then on to Winfield. The next-door neighbor was not home when we arrived, but I was certain he would be back by the time we got back from Old Alexandria. Alas, he was not. They were out of town. So we all bunked at the parsonage. I gave the girls my bedroom (the only room with a bed in it) and I agreed to sleep on the sofa in the living room. I maintain to this day that my reasoning was to give them the comfort and privacy of the bedroom. Pat insists it was because the heater was in the living room and I was toasty warm while they nearly froze in the bedroom!

The services went well and they sang beautifully and by Sunday afternoon we were headed back to St. Louis. By the time we got back to St. Louis, we had decided to double date on Tuesday and I arranged a date for Daggie with a college chum of mine home for the holidays. It is safe for me to say that the unplanned meeting at the Campbells and the weekend at Winfield parish with Pat and Daggie, changed my future. Within three months, Pat and I were engaged on her birthday 8 March and married on 5 September 1954.

(For those of you who wonder about my old fashioned ways, I visited Pat's Dad at the Union Railway Station in downtown St. Louis to ask for her hand in marriage. I showed up at the baggage counter where he was in charge and before he could look up to see who was next in line, I opened the ring box and placed it in front of him and asked if he could check it for me! He looked at it and grinned and we talked about my ability to support a family while still in school! He agreed that we would be a happy couple. He and I shook hands on it. Pat had not seen the ring yet, until the following day when on the way to visit my family, I formally asked her to marry me and put the ring on her finger. I'm embarrassed to say that it wasn't as large a diamond as she deserved, but it was all I could afford! And I could only afford that much because the St. Louis Jewelry Company gave discounts to ministerial students! Years later Pat had the diamond reset in a small tie tack for me and I acquired a larger engagement/wedding set for her.)

She is and has been the most remarkable thing that has happened to me in my life. She has been the most considerate, most effective, and most loving pastor's wife that has ever been. She has taken in stride every move around the country and the world that ministry has taken me and been a most valuable helpmeet in the process. When I joke and tell folks that the bishop once said she was the sweetest thing about me, it is really not a joke. He did and he was right. She is and has been. Little did either of us know at the time that we would be led in ministry to many places and situations around the world. Our three children will testify to what a wonderful mother she has been and the grandchildren will double the compliment. Every parish and community where we have served, Pat has been the quiet, loving Christian that has touched many lives. (If I go on much more than this, she'll never let me publish it!)

CHAPTER FOURTEEN

I t would have been the proper thing for us to be married in Pat's home church. However, when we set the date for a Sunday afternoon, she was informed that they didn't do weddings on Sundays! As a result, we made the decision to be married a block away at Lafayette Park Methodist Church where I had served as associate pastor. Her pastor, O. R. Shields, did agree to participate in the wedding, so he and Alfred Watkins conducted the service. (A reason for marrying on the date we chose was that I had only one Sunday off from my pastoral duties and my third and final year of graduate seminary studies was beginning by mid-September. By preaching twice that morning - Labor Day Sunday - and having the following Sunday free, we had adequate time to have a honeymoon before I plunged into senior studies.)

St. Louis can be hot and humid on most summer days. Labor Day Sunday of 1954 was no exception. The temperature reached low triple digits! Perhaps 102 degrees! The Church had some large fans set in the two upper corner balconies, but no air conditioning! The church was packed with our friends from the two congregations plus the congregation at Trinity that I was now serving and our two extended families! The service was a simple one following the Methodist book of worship order for weddings. When the service concluded, we passed through the traditional crowd throwing rice at us and got in the limousine from the funeral home across the street! I mentioned earlier that Laymon Cooper, the owner, was a good friend of Pat's family, active in the Baptist Church, and of course, I knew him from conducting services when I was serving at the Methodist Church right across the street from the funeral home. We rode around the area in style, until it was deemed that the crowds would now be in the fellowship hall downstairs at the church. We returned there for the reception. Although we had received many wedding gifts sent to Pat's home prior to the wedding, there were numerous more brought to the church on that day. We opened and registered as many as we could until the hour began to grow late for our departure.

Our plan was to drive to a place in Southeast Missouri for the first night of our honeymoon, and then on to Jackson, Mississippi for the second night. Our goal was to arrive in New Orleans, Louisiana at a decent time the third day. There we would go to the home of F. J. Aragon, a seminary classmate of mine, still home for the summer break. F. J.'s parents were in the wholesale floral business and had a lovely cottage at the beach in Long Beach, Mississippi. As a wedding gift to us, they were giving us the use of the cottage for our vacation time. We arrived at their home, got the key and were on our way East along the Coast to Long Beach. The cottage was a beautiful little house, three bedroom, full kitchen (which they had furnished with all the groceries we could use) and was only four houses from the coastal highway, across which was the beach. It was a marvelous gift to us; and a great time to relax and enjoy each other. Each day was a time of true vacation without concern for pastoral duties or office work.

(We returned to New Orleans the following weekend in time to attend services where F.J. was functioning as an intern. I still remember his stately procession with the choir at the beginning of the service. Robed and dignified in his appearance, the mood changed a bit when he sat down and we saw the bright red socks he was wearing!)

During our time in New Orleans, we had the opportunity to visit the cemetery where my Grandfather Wolf Jacobs was interred. The grave was at the edge of the cemetery up against a fence. It obviously needed some attention and we mentioned that to the staff there. They promptly dispatched someone to look after the cleanup effort. We also visited the antique shop where he had worked for many years. William Feldman and Sons was still in existence in 1954. When we visited, the sons were present and, when they found out my relationship to Wolf Jacobs, encouraged us to stay until their Father returned. He had gone, as was his practice every day, by trolley car to visit his wife in a nursing home fairly close. He would be back after lunch. Since they assured us he would be back soon, we remained, looking around the shop at beautiful furniture items far beyond our budget! Soon he returned and the sons asked him rhetorically, "Papa, I bet you can't guess who this is?" He looked at me for a moment and then said, "You must be a Wolf Jacobs grandson!" I had never thought I looked much like my grandfather, but obviously Feldman thought so. Years later, our son Tom, visited New Orleans and not only took pictures of the graveside, but also pictures of himself standing in the store in the same position as Wolf Jacobs had stood in a vintage picture. On another occasion a group of the granddaughters who called themselves the JAWS - Jacobs Adventurous Womens Society - also visited the cemetery.

We arrived back in St. Louis in time for Pat to return to her job at the insurance company, and myself to the work of the church and then to my senior and last (third) year of study at Eden Theological seminary. It was time to choose my topic for dissertation as well. After some careful thought, I chose to write my thesis on "Pastoral Counseling for Christian Baptism". This allowed me to enter into the realm of interpersonal relations and pastoral counseling and, at the same time, develop a theology of baptism for both adults and children. It gave me professor-assigned guidance in both the pastoral care department and the systematic theology department. When it came time to complete the dissertation and defend it, I did so before Dr. Pflug (Christian Education Professor), Dr. Biegeleisen (New Testament Theology Professor) and Dr. Arndt (Systematic Theology Professor).

In addition to my work with the church and my studies, I had an opportunity to direct the nurse's chorus for the St. Louis City Hospital School of Nursing. This came about because Pat had begun nurses training there right out of high school. Probably because of the conditions at City Hospital (a charity institution in those days and not very modern in equipment or program) she left before completing her work. But she had maintained a good relationship with the woman who was the director and when she found out they were looking for a director, she recommended me. I applied, was interviewed and received the appointment. It meant a rigorous rehearsal with the chorus each week and several opportunities to perform during the year. I was paid $30 per month for this task! (When the check from the city of St. Louis arrived each month, Pat referred to it as my 'graft money'.) The high point of the year was the Christmas concert that included a number of nursing school choruses (all female in those days) each performing one number and then all the choruses together under the direction of the Professor of Music from Washington University in St. Louis. So, I guess, my claim to fame, is that I directed the St. Louis City Hospital School of Nursing Chorus on the stage of Kiel Auditorium, the City performance theater!

I had been living in the parsonage next door to the church on 13th and Tyler in the heart of what would have to be described as a slum neighborhood. My sparse bachelor furnishings had to be expanded for our life style as a couple. This was especially true because we entertained from time to time. The area had originally been settled by German immigrants, hence the German Methodist Church. Then the neighborhood became Irish and was nick-named Kerry Patch. After that it transitioned into a large Polish neighborhood (and we had some of them in the congregation). From that it had shifted more toward a black neighborhood but was changing again. Its run-down nature gave it a different flavor. It was not uncommon to find a drunk sleeping on the front steps of the church or the parsonage on any given morning. We held both morning and evening services each Sunday, Sunday School in the morning before church and Methodist Youth Fellowship before the evening service. In addition, we had a prayer meeting on Wednesday night followed by choir practice. The choir had been struggling without leadership and so I found myself directing it as well. I took seriously the charge that had been given me by the bishop and Dr. Luetzow so, during the first month I was back from our honeymoon, I went to the City Hall and obtained the city plat for the area about ten blocks in all directions from the church. My intention was to visit every house in the area, find out if they went to church and where. If they did not go to church, then I would ascertain if they considered themselves Christians and invite them to Trinity.

I received a phone call from the bishop's office one day. His secretary informed me that the bishop would like to come and preach for me. She gave me the date he had in mind. "Certainly", I responded. I'd love to have him come to preach. I mentioned to her that this was a first Sunday in the month and we would normally have Holy Communion. She responded by telling me that would be fine. The bishop would be pleased to be there on that date. After a discussion with Dr. Luetzow, Pat and I decided to invite the bishop and his wife for the noon meal following the services that day. I knew that the bishop's wife normally drove him everywhere anyway, so this would be ideal. I have to tell you Pat had some concerns. Growing up in the Baptist Church, she wasn't exactly sure how one entertained a bishop! We finally decided he was a Methodist preacher and fried chicken would surely be in order. We included Dr. and Mrs. Luetzow in the dinner invitation.

Two interesting events occurred on the aforementioned date. First of all, when he arrived at the church and I was going over the order of service, he informed me that I was the pastor and should be the celebrant at Holy Communion. He would assist me! Then when we were having our noon meal in the parsonage, the bishop lost a small pickled onion off the relish tray to the floor. Though I would have ignored it, he insisted on retrieving it from the floor. After the meal, he kept insisting they were going to help with the clean up in the kitchen. Pat finally persuaded the bishop and his wife that this was not necessary!

Within a matter of weeks I made an alarming discovery. The city plat showed houses where there were none! Old houses had become boarding houses, then tenements, then were bought by trucking companies and torn down and the lot converted into parking space for trucks. This was an ideal situation for many of the trucking companies because of the proximity to the riverfront, the rail yards and other commercial warehousing between the church area and the river. It was clear that most of these had been taken down and converted into parking without notifying the city of the change. The reason became clear. The taxation on old, run-down, housing was considerably less than for commercial parking areas. Companies therefore didn't report the demolition, but continued to pay the lower property taxes unless the city appraiser found out the change.

In my exploration of the church's possible future, I also determined that immediately West of the church the new interregional highway had been constructed. This was a 'freeway' construction design with access only after many blocks. Otherwise, it swept from the South side of St. Louis parallel to 12th street running north and south and then Northwest to the St. Louis Lambert International Airport. Such highways divide neighborhoods just as much as a river. People who live on the west side of such a highway are not apt to drive North or South until they come to an access crossing and then drive back to where the church is located just across from where they began.

In addition to these problems, I found that through the reunion of the Methodist denominations (South, North, and Protestant) we likely were over-represented in the area. Just a few blocks North of Trinity (which had been an old German Methodist Church affiliated with the Methodist Protestant denomination) was St. Paul Methodist Church that had been a part of the Methodist Episcopal Church (North). Furthermore, two miles South and slightly West was the Centenary Methodist Church, the mother church of Southern Methodism in the area. If I traveled a few miles South from there, I would find Marvin Memorial Methodist Church, another of the old South denomination. I set to work, in addition to my seminary classwork, my dissertation, and preparing two sermons and a prayer meeting message each week, to write a document that made the case for the future of Trinity Methodist Church. Meanwhile, following the habits I developed while an associate to Alfred Watkins, I tried to visit as many prospective members as I could each week.

By late summer of 1954, I was prepared to meet with the City Mission Society of the Methodist Church, Dr. Luetzow and Bishop Holt to present my findings concerning the future of Trinity Methodist Church. Given the items I've listed above, you should not be surprised that I determined that the congregation should be reconstituted elsewhere in the city, the building sold, and what few members still living in the local area transferred to one of the other nearby Methodist Churches. The only area where a number of the members now resided was in Southwest St. Louis County. My paper was over 30 pages of typewritten documentary and maps.

When I finished my presentation, Bishop Holt spoke first. "Bill," he said, "you have done an outstanding job of research and commentary on the future of Trinity Church. But, I have a problem. You have taken in 30 new members this past year, the church has paid out its apportionments for the first time probably in twenty years, and your attendance each week has increased in all categories."

I nodded my agreement to what he was summarizing. It was true. We had received new members from the visitation work I'd accomplished. Our attendance was up and because of that, our finances were in better shape than they had a right to be!

The bishop continued with, "As a result, I'm going to reappoint you to serve another year so that you can convince the folks here that it is important for them to re-locate the congregation." At Annual Conference, October 1954, I was reappointed as pastor of Trinity Methodist Church.

My workload increased when right after Christmas, 1954, the pastor at Marvin Memorial Methodist Church (remember - a few miles south) had a heart attack and died. I was called by Dr. Luetzow and asked to take that responsibility for the time being. It meant preaching there on Sunday morning during the Sunday School hour at Trinity and otherwise looking after the flock and its needs. Pat often says that when we were dating, we rarely went anywhere until after 8:30 or 9 p.m. because I was busy visiting or in a meeting. By the time I got home, it was time for studying. After our marriage, things did not get any simpler for us. In fact, as I got into the last part of my senior year, it was not unusual for me to be up well past midnight, writing or studying. I was able to complete my studies at Eden and graduate in May of 1955. I had successfully passed the comprehensive exams and had defended my dissertation before a committee of three professors. With this completion, I was able to apply for full ordination as an elder in the Methodist Church. I had been ordained a deacon the year before and enjoyed the status of a 'clergy member on trial' during the year. Later this term was changed to 'probationary member' and still later to candidate member! Normally, full ordination would require a minimum of two years of pastoral work beyond seminary, however, because I had been serving churches since January 1949, this requirement was waived.

Pat's life took on an additional complexity that year as well. In July of 1955 our son Andrew John (Andy) was born. Pat gave up her job at the insurance company a few weeks before the blessed event. Andy arrived at 8 pounds 9 ounces, strong and healthy. Pat chose to nurse the baby and this placed an additional physical demand upon her. He was born in a hospital that extended a 'clergy' discount to patients. They discounted the hospital stay for Pat and Andy by 15%. As I remember that brought the eight-day stay to a cost of about $135! In addition, the doctor (Riley) charged nothing for what he declared was second-generation babies. He had delivered Pat when she was born! Since we had no health insurance of any kind at all, these benefits were greatly appreciated!

Maternity wards in those days had very strict rules about visitation. Dads and other family members were not allowed in labor or delivery rooms. Mostly you waited until they came and announced the birth and sex of the baby. Within an hour, you could go visit the baby through the glass of the nursery! You could visit the mother only at strict times. The rest of the time the maternity ward was in lock down! This was especially true of the times when the babies were 'on the ward'. As a result of these restrictions and the requirement for Pat and Andy to remain in the hospital for eight days, I was able to visit her once during the day for a while and see Andy through the glass!

On the day that she and Andy were to be discharged from the hospital, I made my way to the cashier's office and wrote a check for the $135. I knew the doors to the maternity ward would be locked at that time of the day, but knowing the hospital fairly well from having visited patients through the years, I slipped around the back stairs and hallway and came to the maternity ward where I made my way to Pat's room. Andy was there with her and they were both dressed to leave. While I was enjoying the opportunity of holding him for the first time, one of the nurses assigned to the ward came into the room. She looked aghast! What in the world was I doing in the ward when the babies were out on the 'floor'? And, I was holding the baby?

I quietly explained to her that I was the father of the baby and this was my first chance in eight days to hold my son. Furthermore, showing her my receipt from the cashier, I had paid for this baby and was going to take him and his mother home with me! She huffed a little more and left us! (My! How quaint that all sounds in the context of the way maternity wards are operated today!)

The work at the church of convincing folks that the future of Trinity Methodist Church lie somewhere other than the declining neighborhood went well. The City Mission Society had bought eleven acres in South West St Louis County for the establishment of a new church. The property had been a riding stable but the entire area was now developing into subdivisions. The plan was that Trinity would be re-located there and re-named Concord Trinity Methodist Church (Concord Village was the general name being given to the area). The old building would be sold for whatever it could bring and the funds directed to the new church. A few of the members of Trinity already lived in that area and would become charter members of the new congregation. Others might transfer to whatever Methodist Church seemed appropriate to them based on their current residency. On the new property were several buildings. One was the caretaker's home. It was a very nice cottage right inside the gate to the property and would become the parsonage. Another building served as the offices. Here were three nice size rooms that would become the children's building. Another building had been a kind of dance hall and bar. It would be reconfigured into Sunday School space and the final building was a huge barn that could be remodeled into a worship area. Pat and I had been given the keys to look over the area including what would become our parsonage. We visited there and tried to visualize how we might fit into this nice cottage. It seemed very nice compared with the old three-story building next door to old Trinity! At a charge conference in August, the congregation of Trinity voted to pursue the offer from the City Mission Society. Dr. Luetzow commended me on my fine job and told me I would be assigned as founding pastor of the new congregation at conference.

CHAPTER FIFTEEN

During my second year at Eden Seminary, I felt a calling to serve as a military chaplain. Because my mother had several brothers who had served in the Navy, as had my brother Gene, I felt like that would be my branch of service choice. As a youngster, I used to read the National Geographic magazine at school and saw ads for military schools and especially some that listed Navy prep schools. These were designed, supposedly, to equip you for the possibility of an appointment to the Naval Academy, which I thought would be a great education. After I had accepted my call to ministry, I put those thoughts away for a while. But, in seminary the idea was refreshed. I have indicated earlier my knowledge of the Air Force Chaplaincy through Professor Floyd Patterson. Now, I went to the Navy Officer Recruiting office and inquired about the future possibility of the Navy Chaplaincy. To my surprise, I learned of a chaplain probationary program the Navy had developed. It permitted seminarians to apply for a commission as a Chaplain, Ensign, (Probationary) while still in school. I looked into the matter more thoroughly and filled out all the necessary paperwork. Soon, I was contacted and, after passing the physical examination, was so commissioned.

(I took the physical at the Federal building in downtown St. Louis and then had to report back to the office for officer recruitment. Lunchtime intervened and I stopped at a drug store to get a sandwich and a cup of coffee. While I was sitting there an old friend from college days came by and we sat and visited over several cups of coffee until I realized I was going to be late for the final part of my physical with the doctor. So I rushed out of the store and ran to the Federal building to finish my physical. Well, my blood pressure was high! This had never happened to me before, so I was surprised. However, when the doctor found out that I had just had three or four cups of coffee and ran seven blocks, he was not surprised! He did require me to go to the seminary doctor for three days and have my blood pressure checked each day and the results forwarded to him, where he passed my physical as ok.) The appointment as a chaplain probationary in the US Navy Reserve required me to participate in a meeting of reserve chaplains once a month and gave the possibility of two weeks of summer training at a Navy base somewhere in the United States. I began immediately meeting with the small group of reserve Navy chaplains, primarily men who had served in World War II. I didn't have a uniform, but they all wore civilian clothing when they met so this was not a problem. I was told that when I got an assignment to a summer encampment, then I could acquire the necessary uniforms.

Upon graduation and full ordination, I would be promoted to Chaplain, Lieutenant Junior Grade in the United States Navy. In the summer of 1955, now a seminary graduate and scheduled to be fully ordained in October, I was exploring the possibility of active duty sometime in the future. The Methodist Commission on Chaplains, located in Washington, DC was the appropriate endorsing agency for such a position. They had granted me full endorsement for the probationary program so I felt certain there would be no problem in gaining endorsement for full appointment. To my surprise, in early September, 1955 I was contacted. Fred Heather, then serving as the Associate General Secretary of the commission and himself a World War II Army chaplain told me that according to the latest information, there would be no available slot for me in the Navy for active duty for up to the next five years.

Chaplains served in the Armed Forces at that time on the basis of what was referred to as the denominational quota system. This was based on regular auditing of the percent of religious affiliation of personnel in the particular service by denomination. Hence, the Methodist quota in the Navy was full and accessions stood at zero. Fred told me that unless there was an unexpected death or retirement of a Methodist chaplain in the Navy, there would be no active duty slot for me in the Navy. However, he pointed out that the Methodist quota in the Air Force had been recently re-calculated and they were short 23 chaplains in the Air Force. This had evidently occurred because they had been counting all the various varieties of Methodists against the Methodist church quota. (This included such groups as the Wesleyan Methodist, Free Methodists, the three denominations of Methodists that were primarily African-American membership - Colored Methodist Episcopal or CME, later called Christian Methodist Episcopal; African Methodist Episcopal or AME and African Methodist Episcopal Zion.) When the Air Force realized that each of these denominations had their own quotas, the Methodist Church was determined to be short 23 spaces. Now the Commission on Chaplains had the responsibility to try to fill these spaces.

I explained to Fred that I was in the Navy Reserve already. He informed me that he knew this, but would I be willing to fly to Washington, at their expense of course and meet with a committee to discuss the possibility of my switching to the Air Force and going on Active Duty. After a discussion with Pat, I agreed to do that. I flew to Washington and met with the commission. They had brought 21 of us in for interviews. At the end of the two-day orientation and individual interviews, they informed 14 of us that they would like to pursue getting us on active duty. The other seven were told they were good candidates but they didn't think they were ready at this time to apply for active duty. I was the only one who was not in the Air Force Reserve.

At the end of the interview and briefing program, Fred Heather took me into his office and told me the committee was impressed with me and really wanted to know what it would take for me to switch from the Navy to the Air Force and go on active duty. In the course of our conversation, it became apparent that it might take as much as six months for me to get the paperwork taken care of that would allow me to resign from the Navy Reserve effective one day prior to accepting a commission in the United States Air Force Reserve as a chaplain, first lieutenant and report to a class at the Air Force Chaplain School. I shared with Fred the story of the move of old Trinity to St. Louis County and what appeared to be my appointment in October. I told Fred that I was sure that if I returned home and informed my bishop that I was going on active duty in the Air Force in the spring, he would appoint me (at the October Conference) to the Air Force Chaplaincy, and not to the startup of a new church. That would leave me without a job or salary until my reporting to the Air Force. I wanted to be upfront with Fred and so I added, I have a wife, a baby, and a car payment and I can't afford to be without a salary of some kind.

Fred asked me about the time of my flight back to St. Louis. I was flying back on Eastern Airlines 'red-eye' that left at midnight. "What," Fred asked, "if the commission had a job for me in Washington during the time I was awaiting my discharge from the Navy and reporting on active duty in the Air Force?" After further discussion, he told me he wanted to take me to Silver Spring, Maryland (suburb of Washington, D.C.) to the Marvin Memorial Methodist Church where he was involved as a teacher of a very large adult class. They were in need of an associate pastor immediately, and he believed they would be delighted to have me on board until I reported the following April to chaplains school. I agreed to go with him, reserving any decision until I returned to St. Louis and could discuss it with Pat and we could pray about this abrupt change in plans. Of course, I would have to consult with my bishop as well.

Marvin Memorial was a congregation of about 2200 members, many of whom were involved with the government in some way. The senior pastor was having some difficulties resulting partly from the death of his teenage son in a drowning accident that summer. The bishop wanted to assign someone there but didn't want the senior pastor to feel threatened by a younger, more vigorous associate. I would not be a threat since it would be known up front that I was there as interim and was reporting to the Air Force right after Easter. The staff included a director of religious education, however, she and the senior pastor clashed on a number of issues. The Adult Class that Fred taught was having their annual Crabfest. It would be an opportunity for me to meet the senior pastor, be interviewed by a committee consisting of the chairman of the Board of Trustees, the Chairman of the Official Board and the Lay Leader. If all this went well, and I wanted to take this opportunity, I could come at the end of my Missouri Annual Conference and stay until I reported to the Air Force sometime in April. The church would pay for my personal move (not household effects) and provide me with a furnished apartment with utilities paid and a salary and car allowance for the time I was thus employed. Since I would be entering active duty from Maryland, the Air Force would provide for my transportation to chaplain school in San Antonio. The church would provide for Pat and Andy to return to Missouri while I was gone to chaplain school. In those days, the Air Force Chaplain Course was located at Lackland AFB, San Antonio, Texas and was a nine week course during which time the chaplain candidates were to live in the dormitory (military barracks) on base in a temporary duty status (TDY). Families would not be permitted to travel until the chaplain successfully completed the course and then they would be able to accompany him (there were no female chaplains at the time) to the first duty station. I agreed to be in touch within a few days after I had returned to St. Louis and followed my need to consult, pray, and decide.

Fred Heather took me to the airport that evening so that I could make my flight back to St. Louis. Pat and Andy had stayed with her folks while I was gone. Pat and her Dad met me at the airport and we headed back to her folk's home. Since it was the wee hours of the morning and we didn't want to awaken everyone so early, we stopped at my favorite Pig Stand Restaurant for breakfast. I outlined to Pat and her Dad what had transpired. I still remember Pat asking, "You would go to San Antonio but we couldn't go there? And then, after nine weeks, where would we all go?"

"I honestly don't know. It could be Timbuktu for all I know." The next day, Pat and I discussed the issues involved further and prayed together about the decision. Then I called Dr. Luetzow and told him what had occurred. He suggested I needed to discuss this with the bishop in person. So I called his secretary and made an appointment to meet him that very afternoon. His office and the district office were in the same complex and so when I arrived, Dr. Luetzow offered to meet with the bishop and myself. I quickly agreed to that. When we met with Bishop Holt, I began by reminding him that I had been a Navy Reserve chaplain for some time and felt called to serve in the military chaplaincy. Then I told him about my experience in Washington, D. C. and Silver Spring, Maryland.

"Bill," the bishop asked, "what do you feel the Lord is leading you to do in this case?"

"I really feel drawn toward service as a chaplain."

"You know that I was going to appoint you to begin the new church in Concord Village?"

"Yes, sir. I do. I have wrestled with this in my mind ever since my visit in Washington and Pat and I have prayed about it and discussed it."

"I believe there are larger circuits of ministry going to be available to you in this conference, not just starting that new church. But," he continued, "if you feel called to the chaplaincy, I want you to know that you will go with my blessings."

I couldn't have asked for a more gracious visit than the one with Bishop Holt.

I went home that afternoon and called Fred Heather and told him that my decision was to accept the offer in Silver Spring. I would depart St. Louis right after conference and we would be there in early October.

Fred told me that Bill and Jean Strahan would welcome us as our hosts until we found an appropriate apartment. Bill was a Dentist and Lay Leader of the congregation. He'd spent a tour in the Navy as a Dentist. They had a lovely home a few blocks from the church and his office was attached by a breezeway to the home. Although Pat had not met them, I assured her that my visit with Bill and Jean at the crabfest gave me a good feeling about them.

CHAPTER SIXTEEN

The day after conference, when the appointments were read and I was assigned to the United States Air Force as a chaplain, we departed for Silver Spring, Maryland. We had bought a 1954 Ford Ranch Wagon the year before and it was very comfortable for travel. We had a fold up car bed for Andy. This is before seat belts were installed in automobiles, and we extended the side of the support of the car bed that didn't rest on the transmission hump with a taped on leg. Andy did quite well in the little bed. When we stopped for the night somewhere in Ohio, we decided to leave the bed in the car and not interfere with the support system we had built. Instead, Andy slept in the bottom drawer of a dresser in the motel room. With his blankets tucked around him, he was quite cozy.

The next day we arrived in Silver Spring, Maryland and went immediately to the Strahan's home where we were genuinely welcomed. They had two children with their own rooms and they had a guest room to which our things were carried. They also had a big boxer dog named 'Honey' who looked honey colored but we soon learned did not always smell the same. She had a bad habit of breaking wind with an awful odor. Bill or Jean would be embarrassed and run her out to the breezeway to air out!

They had found an apartment in a house where the owner lived in the downstairs while we would have the upstairs. We moved in, but it was short lived. Within the first day, the wife was upstairs in 'our area' telling us not to move anything. She wanted her family pictures to remain where they were, etc. Pat was pretty distraught and we moved out almost before we had a chance to settle in! We found a furnished apartment on Piney Branch Road that was much more to our liking. It was on the second floor but was very new and quite comfortable. The church paid the rent and the utilities in addition to my salary. Various church members brought what additional furniture was needed to make it a comfortable place for us to live for the next seven months.

I discovered within the first week that part of the problems at the church involved the senior pastor's depression over the loss of his teenage son. But there was more to it than this. He had lost his first wife after five years of painful cancer. After a few months, he re-married, this time to the widow of a seminary classmate of his. She had a son. He had two daughters as well as the son that had died. But they were really not a couple. Each morning he would arrive at the office and frequently spend most of the morning sorting through family pictures and other memorabilia, putting things in large stacks on his desk. When he got ready to go to lunch, he would put the stacks away and the process would get repeated the next morning.

In addition to his personal problems, it seemed as though he and the (middle aged single) religious education director didn't speak to each other very much. She would send notes from her secretary to his secretary and he would send notes back the same way. Rarely would they actually encounter one another. I became the go-between rather quickly replacing the exchange of notes. There were two morning services and an evening service. After I had preached the first Sunday services, both morning and evening, he scheduled it so that I would preach in the morning and he in the evening and the next week we would swap places. In addition, I worked with the youth and young adults. The Sunday School was in the dominion of the religious education director and there was an excellent choir director and organist. I quickly fell into the habit of making visits to any newcomers or visitors and occasionally taught an adult class.

I touched base regularly with the Commission on Chaplains and my paperwork proceeded without a hitch. By the first of March, I was out of the Navy Reserve and commissioned as a Chaplain, First Lieutenant in the United States Air Force with a reporting date to Chaplain School in San Antonio, effective April 20, 1956. Easter was the first Sunday in April and immediately thereafter, Pat and Andy flew back to St. Louis. Later that week I departed and drove back to St. Louis. We stayed with Pat's folks until it was time for me to drive to San Antonio. Pat and Andy remained with her folks throughout the time I was in Chaplain School.

There were 28 students in the class of the Chaplain School for that cycle. Nine of us were Methodists! There were two Catholic priests and two rabbis and the rest were split up among the various denominations. Surprisingly, one of my seminary classmates, Art Greer, an E&R pastor was in the class. Art had never mentioned the chaplaincy when we were in Eden together, but here he was in the Air Force! We were assigned two to each dormitory room, alphabetically. Our day began with muster at 0715 each morning in front of the barracks. (It really was considered a barracks and not a dormitory even though we had semi-private rooms and not an open bay arrangement. The shower and bathroom facilities were down the hall.) We lined up by height and we marched everywhere we went during the duty day, in whatever had been posted as the uniform of the day. This might mean shorts and knee socks, in the tan (505) tone. It could mean long trousers in the same color. The shoes and the socks were always black and the shoes needed to be shiny!

We had a military instructor, an old grizzled sergeant named Sam Brown, who drilled us and marched us around. He discovered immediately that one of the priests was very tall and had his own 'gait' and long legs that put him out of step with the rest of the flight. So he named him the right guard, to march out to the right of the rest of us. He told him not to get too far ahead of the flight and told the rest of us not to pay any attention to him or we would be perpetually out of step! One of the rabbis was short and had a strange sort of galloping motion to his step, quite out of step with everything else. The sergeant assigned him to bring up the rear of the flight and try to keep up as best he could!

While we were off to breakfast they would inspect our rooms. Beds had to be made with the top blanket tight enough to bounce a coin. All uniforms and civilian clothing was assigned its right place in our closet and shoes were arranged neatly directly below the clothing items. All shirts and jackets were to be hung neatly on hangers with the left sleeve out! To this day I still hang all my shirts that way!

The rabbi who had the difficulty in marching had been married just prior to coming to chaplain school. Although he was not permitted to have his wife with him, he had brought her to San Antonio and rented a unit in a nearby housing area. Each day when our official release took place at 1630 (4:30 p.m.) he would depart for a visit to his wife. He rarely got back before the wee hours in the morning, had difficulty getting up, and could not get his bed made to pass inspection. Finally, his roommate told him, since there is no attendance being taken except for the daily muster, why not just stay with his wife and get back in time to make the muster call at 0715. Furthermore, his roommate offered to make his bed to pass inspection and it would always be ready since he wouldn't be sleeping in it. (The roommate really was tired of their 'room' getting a demerit because the rabbi's bed wasn't made correctly.) This arrangement worked out fine the remainder of our nine weeks there.

In an effort to 'prepare' us for what was coming, there were lectures on Air Force History (we saw all the movies about the war in the Pacific for instance) Customs and Courtesies. Most of these were given by one of three young captains who were training officers for a number of the courses at Lackland at the time (judge advocate course for instance). One of the first appearances of these captains began with one of them trying to impress the class with the fact that they had 'x' number of years of service plus all three had master's degrees in something or the other. Chaplain Bill Campbell (one of the two priests in the class,) surveyed the class that evening and the next time the young captain was on the schedule, Campbell stood up and informed him that he had surveyed the class. Of course, every chaplain had at least two degrees and several had three degrees. In our class were a number of veterans, including one who had been a Marine sergeant in World War II and another who had flown in that war as well as Korea (with spurts of education in between that led to his ordination). In any event, Campbell told the captain, "you needn't try to impress us with your degrees or your service careers. Just tell us what you know about the subject!" If was a bit impudent, but the captain had been audacious in his claims to try to impress us, and so most of us thought he deserved it.

I need to insert two interesting experiences that occurred in my sojourn at the chaplain school. When I had been in Silver Spring, Maryland prior to reporting to chaplain school, I met Chaplain Vernon Goodhand who was in the office of the Chief of Air Force Chaplains, working for the Chief - Chaplain, Major General, Charles Carpenter. Chaplain Goodhand, a Methodist, was on the review panel that interviewed me on behalf of the commission on chaplains. Before I departed the Washington area, I had the opportunity to visit him in his office at Bolling AFB. He had orders at that point to report to Lackland as the Center chaplain and asked me to be sure to look him up when I arrived for chaplain school.

On the first day in which I had any free time, I went to the Center chaplain office and met with him. He introduced me to several of the chaplains on his staff. Over the course of the nine weeks I was in the chaplain course, I spent most of my weekends helping out in the center chaplain office. I accompanied the duty chaplain on calls, I counseled with several young airmen, I gave the Methodist denominational talk and individual interviews with incoming airmen on two Saturday mornings and participated in Sunday services in the basic training chapel. I was the only one of our class so involved, although I believe the two rabbis and the two Catholic priests also participated in their denominational activities in the basic training area.

I might not have completed chaplain's school because of a physical problem! Actually, I had passed all my physicals when I applied for the Navy reserve and again in Washington when I was commissioned in the Air Force Reserve. When I arrived at Lackland Air Force Base, I went through all the physical process as well with no problem. Five weeks into the course of nine weeks, I received a letter from the chaplain school commandant. This was my first encounter with military protocol that seemed a bit over the top. It forwarded a letter from the Center Surgeon's office informing me that I was overweight and should report immediately to that office to receive guidance in terms of my exercise program and my diet. The letter had gone from the surgeon's office to the Center Commander's office, to the Commandant of the Officer Basic Training Schools, to the Commandant of the chaplain course to me. It requested that I respond by endorsement as to my handling of this request. I reported to the surgeon's office. There I was shown into the office of the surgeon. I still remember Colonel Jules Chapman, MD. He was about as big as a minute and skinnier than anyone I'd known!

It seems as though when I was given my physical on arriving there, I weighed in at 213 pounds and my maximum allowable weight for my height was 189 pounds. (Let me note that my 'playing weight on the college football team was usually 203, so after three years of seminary and some additional time I had gotten heavier.) The doctor examining me upon my reporting in had written on the medical form, 'this officer is in excellent physical condition and I waive the weight requirement.'

The surgeon said he was not waiving anyone's weight requirement. I should report immediately to the gym for an exercise regimen and to the hospital for a diet plan. When I tried to explain that I had already lost weight (due to marching around in the Texas heat!) and that I would lose the rest. He told me he didn't care if I had to cut off an arm, I would not be allowed to graduate unless I met my weight requirements. There would be no waivers! I saluted and departed. I was given instructions that I was to be back every week for a 'weigh in' and should do as the surgeon had said about the gym and the diet plan. I ignored the latter aspects of the advice. Two weeks later I weighed in at 188 and 1/2! (The first week I weighed in I was already down to 194.)

I reported to the surgeon's office with the official weight slip in hand and asked to see Dr. Chapman. The warrant officer who was medical services and acted as administration chief in the office looked at the slip and thanked me and told me I didn't need to see Dr. Chapman. I informed him that I had been told to report to the doctor and I wanted to see him. He checked in the next office and then ushered me in where I reported in military style to the doctor. He looked at the slip and waved his hand and said, "O.K. You don't have to report back here again."

I asked him if I could please have a letter indicating that I had met the general weight requirements without benefit of waiver. He told me I didn't need that. I told him I didn't need the first letter that came to me by way of six offices and to which I had to reply by endorsement. Now, I wanted it clear that my records would show that I had met those requirements. He turned to the warrant officer and said, "Oh, prepare a letter for him."

I said, "Please make it for the Colonel's signature since he signed the one that came to me originally, and I'd like six copies so that each level that got the original letter will have one of these as well."

The Colonel wasn't very happy with me, but I felt that if he was going to tell everyone along the line I wasn't qualified then now I needed him to let them know I was qualified. The letters were prepared and the Colonel signed each of them. I saluted him and thanked him and said goodbye.

We were to 'pull duty chaplain' each evening, but only for our class. So one of us would put on his sleeve the Chaplain OD (Officer of the Day) armband after the last class and turn it in the next morning. The only requirement was that at midnight, the duty chaplain was to make an inspection of the barracks building and the adjacent class room/office facility. Supposedly this was for fire safety. Taking a flashlight, the duty officer would visit the basement in each building to insure the basement was still there and annotate his duty log as to the time he'd made the visit. That was it! In the basement of the class room/office facility was a casket that was used by the class when we did a 'mock military funeral' as a project. Different chaplains would play the part of the various elements of the military funeral on that day. (They used my blue Ford ranch wagon for the hearse! Otherwise, they would have to arrange for a station wagon from the motor pool.)

A group of the chaplains got together and decided to play a trick on one of the others. The night he was to 'pull duty' one of the others climbed into the empty casket and when the unsuspecting 'chaplain OD' came down the stairs of the class room/office facility and shined his flashlight around, the guy raised the lid of the casket and sat up! The 'duty chaplain's' screams were drowned out by the laughter of the rest of the pranksters by the time he got up to the ground floor!

Each student chaplain was to be interviewed by each of the four chaplain instructors independently. And, of course, they each wrote or filled out some kind of evaluation on each chaplain. My interviews with the commandant, a full Colonel, went well. As did the interview with the deputy who was a Catholic chaplain. My interview with the third instructor was marked by a somewhat humorous event. There had been clear instructions to the class that coffee or snacks were to be confined to the break room in the class room/office facility. None were to be taken into offices or classrooms. The Commandant had been adamant about this on the first day and reiterated it several times. So, you can imagine my surprise when the chaplain interviewing me asked if I'd like a cup of coffee. He had noted my enjoyment of coffee in the break room. I asked him, "Oh, will we do the interview in the break room?"

"No," he said. "We'll have a cup right here." He got up and closed the door and opened the file drawer in his desk where he had a coffee pot and several cups! The pot had a cord that ran out of the back of the drawer and was plugged into the outlet on the wall by his desk. I suppose I showed my surprise, and he put his fingers to his lips and said, "This is our secret. Don't tell the old man. He'd have a fit if he knew I kept coffee in the office." We enjoyed our coffee together and our interview!

The interview I had toward the end of the program with the youngest member of the staff (a First Lieutenant himself) was not quite as much fun. He made the mistake of asking me point blank, in confidence he said, what I thought about the curriculum in which we'd been involved and the activities assigned. I made the mistake of believing him - that it was in confidence! I should have known better. So, politely, I informed him that I thought the first four or five weeks were of value. We'd gained information about the chaplaincy, the Air Force history, customs and courtesies, etc. BUT, I thought we'd been marking time ever since. We were now in the seventh week with two more to go before graduation. I had gained more in my 'non-class' time helping out at the center chaplain's office than in the classroom! I thought the marching around and saluting and some of the other activities seemed designed to stretch out the time rather than contribute to our ability to function as chaplains.

I have no idea what he wrote in his evaluation of me. I only developed a suspicion of this some months later. In the first visit of the staff chaplain from my higher headquarters to my duty assignment in Minneapolis, I got a glimpse of this. Chaplain, Lt Col, Tom Shea, a Catholic priest was assigned to Central Air Defense Force (CADF) at Richards-Gebaur AFB in Kansas City. He came to Minneapolis where my assignment was to the 31st Air Division (Air Defense) to visit radar sites throughout Minnesota, Wisconsin, North and South

Dakota and two provinces of Canada. (More about this assignment later.) Father Shea wanted to accompany me to the two Canadian sites (Beausejour, Manitoba and Sioux Lookout, Ontario) since he had never been to either of them. We had a very good week's trip to the two sites, flying to Winnipeg and then taking the Canadian National Railway to Sioux Lookout. Returning by rail, we were picked up by staff car from Beausejour and made our visit there. They returned us to Winnipeg to fly back to Minneapolis. On the return flight, Father Shea told me that he thought I was all right and would be a valuable chaplain to the Air Force. He then said, "You know, the evaluation from the chaplain school sort of warned me to keep an eye on you because you were a bit of a rebel."

An after thought to the experience at the Chaplain School would have to include that some years later they moved the course to Maxwell AFB, Alabama and shortened it to about five weeks! Here as a part of Air University, it was considered the chaplain basic course and was orientation and not training.

CHAPTER SEVENTEEN

at and Andy stayed with her folks during my sojourn in chaplain school and Pat left Andy there and took the train from St. Louis to San Antonio so that she could be there for my graduation from the course. The day before her arrival we received our assignments. That's when I discovered I would be going to Minneapolis and assigned to the 31st Air Division, Air Defense. Chaplain Carpenter, the chief, came for our graduation and expressed genuine interest in each of us, and our assignment. He had recently been to Minneapolis to attend the General Conference of the Methodist Church, which also was his denomination. He told me what a wonderful place it was and how I would enjoy being there. Little did I know how little of Minneapolis I would see!

Pat and I drove back from San Antonio to St. Louis. I had ten days leave before reporting to my first duty assignment. I had been told by one of the instructors that I might want to check at Scott Air Force Base, near St. Louis, to see if there were any flights to Minneapolis. It would give me a chance to arrange for housing before moving my family. I learned almost immediately upon getting my assignment there were no family quarters on base and that I would have to rent or buy in town. As soon as I arrived back in St. Louis, I called base operations at Scott AFB and discovered they had a flight on a C-47 (military version of a DC-3) going to Minneapolis, up and back the same day the following week. This was a great opportunity for me.

On the anticipated day I went to Scott and was manifested on the flight. When I arrived in Minneapolis, I discovered that the Air Base was on the edge of the International Airport. In fact, Wold Chamberlain Field had been an Air Base before it became the city airport. The 31st Air Division had their offices in a small compound across the 'beltline' highway from the airport, an area known as Snelling Air Force Station. Old Fort Snelling was just down the road from there as was the Fort Snelling Military Cemetery. I'd been encouraged to travel in 505's (khakis to most folks) but take along a class A uniform (Class A referred to trousers, coat called a blouse, blue shirt and tie) to wear while there. This I did.

I had the opportunity to meet with the staff chaplain (who would be my boss) Chaplain, Major, Ransom B. (Bud) Woods. He told me that although he and I were the 'site' chaplains, he had been sharing some of the TDY (temporary) duty time with the two chaplains assigned to the base (475th Fighter Group) program. Both Captains, Ken Hamstra and Jim Dean would go about one week per month to cover some of the sites. Now with me on board, that would continue and it would allow me to also spend some time in the base program in order to get experience in base chapel activity. The base Catholic program was covered by Father Bob Vashro; who was an Air Force National Guard Major and the dean of students at a local university. He came for daily mass most days and on Sunday morning as well. Part of his duties covered his Air Guard responsibilities and partly he was hired as a contract auxiliary chaplain.

With some guidance from these folks and a local real estate agent, I located a new house being built that we could buy for $650 down payment plus a $25 credit check fee. It was a nice three bedroom home, two bath, single car garage and not too far from the base. I had brought my checkbook with me and so I signed the paperwork and wrote the check. I had come on active duty in what the Air Force called a three year stated tour. The chaplains told me that with chaplain school behind me, I probably would spend the entire time there in Minneapolis, unless I were to be offered and accept an extension or become a 'reserve indefinite'. It seemed to me more prudent to buy a house and perhaps sell it for a small profit than to pay rent. Pat and I had discussed this before I left and she agreed.

The flight back to St. Louis was uneventful. I changed back into my khakis (505s) for the flight. When we got back to Scott AFB, I grabbed my clothes hanger from the rod in the back of the plane and got off quickly. Pat's dad had brought her over to pick me up. You can imagine my dismay when I got home and started to hang up my other uniform to discover that the trousers had slipped off the hanger (evidently in the plane) and all I had was my class A blouse (jacket). Pat teased me for years about how on my first trip away I lost my pants! I was glad that I had bought this set of uniforms with two pair of matching trousers!

We made a decision that I should drive to Minneapolis and get settled in since the house was not yet finished and then take leave to come back and get her and Andy. When I arrived and signed in, I moved temporarily into the BOQ (bachelor officer quarters) where I had a bedroom and bath and shared a kitchenette with another officer. Within two weeks, and before the new house would be ready, we had a visit from the Air Defense Command Chaplain, headquartered in Colorado Springs, Colorado. He told me not to get too comfortable because I was number three on the overseas list in the command. "The chief's office likes to get one overseas tour out of you fellows on three year stated tours before you get out of the service. This usually means you go remote after you have been on active duty about a year. The alternative to this is to offer you an accompanied tour, but you have to either apply for indefinite status or at least extend your stated tour."

I thought about that a long time and finally asked the other chaplains there if this was true. They all agreed that they had experienced the same thing. With that information, I called Pat to see what she thought we ought to do. I didn't want to own a house in Minneapolis (actually the suburb of Bloomington, Minnesota) if I was going to leave within a year and go overseas. We decided it might make more sense to rent for the year I would be there rather than buy. I called the agent with whom I had been working on buying the house and told him what I had learned. He agreed that if I would put it in writing, they would cancel the contract and refund my down payment. When I did this, he not only refunded the down payment but actually gave me back the money I had paid for the credit check, which he would not have to do since the contract said that it was non-refundable!

Then I began looking for a place to rent and found one just a few blocks from the house we were going to buy. It was almost identical to the new house except that it was several years old. The house belonged to a sergeant who had been sent to Goose Bay, Labrador. He was willing to rent to me for $125 per month. I would pay my own utilities, of course. Any major repairs, he would pay if I just notified him at the time. He did pay for a septic tank repair during the first year. In fact, he also paid for the materials for a fence around the yard that I installed so that the puppy we later acquired wouldn't run away!

With a house ready, I made arrangements for leave time to go to St. Louis and bring Pat and Andy back with me to Minneapolis. The government shipped what little furniture we owned from St. Louis. We met a gentleman through some new friends who was in the furniture business in the area and who liked giving GIs a good deal. We bought several things from him over the next couple of years, always at a good discount! Soon we were established in our situation in the rent house.

Within a matter of months of arriving, the senior chaplain, 31st Air Division, received an assignment overseas. When this occurred it was several months before his replacement arrived. During this time I organized a 'first ever' conference for all the auxiliary civilian chaplains (pastors and priests) who were serving at our remote sites in the four states. We brought them into Minneapolis at Air Force expense, housed them on base, and gave them briefings and tours so that they would be in tune with what we were doing and their significant part in it at the site near their community. With Chaplain Woods gone, I spent more and more time in temporary duty visiting the sites and less and less time in any of the base activities. Part of this was a relief, because the first three Fridays we were in Minneapolis (before Pat and Andy had joined me) we had aircraft accidents. In two of these I was duty chaplain and responded accordingly. One of these was an air-to-air collision of two fighter aircraft 'running intercepts' on each other. The second was a horrible accident in which an F-89 slid off the end of the runway and into an automobile parked in a no-parking, low flying aircraft area. In the automobile were a grandmother and three children, 'watching' the airplanes. All were killed along with the pilot and radar controller in the back seat. The third one, I did not respond initially, but I did wind up being the chaplain responsible for meeting with the family and eventually conducting a memorial service and burial at the Ft. Snelling Cemetery.

This gave me experience in working with the family of a deceased military member. It was an unusual situation because the pilot had recently divorced but had not changed any of his paperwork concerning survivors' benefits. As a result, there was a huge clash between his ex-wife and his mother. Each claimed that they were the appropriate beneficiary, not only of his insurance, but also of the right to determine where and how he would be buried! I stayed out of the insurance aspect of the situation and allowed the lawyers and the military advisors to handle all of that. However, I couldn't stay out of the other aspect of the situation since we had to make some decisions about burial. I was able to convince them both that he had indicated a desire to be buried in a national cemetery and since Fort Snelling was in the immediate area, this made sense. So we proceeded with a service at the Fort Snelling Chapel and burial there in the national cemetery. I was relieved that my part in the matter resulted in some amicable result.

After a ninety-day gap, the new senior chaplain arrived. He was not happy to be there and within the first three months was in an auto accident that left him in the VA hospital with multiple injuries. During this period, I continued to be the staff chaplain and make almost all the site visits. This meant I was 'on the road' most of the time. I was in Gettysburg, South Dakota when I received word that Pat had been taken to the hospital because she was having a miscarriage. The chaplain from the base level who called me with the information told me, "These things happen all the time. She'll be fine. You don't have to come back from your TDY."

I thanked him and hung up and immediately signed out at the orderly room and headed for Minneapolis. Perhaps these things happen all the time, but this is the first time it had happened to Pat and I wasn't staying 400 miles away! Pat came through the physical part of the problem with little difficulty but such events always carry their own scars emotionally, not only for Pat but for myself as well.

Before the 'new' staff chaplain got out of the hospital, I got a call from Chaplain Shea at Central Air Defense Force (our next higher headquarters) saying that the senior fellow was on the RIF list. (Reduction in force programs have occurred at various times, this one in late 1957 and included over 100 senior chaplains. The one involved in Minneapolis was a major. He later re-enlisted as a staff sergeant to finish out a twenty-year career!) Father Shea said that he was coming to Minneapolis himself to inform the chaplain in person rather than on the phone since he was hospitalized. This occurred. It was a devastating blow to the chaplain. Over the months ahead, he managed to get himself extended several times in order to not be discharged, remaining away from the office on 'convalescent status.'

At one point, the commander of the 31st Air Division called the Chief of Chaplain's office to see how much longer it would be until the discharge took place. The chief's office was surprised that he was still on active duty. They thought he'd been released months before. During this time, he was either in the hospital or on convalescent leave and did no actual duties. I continued to visit all the sites as well as attend the division headquarters staff meetings when in town.

During this period I was asked to counsel with a young airman in the base 'stockade' or confinement facility. He was a clean-cut young man whose nickname covered his origin - "Kentucky". When I read the charges against him prior to visiting with him, I noted that he had worked in the motor pool as a driver and taken a battery from the shop to put in his own automobile. When he was confronted with this he admitted he had done so but intended to put it back as soon as payday allowed him to buy a new battery. The one he'd 'borrowed' was actually old and on a re-charger when he 'borrowed' it. At the time of his 'arrest' they inspected his wall locker and found he also had a government issued 45 caliber pistol (for which he had no authorization) and a government issued jacket he had not signed for. So the charges were pretty serious!

During our visit, he confessed these things and more to me and also that he knew he'd not been living in accordance with the moral principles by which he'd been raised. He wanted to make a clean start with God as well as the Air Force. We prayed together and he confessed all these things to God as well. In our discussion afterwards, I indicated to him that confession was a good thing for him so that he could get a clean start with his life.

The following week I received a call from the major who was the staff judge advocate (lawyer) in the headquarters. He told me I was crazy to tell anyone that confession was good! "Kentucky" had signed a written confession for all these things and more with the Office of Special Investigation (OSI = the Air Force FBI or the TV popularized Navy NCI). It was going to make it impossible to defend "Kentucky" when he went to trial. I explained to the major

that I had only meant for him to confess to God and it had nothing
to do with the legal proceedings that were pending!

He remained in the stockade for several more weeks, however,
when I returned from one of my site visit tours I got word he wanted
to see me. I went to the facility and visited with him. He explained
that he wanted to get back to work and prove that he could be a
good airman! Afterwards, I spoke with the headquarters squadron
commander and asked if there was a reason for him to continue to
sit in the stockade until his case was resolved when it would make
more sense to put him to work somewhere. The commander agreed
and the following day, "Kentucky" was 'sprung' from the stockade
and assigned back to the motor pool. The second day he was back, he
happened to be the only airman available to drive General Matheny
somewhere in the staff car. His appearance and bearing were so
good, that the general asked for him the following day to be his
driver on another trip. The executive officer called me and asked if
I would be willing to speak to the general about this young man's
record. I suspected at the time that the 'exec' thought he was a 'risk'
of some variety. I agreed to do so and made an appointment with
the general. When I told him the story about "Kentucky" and his
'confession', the general (a strong Roman Catholic) laughed and
said, he's my kind of airman. Subsequently, he was assigned as
the general's regular driver, however, "Kentucky" was concerned
because his case was still pending! I spoke with the judge advocate
about this and asked if there was a way to resolve the issue. His
answer to me was, "I've just got an assignment to Thule, Greenland.
When I leave the paperwork on Kentucky will disappear with me.
There will be no case!" This occurred in the following months and
"Kentucky" finished out his enlistment as the general's driver! As in
many situations in which a chaplain is involved, I never knew what
happened to him after he was discharged, although I heard he'd
gone back to Kentucky!

In January 1958, I received a call from Father Shea informing me
that I was designated to attend a month long seminar in Family and

Marriage Counseling at the University of Texas, Hogg Foundation in Austin, Texas. Evidently, the chaplain tapped for this program also had been on the RIF list and so was ineligible to attend and I was the alternate. Pat had become pregnant again and the baby was due the middle of February. I still remember telling Chaplain Shea that I didn't think it was a wise thing for me to be gone, especially since we had lost the baby the year before. He informed me gently, 'war is hell'. You have to go.

So on January 15, 1958, I flew into Austin, Texas to attend the first seminar the Air Force sponsored with the Hogg Foundation at the University of Texas. I remember the last words Pat said as she put me on the plane, 'you better learn a lot about marriage counseling, you may need it when you return!'

The seminar was attended by 30 chaplains from around the Air Force and was conducted by Dr. Bernice Moore and Dr. Glenn Ramsey. Dr. Moore was a staff professor in family counseling at the University and Dr. Ramsey was a psychiatrist in private practice in Austin. The seminar was extremely well organized and quite good. Many of the other chaplains in attendance were good colleagues through the years, although I was never stationed with any of them subsequently. I called Pat at least once a week to see how she was doing and got good responses. On February 14, 1958 (Valentine's day) the seminar ended and I was on the first commercial flight I could arrange from Austin to Minneapolis by way of St. Louis, arriving late at night. Pat had a neighbor boy staying with Andy and she met me at the airport. We got back to our 'rent house' at nearly midnight. I was tired and dirty from the trip and decided to take a shower before going to bed. As I got out of the shower, Pat informed me that her water had broken and we needed to go to the hospital.

I went next door and awakened the neighbor and their teenage son came back over to care for Andy and we were in the car and on our way. By the time we got to the area of the hospital it was nearly 2 a.m. and dark and everything was covered with snow! I had only been to that hospital on one occasion and couldn't be sure where it was! Believe it or not, a man was out walking a dog at that hour - and when I asked about the hospital, he directed me to the next block and turn right and it was only two blocks from there. We made it fine. That morning around 7, the doctor came to inform me that we had a beautiful little girl in our family. Pat had told him she wasn't having that baby till I got home and he commended her on her self-control! So Tamara Jane (Tami) joined our little family.

I resumed my site visitation, now covering all the sites by myself every month. I would be gone for two weeks at a time, home long enough to file my paperwork and receive another set of orders and head out in a different direction. The Air Force was in the process of 'augmenting' the regular officer ranks. Regular officers had certain advantages over against Reserve officers, presumably, in promotions and assignments and protection from future RIF events. I was notified that I had been selected for promotion to Captain and augmentation to the regular corps. I would have to make my decision within 30 days. Pat and I talked about it and we prayed about it as we did all such decisions. Then came a fateful Sunday afternoon. I had returned home on Saturday and planned on Monday to file paperwork and get new orders for the month and depart. We were on a nice Sunday afternoon drive. As she often did, Pat asked about my upcoming itinerary.

"I'll leave on Monday after I get my paperwork set up, and drive to Gettysburg, South Dakota. I'll be there for two days and then on Thursday drive to Finley, North Dakota. That Sunday I'll be at Grand Forks (a new Air base that did not yet have a chaplain assigned but was in the process of converting from an ADC (Air Defense Command) installation to a SAC (Strategic Air Command) installation. After that on Tuesday I'll come back to Wadena, Minnesota and then to Willmar, Minnesota."

About that time, Andy, who was standing in the middle of the back seat - no seat belts in those days- asked, "Daddy, then are you coming to visit us for a while?" It was a defining moment. My son saw me as a visitor who came now and then. Although it took me several days to make the decision, I think the seeds were planted right then.

I discussed my situation with the commander of the 31st Air Division. I went to personnel and declined the promotion and the offer of a regular commission and requested release from active duty on the ending date of my three year stated tour, which would be in April 1959. When it was approved, the date of my release was moved back to 1 March since the division was shutting down on that date. The Air Defense Command was in a major reorganization program in which they were establishing 'SAGE sectors'. (SAGE = Semi-automatic ground environment, a new and highly automated radar system that would put many of the sites out of business.)

Within a few days, I wrote my bishop in St. Louis to inform him of my release from active duty on 1 March and requested a pastoral assignment. The bishop had changed since my departure with the retirement of my previous bishop and the election of a new man. He wrote back and assured me there would be a place for me when I arrived, to come by his office as soon as I was back in St. Louis. (Those of you who understand the Methodist system of appointments will know that once a pastor is ordained and a full member of a conference, he is subject to a guaranteed appointment to a church within the conference. This is under review in Methodist circles today and may be changed by the time you read this.)

One sergeant was left in the office along with myself. We closed out the 31st Air Division as an entity. He was reassigned to Richards-Gebaur in Kansas City after I made a special request for him. Initially, they told him he was going to Grand Forks, North Dakota. He came to me and asked if I would help him get it changed. His reasons were that as an African American he knew there was no black community in Grand Forks, however, there was a large black community in Kansas City and he and his family would be more at home there. One phone call to the personnel people and they were able to change his assignment.

Meanwhile the base at Wold Chamberlain Field, 475th fighter Group, 432nd Fighter Squadron was also undergoing a change. The unit would be phased out, the aircraft turned over to the Minnesota Air National Guard (currently flying older aircraft from an old and smaller field in St. Paul). Chaplains assigned to the new SAGE sectors (for my area of responsibility it would be Grand Forks and Duluth) would provide the site coverage. The Air National Guard had chaplains who would provide the local coverage for the base. (This included Father Bob Vashro who also had been our civilian Catholic chaplain for several years and was a Major in the Guard.) On 1 March 1959, I was released from active duty, had our household goods shipped to St. Louis to be held for us and collected my final paycheck and travel allowances. We departed for St. Louis, planning to stay with Pat's folks until my assignment by the bishop gave us a parsonage to move into.

CHAPTER EIGHTEEN

The day after arriving in St. Louis, I called the bishop's office for an appointment when I might discuss with him where I was to serve. When I arrived the next morning, he was most cordial and then told me there wouldn't be anything available until conference the end of May when annual appointments would be made. It was almost as though he had not written me the letter that implied there would be a place for me to serve upon my return. I explained to him that had I known this, I might have extended until the May date (although I have no idea if that would have been possible with the closing of the headquarters). He apologized for any misunderstanding and assured me that my name would be on the list for an appointment at conference.

I left his office somewhat disheartened as to the next couple of months. Obviously, we could avoid any major expenses by staying with Pat's folks. On the other hand, we would have normal expenses of buying baby food and maintaining our automobile. I felt like Pat and I needed some time just to relax and had always wanted to make a visit to Mexico and this might be the time. I had funds from my final paycheck that included unused leave pay as well as travel allowance. When Pat's folks offered to take care of Tami (our daughter) while we made a trip to Mexico (Andy would go with us), we decided to do it.

We had a great time in Mexico for the most part! (Well, Andy and I had a great time. Pat not so much as you'll soon see.) We stopped in Austin, Texas on the way and chatted with Dr. Glenn Ramsey. He had made many trips to Mexico and gave us some valuable advice about our plans. We drove to Laredo, Texas the next night. (Pat can tell you that she didn't sleep a wink all night counting the cockroaches on the wall!) The next day we drove to Monterey where we'd been told we would find a Methodist mission program with an orphanage. We had a chance to tour that facility. Then we went on to Saltillo, which is beautiful and friendly. Dr. Ramsey had suggested that if we parked the automobile on a public street and some boys offered to watch it for a dollar, we should agree to do so, not giving them the dollar until we returned. (Otherwise, he suggested they would steal our hubcaps. This way, they would protect us from some other boys stealing them!) We found exactly what he had described as the case and agreed to pay the boy a dollar for watching our car.

The next day we drove to San Miguel de Allende, a town that had attracted a considerable number of American artists and writers. It is a colonial town, with a beautiful town square and cathedral at the plaza in the center of the town. We stayed at a recommended motel right on the plaza. The accommodations were more than adequate. The following morning was a Sunday and we awoke at sunrise with a huge explosion noise followed by several others! I thought the civil war had begun and we were in the middle of it. Later we were told by the clerk that they did this at sunrise every Sunday in order to scare away any evil spirits that might be lurking and trying to keep folks from attending church!

I set out with my phrase book in hopes of finding someone who might direct me to any Methodist church in the area. When several seemingly nice folks couldn't understand what I meant by

Methodist, I switched to Protestant. Then I was told unequivocally, 'no Protestante aqui - todas Catolica.' No Protestants here, all is Catholic! We enjoyed our visit there and proceeded on to Mexico City, again staying in a motel that Dr. Ramsey had recommended. It was also a very nice facility. Unfortunately, the second day there, Pat became ill. We soon learned her illness variously was referred to as the touristies or Montezuma's revenge! She was so ill, that we asked the motel clerk to call the English speaking doctor who was available to them, who came and diagnosed our problem exactly as the clerk had suspected. She was asked if she'd been careful about drinking the water. "Oh, yes." She had drunk ice tea! Although the tea was boiled and therefore safe, the ice cubes in it probably were not! Pat stayed in the motel room for the next several days while Andy and I made short day trips to places in the city. Pat was just about over her problem when we left to drive back to St. Louis.

When we arrived back in St. Louis, I discovered I had received a telephone call suggesting I contact the Reverend John Taylor at the Conference Secretary of Education office. I had known John when he was pastor of the Methodist Church in Maplewood and was active in the various Methodist Youth Camps at Epworth Among the Hills, the conference youth camp in Arcadia, Missouri. The office of the Conference Secretary of Education was at that time responsible for most of the conference activities outside of the bishop's office and the offices of the various superintendents. This included directing the organization of the summer youth camps as well as the organization of the annual conference activities.

When I reached John at his office, he asked me if I could come by and visit with him about a possible job. We had a good visit in which he told me he did not have a conference youth director anymore and, as a result, none of the summer camp activities had been organized and staffed with the volunteers that would be needed for programs. The camp had a permanent staff for maintenance, food service and other portions of the summer program. He offered me the job of being the temporary conference youth director to set all this up and organize it as well as the annual conference sessions and reports. I would receive an appointment at conference time and he knew this, but hoped then to be able to find a permanent youth director for the conference.

I immediately agreed to the offer. I spent the next couple of months in getting pastors and lay folk to volunteer for work in the various youth camps all summer long. In addition, I set up a system for annual conference reports from the various committees and boards. Previously, each of these had shown up at conference with their material and distributed it as they were called upon to present their report in the session. They were in various sizes and types of paper. Now, we would request that they submit their reports to us in advance. We would produce them in a uniform format and organize them in a booklet that was bound with a file folder. As a result, pastors and lay representatives could refer to this while at conference and take them home to place in their files. It was very successful. In fact, a number of conferences copied that technique and for a number of years that is how reports were handled.

Let me take an aside here and mention how important were the times I spent at Epworth Among the Hills, on the outskirts of Arcadia, Missouri. (The Epworth name, by the way, is found frequently throughout Methodism. It is the name of the parish Samuel Wesley, Sr., father of John Wesley, Methodism's founder, was serving when John was a small child. The parsonage - or manse as it is sometimes called - caught fire when John was but five years of age. There was always a rumor that it might have been set deliberately to drive Samuel away from being the parish priest there since he may have not been well liked! John was saved from a second floor window escape by parishioners and referred to himself occasionally as a 'brand plucked from the burning.')

The campground at Arcadia, Missouri was the location of summer youth camps for the St. Louis Conference of Methodism. Also held here were retreats for women, men and occasionally for pastors and even pastoral couples. Many members of my family older than myself attended camps there through the years. One of my sisters (Evelyn) composed the words of "I Love Arcadia" which was sung there frequently in my early years. Because I moved from being a youth to being a pastor in a seamless manner, I attended Arcadia as a youth and then as a counselor without much of a break other than my three years of active duty at that time! I've mentioned previously my spiritual experience there around the campfire. I had many similar experiences through the years. I also served as the recreation director at one youth camp, which included directing folk dances and square dancing on the huge tennis courts that had multiple usages. (One bunch of kids called me the slob on the slab that year! I think it was meant as endearing?)

A highlight of most weeks at Arcadia included a trip to Pilot Knob, a mountainous outcropping in the granite hills that was not too far away. It earned its name from being used as a lookout post by troops during the Civil War. Campers and counselors would be bused to the foot of the mountain and there would begin the climb to the top. Some years this was an early morning experience in order to observe sunrise. Other years it might be a late afternoon experience in which the sunset was observed. In either case, a stop half way up the mountain trail was made at the opening of a cave that was nicknamed 'Devil's Icebox' for the cold air that poured out of its opening. Campers were given snack sacks to consume at this cool respite on the climb.

When reaching the top of Pilot's Knob, the events included group singing of some of the favorite songs, moving from popular ditties to more spiritually related songs. Then, just as the sun came up (or went down) the spiritual message was delivered by one of the camp leaders. I had the opportunity through the years to be both recipient and deliverer of these messages. They were always inspiring. (Hopefully, mine were as well as those I heard.) The descent from Pilot's Knob (whether in the morning or the evening) was always in silence until back on the bus. Sadly, the campsite has been sold to private folks now and Methodist Youth Camps are no longer held there.

Annual Conference in 1959 took place in Sikeston, Missouri in late May, with pastoral assignments effective the first week in June. When I arrived at conference I was contacted by several of the superintendents about my possible assignment. At first, it appeared as though I would be appointed to the church in Manchester, Missouri, a burgeoning suburb of St. Louis. Then Dr. Harvey Anglin, Rolla District superintendent told me that was off the table because one of the senior pastors in the conference was coming off a district job and wanted to go there. So, I would be sent either to Cabool or Houston in his district. At his suggestion I met with the lay delegate from Cabool. I have to admit, I was not impressed with him.

The next day I was asked to meet with a delegation from Houston, Missouri. There were several of them and they were eager to talk with me about their church and their community. I agreed with them that they had much to offer there in their church. And when conference appointments were read, I was assigned to the church in Houston, Missouri. This is a county seat town in the largest geographical county in the state, hence named Texas County! We spent the next year there in that community in the foothills of the Ozarks forty miles South of Fort Leonard Wood, a large Army post.

The parsonage was somewhat small and old, but the parsonage committee quickly offered to provide paint to refresh the walls. We found the congregation was a very warm and welcoming group of Christians who took us in as a part of every family. Many of the older women doted on our two children, Andy then five and Tami, a little over two. The membership comprised mostly of the business and professional folks in town. As an example, the choir director was the Chevrolet-Oldsmobile dealer. (He had been college trained as a musician, but his father died and he came home to help his mother run the dealership.) In the choir at tenor was the Plymouth-Chrysler dealer and at bass, the Ford-Mercury dealer! There were several college-trained organists in the congregation. One of the local physicians, Paul Beckman was also in the bass section of the choir. The county attorney and the county judge were members. The bank president and his father and uncle who had been in the bank were members. The state representative was a member. Educators, owners of the small businesses on the main street, as well as doctors and lawyers seemed all to be Methodists.

I set about as usual to make as many house visits as possible. I ran into a problem in finding people's homes. It seems they had recently named all the streets in town in preparation for home delivery of mail. But few folks seemed to remember which street was named what! I would ask someone about Oak Street and would get a frustrated look and a response that asked, 'what street did we name Oak?' Eventually, they would ask whose house was I looking for. 'Oh', the answer would come, 'they live in the old Perry house.' Of course, I had no idea where that was. Then would begin the routine, 'do you know where so and so lives?' 'No'. Oh, finally we would get to the real question, 'do you know where the courthouse is?' Of course, I knew where the courthouse was. So I would get instructions on how to find the house from the courthouse. Within a few weeks, I could find my way anywhere in town, but had to go back to the courthouse to get to the next spot!

The parsonage was located on the side street directly behind the church building. The church was at one end of Grand Avenue (the main street) and the County Court House was at the other end. (The street went a few blocks in either direction at the ends.) If I walked from the church down the street and looked in at most of the business places until I got to the court house, I would have visited a large number of my members. Leaving the courthouse, I could cross the street to the Post Office and get my mail (they still did not have door to door mail throughout the town, though they were working on that), go next door to the drug store and meet with several more members. In fact, some of the men vied to see who would buy the preacher's coffee on any given morning. Visit the Five and Dime, and walk back toward the church on the other side of the street and I would have visited with many more of our members.

At one point later on, the district superintendent asked me if I would be organizing a Methodist men's group there. I told him they already had one that met once a week for lunch. It was called the Chamber of Commerce! We had many wonderful experiences there in the following year. We began a new building fund to replace the old church that was small and had many maintenance problems because of its age. (In a recent visit to Houston we were able to take pictures of the building that was constructed a couple of years later as a result of that fund.) It would be possible to write an entire book just about our experiences there and perhaps we'll do that some day. I discovered from the newly appointed District Superintendent (Chester Yoes) that I was the only seminary-trained pastor in the south end of the district. He appointed me to be the youth coordinator for the district and utilized me as an assistant in other ways in the south end of the district that stretched to the Arkansas border.

Our children, Andy and Tami, enjoyed living in the parsonage with Dad home most of the time. We did have to adjust to being a parsonage family! For those who are not aware of this lifestyle, a fishbowl would be privacy compared to being the pastor of a church in a small town. Every event is magnified and reported almost instantly! For instance, Pat went to see the doctor in the small town because she was having some sinus infections. By the time she got home, the word was out around town that she had seen the doctor and was pregnant. (Not true.) One of the ladies in the church met her on the street and congratulated her on the wonderful news! She didn't deny it, but let the story run!

The preacher's children are more in the spotlight than those of a chaplain (who have the double blessing of being PKs - preacher's kids, and officer's brats.) Early in our time at Houston, Andy was standing during the singing of a hymn. When it came time to sit down, he was slow in releasing his grip on the back of the pew in front of him. The lady sitting there was rather large and in returning to the pew couldn't just sit down … she plopped down. In a rather loud voice as his hands suffered from her weight, Andy exclaimed to his mother, "Oh, that fat lady just killed my hands." Fortunately, she took no offense but apologized for not being able to sit down without just plopping and hoped his hands weren't really killed.

We had morning and evening services at the church each week. Since the parsonage was right next-door (really down the hill behind the church but in the same block) we always walked to church. One Sunday evening I had gone on with Andy in tow. Pat stayed a little longer getting ready. At the last moment, Tami was in the bathroom doing what a three-year child should do before venturing forth in the world. Pat finished getting ready and hurried up the hill to the church with Tami. When she arrived, one of the sweetest of the older women remarked how pretty Tami was (and she always was) and asked to hold her. When she took Tami in her arms she suddenly got a strange look on her face and remarked loudly, "Why, Mrs, Jacobs. This child has no panties on!" Ah, yes, the rush of getting away to services left one thing uninspected!

I needed to maintain my reserve status as a chaplain and discovered that one of my church members was an Army reserve Lieutenant Colonel in command of an engineering battalion at Fort Leonard Wood. He asked if I would like to be his chaplain. He had a reserve slot but no one serving. It meant a meeting once a month, plus one weekend a month at Fort Leonard Wood. I could spend the Saturday at the fort visiting with troops and then return on Sunday afternoon to conduct a worship service, so it wouldn't interfere with my Sunday morning activities at the church. I got in touch with the Tenth Air Force staff chaplain at Selfridge AFB, Michigan and received written approval to continue my status as an Air Force Reserve chaplain by serving with this Army unit! I enjoyed my time with them and had a good time on occasion running bulldozers and other pieces of heavy equipment!

CHAPTER NINETEEN

The following spring, I received word that the Chief of Air Force Chaplains was recalling certain selected chaplains to active duty. My name had been selected as one to be re-called if I desired to do so. If I didn't want to be recalled, then I needed to have my supervisor (the bishop) and/or my endorsing agency (the Methodist Commission on Chaplains) to notify the Chief's office that I was ineligible to return to active duty. After prayer and discussion, Pat and I decided that if we were to be called back to active duty we would report. I notified the bishop of this possibility and shared with him that I had always felt a call to the chaplaincy, however my first tour was not really a good try since I was not in a normal chapel setting. I contacted the Methodist Commission on Chaplains with the same information. Then I contacted the Chief of Chaplain's office and asked that if I could be returned to active duty in my status as a Captain (to which I'd been promoted in the Reserves) and the reporting date could be close to the end of May so that I could complete my responsibilities until annual conference time, then I would accept recall.

I received a telegram from the Chief's office affirming my status as a Captain and giving me reporting instructions to Stead AFB, Nevada (near Reno) effective the last day of May. With this information, I informed the local church of my recall and my departure from Houston. In many ways it was a bittersweet departure for we had become dear friends to so many in the congregation and yet, felt compelled to give the chaplaincy a chance where I would actually serve a local chapel responsibility. With official orders transmitted to me also by telegram, I went to the transportation offices at Fort Leonard Wood and they made 'thermofax' copies (Remember the 3M machines before there were real copiers?) and used these to ship our furniture to Stead AFB, Nevada.

With a relatively new Mercury (purchased from the church member who owned the dealership - at a good price because his father had ordered it and when it arrived as a four door instead of two door, he declined it!} we departed for Reno, Nevada, the nearest town to Stead AFB. The car was not air-conditioned (nor were most cars in those days) but a brother-in-law loaned us his evaporative car cooler to use. This contraption was mounted on the passenger side window nearly closed. It had a compartment in which you put water and periodically you pulled a rope to keep the water evaporating! It actually worked pretty well although a bit awkward for any permanent usage!

We arrived at Stead AFB and checked in. They had furnished base housing for us and we moved into one of them temporarily until our household goods arrived. Even then, we were allowed to go to the housing warehouse and pick out what we needed to complete our furnishings. The senior chaplain, a major, had just gone to Travis AFB, California to have surgery and so he was not there to welcome us. The other Protestant chaplain, a Lutheran, Sheldon Hermanson, and his wife Renee gave us a hearty welcome. The senior chaplain never came back to duty, but was on convalescent leave until his orders to an overseas base came! Within a couple of months a new senior man arrived, Marlin B. Morris and we served with him until our own overseas assignment came about eighteen months later.

During the few months that I was the senior chaplain at Stead AFB, I maneuvered an important office shuffle. The Major who had been the senior chaplain had gotten permission to move his office - along with the senior enlisted man - into a suite of offices in the wing headquarters building. It seemed to me that the chaplain ought to be in the chapel that was only a block away. And that meant the senior enlisted man ought to be there also to supervise the various airmen in their duties. After the wing commander had 'looked' for me in the headquarters offices a couple of times, his executive officer told me about it. I visited with the wing commander and told him my reasons for being in the chapel and visiting duty sections all over the base. He asked if I wanted to move the wing chaplain office to the chapel. I replied that I did. He asked me, 'what if the new senior man comes in and doesn't want to do that?' "Well," I responded, "that would be a good reason to do it before he arrives. The chapel is where folks expect to find the chaplain, not in the headquarters." Meanwhile, I had discovered the Wing Manpower office was cramped for space right across the hall in the wing headquarters.

The Wing commander told me he would think about it. The next day at staff meeting, he asked how soon would I move if he gave permission and I told him by mid-afternoon that very day! He gave me the go ahead to make the move. The Manpower people were grateful for the additional space. My main reason for wanting to do this was that I heard complaints on numerous occasions when I first arrived that the wing chaplain was always sitting in an office in the headquarters when he should have been available at the chapel. Furthermore, the senior enlisted man said he spent much of his time going back and forth to the chapel to coordinate and supervise the other enlisted personnel. It was a good move and worked out fine. When the new senior chaplain arrived and I briefed him on this move, he nodded and told me he was glad I had gotten it done before he arrived so that it was one battle he wouldn't have to fight as the new man on board!

Stead AFB was the location of Air Force helicopter training and the Combat Crew Survival Course for the Air Force at that time. None of the chaplains had been through the Survival Course prior to this time. The Catholic chaplain and one of the Protestant chaplains would fly by helicopter on Sunday afternoon to the field training area in the Sierra mountains nearby to conduct worship services. This would allow the chaplains to observe the training for an hour or so as well. It seemed to me that I would understand this activity better if I attended the course as a student. The Wing Commander agreed with me and I was assigned a slot in the next three-week training program. (As a result, I suspect I am one of few Air Force chaplains who is a graduate of that program!) The program, in those days, consisted of lectures and demonstrations for nine-days followed by a nine-day field phase. This was followed by a three day 'Code of Conduct' phase. The latter was a simulated POW (prisoner of war) camp exercise.

The nine-day field phase was further divided into three days of static camp exercises followed by three days of flight movements. (Flight is the term used in the Air Force for a small unit, similar to the term squad in the Army. Of course, it has other meanings when applied to a group of aircraft.) This concluded with three days of escape and evasion training prior to being brought back to the base for the Code of Conduct phase. Everyone serving in the military today is familiar with the Code of Conduct. What is less known, is the origin. As a result of the war fought in Korea more than 60 years ago, this code would be become part of our military culture. Note that the code was first promulgated by President Eisenhower and has had only a couple of changes since that time. It is reproduced in its entirety herewith. Many of us had a small 'wallet' card that we carried with us at all times.

The Code of Conduct

I

I am an American, fighting in the forces which guard my country and our way of life. I am prepared to give my life in their defense.

II

I will never surrender of my own free will. If in command, I will never surrender the members of my command while they still have the means to resist.

III

If I am captured I will continue to resist by all means available. I will make every effort to escape and to aid others to escape. I will accept neither parole nor special favors from the enemy.

IV

If I become a prisoner of war, I will keep faith with my fellow prisoners. I will give no information or take part in any action which might be harmful to my comrades. If I am senior, I will take command. If not, I will obey the lawful orders of those appointed over me and will back them up in every way.

V

When questioned, should I become a prisoner of war, I am required to give name, rank, service number, and date of birth. I will evade answering further questions to the utmost of my ability. **I will make no oral or written statements disloyal to my country and its allies or harmful to their cause.**

VI

I will never forget that I am an American, fighting for freedom, responsible for my actions, and dedicated to the principles which made my country free. I will trust in my God and in the United States of America.

A new class in the Combat Crew Survival Training program entered each Thursday morning and would graduate on a Wednesday three weeks later.

After I completed the course, I met with the course commander and several staff members at their request to discuss my experience. At that time there were several former POW's on staff, including Ward Millar, who had been a prisoner in Korea and escaped. (His experiences are related in his book entitled "Valley of the Shadow.") Those who had been through the experience of being a prisoner seemed to unanimously endorse the idea that spiritual strength was among the most important aspects of their survival. However, we had no particular spiritual thrust to the program. There was an opening lecture on the Psychological Aspects of Survival. I proposed we follow that with a lecture on the Spiritual Aspects of Survival. Many others in the group endorsed the idea. Within a couple of weeks, I began presenting the second lecture of the first morning in the combat crew survival training program. Following the introduction with the Psychological Aspects of Survival, was my lecture on the Spiritual Aspects of Survival which I entitled, The Will To Survive.

Without going into specific details of the presentation, let me just share that it focused on various aspects of spirituality without delving into sectarian beliefs. I discussed the part that spiritual strength has in survival under adverse circumstances. In this we looked at symbols, discipline and the sense of mission that military

173

personnel must uphold. From learning to analyze and know oneself to accepting weaknesses and building on strengths, the half hour lecture was not intended to solve all the problems of survival but elicit some response as to how one resolves problems of survival through spiritual strengths.

The lecture continued to be a part of the program throughout the time I was stationed at the base, although different chaplains eventually were folded into presenting it and others had somewhat different approaches. One other thing we focused on was developing a nine-day devotional guide for the field phase that presented many of these same ideas in capsule form to be looked at each day. We called it "Unto the Hills" and it featured the picture of one of our instructors dressed in field gear with his eyes upraised to the heavens. Psalm 121 (I will lift up mine eyes unto the hills, from whence cometh my help) was the overall theme. We had these printed and they were distributed on the day before the field phase began. (A side note to this pamphlet involved a discussion of the type of paper on which it should be printed! Some thought it should be on very thin paper so as not to take up much weight in the hiking process. One even suggested onionskin paper, thinking it could be boiled into onion soup! Another suggested tissue paper that could be used for other hygienic needs! One thought the right paper could be used with wild leaves to roll a cigarette. Most thought these were just humorous deliberations on a delicate subject. It wound up on slick paper that was easily readable even in poor light!)

I continued to ride the chopper out to the field every Sunday and to conduct a worship service, as did our Catholic chaplain. While there I would circulate among the various static camps and visit with both students and instructors. On one of these trips, as I was visiting the various groups, I came upon a group that had a large can on a fire pit. When I inquired about it, I was told they were making grasshopper stew! I asked them what they would do with it. They, of course, indicated they planned on eating it. (For the field phase of nine days each student was given two SR-1 packets - survival rations for one day in each packet) and the entire flight of six to eight students were given one live rabbit which they could reduce to a meal! They were also encouraged to live off the land. One of the lectures outlined the various edibles they might find in the wilderness.) "When are you going to eat this grasshopper stew?" I inquired. "As soon as it's too dark for us to see it!" I observed the grasshopper parts bubbling in the pot a bit longer before moving on to another group.

Between the chopper trips to the field exercise and just flying on occasion with different helicopter instructor pilots, I put in quite a few hours in the air. Our aircraft consisted of H-19's, H-21's and the new syncropters, H-43b. Meanwhile, of course, we had all the usual duties of an Air Force Chapel, to include monthly character guidance lectures (mandatory attendance for all personnel in those days and often given as a part of each unit's commander call session.) We also had two Protestant services in the chapel each Sunday, visits to patients in the on-base hospital, personal counseling as requested, the occasional wedding and frequent baptisms. Each week the Personnel section held incoming briefings for those who were new to the base and one of the chaplains would participate in that briefing and then give a cursory examination to the '869' card on the in-processing line. Rather than personnel having to go from one unit to another for processing into the base upon arrival, one day per week was set aside to do these in an assembly line basis. The 869 card was the Religious Interview Guide card. On it personnel would indicate their religious affiliation if any and such things as family data that would be of importance in serving their spiritual needs on base. (I believe these have been done away with?)

Stead AFB, as mentioned, is a few miles north of Reno, Nevada, a mecca for gambling casinos only exceeded in number by the younger Las Vegas community. Most of the casinos in those days had restaurants that served fine meals, often buffets, at an extremely desirable rate. This was either to reward those who were gamblers or to encourage others to become gamblers. We were neither, but enjoyed visiting the restaurants just the same.

I also became involved with the Reno Ministerial Association made up of most of the local pastors in the area. Through that group, I helped to establish the Washoe County Marriage Counseling Center. (Washoe is the County in which Reno is located.) This organization provided counseling for folks who were having marriage difficulties or even those who had arrived in Reno intending to take advantage of the liberal divorce laws in Nevada. At one time, Reno was known as divorce city, USA! On several occasions, we had couples referred to us by their divorce attorney for counseling rather than go through the divorce they contemplated. Many of the pastors in the community cooperated in this endeavor, taking turns providing the counseling on a no-fee basis and without sectarian involvement. A local funeral home gave us free usage of one of their small office buildings that was separate from the main facility.

CHAPTER TWENTY

L
ate in the fall of 1961 I received word that I was scheduled for a one-year 'remote' tour in Alaska, beginning on 1 March 1962. I was not really surprised by this since I had not had an overseas tour in my first three-year assignment in Minneapolis (although I spent one week out of every month in Canada visiting the radar sites, this did not count as overseas.) Alaska and Hawaii are still considered overseas assignments, even though they are both 'states'. Contemplating a year in the remote, snowy, cold arctic led me to believe that I might want to go through the survival field phase in the wintertime. When I first arrived at Stead and went through the course, it was late summer and the weather was ideal in the high mountains. But in the winter trek, the students traveled on snowshoes much of the time and I thought I ought to get that experience as well.

The Survival School commander at this time was Colonel Hollon Bridges. He and his wife Jessie were active in the chapel program, attending services faithfully. I contacted Colonel Bridges and asked if he thought it might be possible for me to attend a winter trek without going through the entire program again. He told me to pick my time and put my name on the list and take the trek. Looking at my schedule in terms of preaching activity and other events, I chose a week and placed my name on the roster for the field trek only. As I did so, I realized this was a special class that consisted of personnel (officers and enlisted) from the First Air Commando unit from Hurlburt Field, Florida. I let their SRO (senior ranking officer) know that I would be doing the field trek with them. He was a full Colonel Day who was commanding this brand new unit just recently established. He welcomed me and told me he wanted me in his flight for the field trek, and in fact, he and I would be E&E mates the last three days. (E&E = escape and evasion.) This was the final three days when students were paired up and the twosome would seek to escape any detection from the instructors who now became the enemy seeking to 'catch' the 'evadees'. Each time you were caught by one of the instructors, your student card was punched and supposedly, these punches would determine how severe your punishment would be when you got back for the POW camp (Code of conduct phase.)

I enjoyed being with the Air Commandos during the field phase. When it came time to split off into our E&E phase, the colonel and I were on snowshoes together 'humping' over the mountain. There were checkpoints along the way on the trek that you had to make in order to insure you were actually making an escape. These were marked on the 'survival' map each one carried. By using our compass and recognition points, we navigated to the various spots where we checked in. Then, on the final morning, students were to 'check in' at the final check point, but not until after 0600 (6 a.m.) Colonel Day was determined that we would be the first ones to check in after it was legal to do so. In order to make this happen, we would need to make our three days as rapidly as possible, hitting all the check points and then be at the final check point before 0600. In this way, as soon as it was legal, we would be the first ones to check in! This meant that we also had to avoid any contact with the 'enemy' in our movements so that we took no hits on our cards.

We made it! But, believe me, I was exhausted and so was the Colonel, though he might not have admitted it! We dragged ourselves on snowshoes over the hills and through the valleys at a break neck speed. Many of the class members did not arrive back at the final checkpoint until nearly noon, which was the final check in time without penalty. Of course, I had an advantage over the colonel. He had to load up in the trucks and head for the POW compound. I was able to go home and nurse my sore feet, ankles and legs!

One other aspect of my tour at Stead that I enjoyed included the POW compound. Permanent party members (those assigned to Stead Air Force Base) were not permitted to participate as students during the Code of Conduct exercise. Someone had decided that if an instructor got tough with us, we might be in a position of authority to make his life difficult later on. It was the only part of the program in which I did not participate as a student. I was issued a Russian Colonel's uniform, and I would visit the compound during the time the students were being treated as prisoners. This allowed me to wander through the camp area and observe what was going on. Most students recognized me from the lecture I had given at the beginning of the course, but avoided speaking to me during my inspection tours. I was concerned less about the treatment the students were receiving as prisoners than how the events affected permanent party personnel. Many of these were young enlisted personnel and we wanted to be sure they were not becoming brutalized in the process of 'mock' brutalizing prisoners. On occasions we did recognize that some were going too far and would quietly insure they were put in less stressful positions for a while.

Pat's parents came to visit us while we were stationed at Stead AFB and this provided an opportunity to take them to San Francisco and to the Yosemite National Park, places they had not been. We also had many visits to Lake Tahoe during this tour of duty. The commission on chaplains of the Methodist Church held annual retreats for Methodist Chaplains and their spouses and we attended these at a beautiful park on the coast at

Asilomar, California.

Although the nineteen months we were stationed at Stead AFB were very meaningful times of ministry and enjoyable as personal family time, they were not without sadness. We had several aircraft accidents during this period of time that resulted in the need to accompany a commander to notify a spouse that her husband would not be coming home. I'm not sure how it is done today, but in my active duty time these notifications were almost always made by the senior commander from the installation, often accompanied by the unit commander and always by a chaplain. Medical personnel might accompany us in case there was thought of needing medical care. Once in a while, the mortuary affairs officer would attend as well, though mostly these came later on. More than once through the years of my service, I had widows tell me they knew when they saw the commander and the chaplain coming up the walk, the news would not be good.

Including my tours at Stead and throughout my career, I was involved more often in notifying the next of kin concerning a death through an auto accident than an aircraft accident. At Stead this included a young doctor's death when he crashed his sports car in a chasm on the way back from town. He had left the officers' club earlier when it closed and made the trip to town by himself to continue drinking. It was this combination that resulted in the accident that resulted in the commander and myself visiting in the wee hours of the morning this distraught young wife. She knew (she later told me) that when the commander and the chaplain were at her door in the middle of the night, the news would be bad. As I tried to console her, she proceeded to curse at me and beat on my shoulders and chest (and my face had I not protected it) because of this horrific news. More than once, I found that the messenger got the frustrated response to bad news. It seemed as though it was easier to beat on the chaplain than the commander!

Another incident stands out in my counseling experiences at Stead AFB. A young Staff Sergeant was sent to me for counseling by his First Sergeant. It seems he had developed a gambling problem that was creating a major difficulty for him and his wife. His addiction led to his going into town frequently and 'blowing' his entire paycheck in a night of trying to 'recoup' his losses. The First Sergeant had counseled with him and with his wife. They had arranged an allotment be paid directly into his bank account each month so it would not be easily available for his habit. These funds would then be available for his wife to use in paying their bills and providing for the family. (There was a time in the military when the equivalent of the housing allowance was always in an allotment to the spouse of an enlisted person. Some felt this denigrated the responsibility of the military member of the family. In fact, I've had airmen tell me, she gets hers to run the family and I get the rest!)

On this occasion, the wife called the First Sergeant to tell him her husband had taken the checkbook early in the afternoon and not returned home. She was convinced that he had gone into Reno to gamble. The First Sergeant had made an attempt to locate him on base and then had a couple of his military buddies go into town to look for him to no avail. By the next morning it became apparent that something serious had occurred when he had not returned to his quarters. His wife was deeply upset by the situation. Never had he failed to return home, even if in the early hours of the morning. Three days elapsed without any contact with him or from him. We arranged for some financial aid for the wife to make a trip to the commissary for needed items to feed herself and their two children.

Then we received the call from the Nevada State Police. The sergeant had been found. As duty chaplain, I accompanied the commander, the Security Police Officer and one of the young medics to the site where he was located. On a remote dirt road off the main highway, about five miles out of town his car was spotted by a highway patrolman. Noting the Air Force base decal on the bumper (where they were placed in those days), he contacted the base. We found him deceased in his car. He had been there, we suspected for at least two and maybe three days. In the car we found both a bank receipt where he had withdrawn most of his funds and a receipt from a hardware store for the piece of hose that conveyed fumes from the exhaust pipe to the barely open driver side window. Three days in the desert heat had created an unbelievable stench in the automobile. The First Sergeant and I made the positive identification and the commander and I were sent off to notify his widow. This was one of the most difficult assignments I had in my career. The only 'identifying' remains task more difficult than this one was when I was sent to the morgue in St. Paul, Minnesota to identify the remains of a young airman who had been in a boating accident in the Mississippi River and his body was found downstream three days later.

On another occasion, when I was serving as duty chaplain, I received a call from the officer of the day (OD), a young lieutenant. He informed me that he was at the Air Police (Later the Air Force changed the nomenclature to 'Security Police'.) squadron headquarters where one of the MPs was threatening suicide. I went immediately to the office. There I found the lieutenant, the first sergeant and the military police senior officer standing around staring at the restroom door. They told me the young airman was in the restroom with his .45 caliber handgun threatening to kill himself. Evidently, he had received a 'dear John' letter from his girlfriend back home and was distraught over losing her. (Dear John became a common term beginning back in World War II when a girl wrote her boyfriend and dropped him.)

When I determined the identity of the young man and realized I knew him fairly well, I went to the door and called to him. "Bob! This is Chaplain Jacobs. Please put down the gun and come out and let us talk about this problem. You know you can trust me." There was a long silence. Then we heard the bolt in the restroom door lock click. Before the knob turned, I realized that I was the only one still standing in the room! Everyone else had either left the room or was hiding behind the desk! The door opened and Bob came out, holding his weapon. I asked him to give me the gun and he obediently did so, handing it to me handle first. I took the weapon from him and handed it behind me to the nearest person who had braved the encounter, put my arms around Bob and took him aside. We spent several hours together as I helped him understand that this disappointment was not worthy of his suicide. He responded quite well to the counseling experience and was functioning normally in no time. There was no squadron punishment or shadow over him as a result of this.

CHAPTER TWENTY-ONE

One Friday afternoon at the officers' club at Stead AFB, the wing commander asked me where my family would be staying while I was on my remote tour in Alaska. I told him that I believed she and our two children would return to St. Louis in my absence. He asked if I had a place there or would they be with relatives. "No, Colonel. When I depart here for leave before reporting to Alaska, we'll go back to St. Louis and try to find an apartment of some sort."

"Not till you are on leave? Why don't you catch a hop back there and get a place nailed down before then?" he suggested.

"Well, sir, I'm not a pilot and I understand because of funds shortages all pilot spots are being reserved for pilots to get in their flying time."

"I'm the commander here. I can waive that!" the Colonel responded. Then he waved to a major across the room. "Hey, Frank. Your daughter still at TCU in Ft. Worth?"

"Yes, sir."

"How 'bout you get a Tbird (T-33 jet trainer - we had several at Stead in addition to our 70+ helicopters - they were assigned for flying status folk to get in their mandatory monthly flight hours) and take the chaplain to Scott AFB (across the Mississippi from St. Louis) so he can look for housing for his family when he goes remote. You could run down to Carswell (then an Air Base on the edge of Fort Worth - now a Navy Reserve station) and visit your daughter for the weekend, go back, pick up the chaplain and come home."

"I'd be happy to do that, sir" the Major responded.

Thus it was on a Friday morning in mid December 1961, Frank and I departed Stead AFB, Nevada for a 'cross-country' flight to Scott AFB, Illinois. Our flight plan called for a stop at Buckley Field (an Air National Guard base near Denver) for re-fueling, thence to Scott. Frank would continue to Carswell for the weekend. He'd return on Monday to Scott for our return trip.

It was close to Christmas time and at Frank's suggestion, I took a box of Christmas presents to distribute to family members in St. Louis, rather than mailing them. The T-33 had a nice 'pod' below the fuselage in which we could carry our overnight bags and my box of gifts. I didn't notify our families that I was coming because I didn't want them to worry about my flying in this little airplane. The flight was without incident until about 30 minutes after our re-fueling stop at Buckley. The sun had dropped and the sky was beautiful. In order to better view the stars, I flipped off the switch that lit my instrument panel since it was reflecting against the inside of the canopy.

My earphones suddenly crackled with Frank's voice as he said, "Criminey! Our tip tank light came on. We just filled those boogers."

Realizing that without the tip tank fuel we would not have enough fuel to make it all the way to Scott, I replied, "I think we better find a flat place and sit down."

"Roger, that," came Frank's reply. Our alternate destination was Richards-Gebaur outside of Kansas City. I monitored his conversation with the operations folks there. Giving our aircraft id, Frank intoned, "We have a fuel emergency and desire approach and landing instructions."

"Sir," came the tower voice, "we are shut down for weather. Big time winter storm sitting right on top of us. Suggest you try McConnell."

"Roger," Frank responded. Then he clicked his switch again and asked me, "Chaplain, can you crank in the McConnell freq. Locate it in the card in the side pocket."

"OK, Frank. First, I'll have to flip my panel lights on."

"Never mind. Take the stick. I've got it going."

I put both hands on the control stick and sought to hold it steady.

Soon I could hear Frank talking with the McConnell tower. They indicated that they had a deteriorating weather condition. Frank noted that he had an emergency. They gave him a vector that would bring him around to final approach at McConnell AFB that was nearly just below us. He took the stick. I released my grip on the stick and saw it wiggle as Frank took control. Then as he banked around to put the aircraft on a final approach, he requested landing instructions.

The response came quickly. "Sir, we are now below minimums. Do you have an alternate?"

"Negatron! I've got a fuel emergency and I can see the runway straight ahead. I'm coming in." Then to me, "Chaplain, I've got it."

We dropped rather quickly and with a wiggle or two, I felt the wheels descend and moments later the aircraft flared and settled on the runway. Frank engaged the tower once again. "Taxi instructions for us now" he said once again identifying our aircraft.

The tower responded with, "Where are you? We can't see the runway because of the heavy fog."

Frank gave them our position and we were directed to proceed to the end of the blue lights and hold. When we got there, Frank opened the canopy and shut down the engine. Because we had declared an emergency, I was expecting ambulances, fire trucks, and who knows what else would be pouring down the runway any moment. It was eighteen degrees, blowing snow and ice fog right down to the ground. Then, we observed an air police vehicle approaching the aircraft as the two of us shinnied down from the wing.

Two young air police jumped from their vehicle and approached us with weapons drawn! The first one in the line demanded to see our identification.

My military ID card was in my wallet, inside the breast pocket of my flight suit, inside my flight jacket. I couldn't maneuver the zipper with my gloves on so hurriedly began the search. My fear was that this young kid was going to shoot me by accident before I could tell him I was not dangerous!

When we had both identified ourselves adequately, the Airdrome Officer, a young captain who had now appeared in his station wagon, asked if we wanted a power start to the engine so we could taxi to a hangar. Frank shook his head. "No. What I want is a ride to the officers' club so the chaplain and I can get some dinner! I don't know where the fuel went that caused me a shortage since I'd just re-fueled at Buckley. So, just tow it in wherever you got a space and we'll look it over in the morning."

The airdrome officer nodded and we both got into his vehicle and he transported us to the officers' club, which fortunately was next door to transient housing. I still remember Frank saying to me over our steaks, "You know chaplain, I'm a Presbyterian, and it wasn't my time to go."

I responded with, "You know Frank, I'm a free will Methodist and I was rehearsing ejection procedures. If it was your time to go, I was going to exercise my free will to punch out! I wasn't going by accident on your call to heaven!" We both laughed a good deal about the ordeal. He also informed me at that time that while I had the stick, we lost 2500 feet in altitude! Fortunately, we were pretty high when the emergency began.

I opted not to call my family and tell them I was delayed in my arrival since they didn't know I was coming. Nor did I want to call Pat and tell her of our ordeal, because I figured she wouldn't worry if she didn't know about it. Unfortunately, my Dad went to the hospital that day for unplanned surgery on a prostate problem. A family member called Nevada to let us know and ask for prayers! But Pat had to tell them that I wasn't home. I was flying into St. Louis to look for housing for them while I was remote. Now, both our families in St. Louis and Pat in Nevada knew I was somewhere other than where they thought. It caused more worry than if I'd made phone calls both directions. But I didn't know any of this until the next evening when I arrived at Scott Air Force Base and called for a ride to St. Louis. Because it was late, I called my brother-in-law rather than Pat's Dad. He came about an hour and a half later and took me directly to the hospital to visit my Dad and have prayer with him before his surgery the next morning.

I spent the next two days trying to find an adequate place for Pat, Andy, and Tami to live while I was gone to Alaska. Unfortunately, I was unable to narrow down anyplace that I thought was suitable and that we could afford. I even looked at the possibility of purchasing a house that we could then keep as a rent place after the year was up. I met Frank back at Scott AFB when the weekend was up and we had a pleasant trip back to Stead AFB. I was disappointed that I had been unsuccessful, but was more aggravated by the fact that I'd had the emergency on the way and in spite of my caution, wound up with folks at both ends worried!

CHAPTER TWENTY-TWO

T he remaining months at Stead went by all too quickly. Andy rode the bus to school each day. This bus left the school grounds and drove through the enlisted housing area and dropped off children and then came back through the officer housing area to discharge students. On one occasion, Andy looked out of the bus and noted his mother's automobile was right behind the bus, so when it stopped he got off, thinking he could ride home with his mother. Unfortunately, by the time he got off the bus, she had turned down a side street to drop off another lady. So Andy was left stranded in the enlisted housing area, some two miles from the officer housing area. He began the walk in the right direction, and someone recognized him and gave him a ride the rest of the way home!

Our housing unit was located on the circle that backed up to the desert! Over the fence behind us was nothing! But we had a lovely lawn and Pat planted some sunflowers in the front between the house and garage. They grew to over six feet tall and had the largest blossoms I have ever seen on sunflowers. Folks passing by often remarked about their size and beauty. We did have to deal with the occasional snake that wandered from across the fence since we were on the backside of the housing area. Behind us was desert! This also resulted in the occasional tumbleweed blowing into the yard. The base commander, a good friend and active chapel participant, wrote me up one time for having more than my share of the tumbleweeds. I promised him that henceforth, I would lift them in the air so they could blow across the circle into his yard!

The base housing at Stead AFB was of two varieties: single family units for field grade officers and duplexes for the company grade officers and enlisted personnel. Ours was a duplex since I was a captain. The structures were 'oversized' A-frames with the duplexes joined at the high point in the center and with garages slightly detached on each end of the building. At the front of the units the high parts were glass windows. Some residents claimed the houses were supposed to be built at a California base and someone mixed up the plans! Anyway, in time most of these high windows had become etched from the frequent sand storms. If any were cracked or broken, they were replaced with pressed wood panels. This was desirable because of the hot sun that came through the windows in the afternoon, especially those facing West. Meanwhile, the base engineers were in a program to replace all of them eventually, but would move ahead of schedule for any that were cracked. One of the men had told Pat that if she tapped a window at the corner with a hammer, it would likely crack and then they would schedule all our windows to be replaced immediately.

The day came when the workmen arrived to replace the windows. One of the men set up ladders and scaffolding. Tami, three and half years of age, watched intently. The workman said to her, "We're going to replace that cracked window in your house." And she replied, "You mean the one Mommy hit with the hammer!" Fortunately, he just laughed!

Since we were living in base housing our departure meant that 'clearing' the base included an inspection from the housing office. Two events coincided with our departure that nearly brought Pat, usually unperturbed by activities around her, to a distraught level! First of all, the morning the moving company arrived to pick up our household goods to be shipped to St. Louis during my remote tour, our daughter Tami came down with the mumps! This meant that we would be traveling several days to St. Louis with an ill four year old, probably not the best traveling companion!

When the household goods were gone, we moved into one of the temporary quarters on base until our actual departure. Pat, with a sick little girl and by herself mostly since I was busy closing out my activities on base, cleaned the quarters ready for inspection. The housing officer, a major and a good friend, thought he'd have some fun and do the inspection himself rather than one of the sergeants in the office. This was fine, of course, with us. The house was spic and span! Our quarters were heated by oil-fired furnaces located in the utility room in the center of the duplex units. When the major was almost complete in his inspection, he went into the utility room and took out a pair of white cotton gloves. He proceeded to open the small door on the front of the furnace and drag his white glove across the smoky glass insert. Obviously, this resulted in a large smudge on his glove and he turned and looked at Pat with a disapproving glance. He is fortunate that she is an even-tempered individual. Some women might have pushed him into the furnace at that point! He did laugh later and said it was just a joke. Wrong joke to play on a woman whose little girl was crabby with the mumps and whose husband was getting ready to move to an overseas location by himself for the next year!

The day was redeemed somewhat that evening when we had dinner with the Bridges (Colonel Hollon Bridges, Survival School Commander and his wife Jessie) who were lovely friends we would meet again in Alaska years later and in San Antonio more years after that.

Our journey to St. Louis for Pat and the children to get settled for the year of my absence was almost uneventful! We were maximizing our travel time in order to get to St. Louis and find housing as soon as possible. Also, we didn't want to be on the road any longer than necessary with a sick child. We got an early start from Reno and headed South through Las Vegas and then East toward Texas. It was wintertime and we wanted to avoid the possibility of bad roads and were taking the 'Southern Route'. We had made excellent time as we crossed Arizona and I felt certain that once we reached New Mexico we could likely make it home to St. Louis in only two more days travel. I probably was over the speed limit as we crossed the border from Arizona into New Mexico, although I had been trying to maintain a reasonable speed. Actually, we were just over the border when we crossed into the Gallup, New Mexico city limits quite a ways out of the city itself. Almost immediately, I saw the flashing lights behind me and pulled over. The Gallup policeman informed me that I was speeding. Did I have reason for my speed. I informed him that I had a sick child and was just trying to get to a motel before it got any later. He informed me that he would have to take me into the police court (open 24 hours a day) to be arraigned where I could either pay a fine or post bond for a later appearance! I asked if there was any possibility that I could get my family into a motel first. He allowed as how he would follow me to the motel. He did. I got Pat and the children registered and then he led me a couple of miles further to the all night court. There a 'judge' or 'magistrate' fined me $60 plus court costs of $6 for my infraction. I could 'post' bond and a trial date would be set for later that month, OR I could plead guilty and pay the fine! Of course, I had little choice and paid the fine and was released to return to the motel.

(Later, arriving in St. Louis I discovered in the latest issue of the Readers Digest a story about the 'speed trap' that was run by the Gallup police department! It was common knowledge among the experts that the city limit had been set quite far out of the actual city at the Arizona border in order to catch unsuspecting motorists who were just crossing into New Mexico. Furthermore, the town was criticized by the article for running this 'scam' of requiring folks to either pay a fine or return some time later for a court appearance. It seemed as though they preyed primarily on out of state license plates because they knew these folks would pay the fine rather than have to return. I called the Auto Association office and asked them if they knew about this problem and they informed me that they had heard from numerous members about it and recommended folks be extra careful in that area as well as several others!)

We arrived in St. Louis two days later without further difficulties, except that we brought a mumpsy little girl with us when getting to the home of Pat's parents. Within a couple of days we had found an apartment in the suburbs of St. Louis that would be adequate for Pat and the children in my absence. Andy, already in school, would be enrolled quite nearby in a good school. The location would be not too far from her parents, nor too far from the highway that led to the farm where my parents lived. The rent was within our ability to pay as well!

Within a couple of weeks, I departed St. Louis by rail to travel to Seattle, Washington and McChord AFB and then air travel to Elmendorf AFB, Anchorage, Alaska. Pat and the children stayed in the St. Louis area for the next year. We communicated by letter throughout the year. Only on a couple of occasions did I make phone calls home. It was $12 for three minutes by long distance and for a young captain with a wife and two children to support that seemed extreme. There was always the possibility of communicating through the military long distance system, of course. However, that was not dependable because once reaching the long line switch in Anchorage, I would be asked my priority. Since it was a personal call, the priority was 'routine' and I would be informed that all circuits were busy! This seemed to be true whether I tried to go from the 'Alaska switch' to the 'Seattle switch' or to the 'Norad switch'. (Seattle Switch was at McChord Air Force Base in Seattle-Tacoma, Washington area. The NORAD switch was at the North American Air Defense Headquarters in Colorado Springs, Colorado.) On a couple of occasions when I got that far, I would have to ask them to call Scott AFB, Illinois. Again, the priority question would stop me cold. Or, on one occasion I was told by the civilian operator at Scott AFB that to call St Louis was long distance and I would have to have a control number! Then came the call I made in which I got through the Alaska switch, through the Norad switch, through Scott AFB operator only to have a man answer the phone! No, he wasn't at my house. He was a sergeant trying the same method to reach his family from Paris, France and somehow our circuits got plugged together! I hung up to let him try to get the operator back. I was unsuccessful later trying to do so. Oh yes. I forgot MARS (Military Amateur Radio System). This was a system of military short wave radio operators, mostly volunteers, at bases around the world who would try to patch one through to their destination. I was never successful at this, even though my older brother in Missouri (40 miles from St. Louis) was a HAM radio operator! On one effort my contact eventually was a HAM operator in Southern California. He couldn't raise my brother on the radio, but took my message and said he would try to get through later. My brother, some time later, let me know that several weeks after my attempt he got a postcard through the mail from the MARS operator with my message!

Pat and I numbered our letters back and forth. The most important reason for this was so that we could always read them in order, since there was no guarantee they would arrive in the order in which they were written and mailed. This may seem inconsequential to folks who have not experienced a loved one deployed or assigned to a remote location. In my case, after I arrived at Elmendorf AFB, located in Anchorage, Alaska, I was informed that my tour would be spent as the chaplain responsible for the Aleutian DEW (Distant Early Warning radar) sites. I had known that I would likely be involved with the visitation of more than one location before reporting, based on information I had received from others. What I had not known was that my sites would be numerous and stretch part way to Tokyo! I had eight sites on my circuit, a larger circuit indeed!

During the year I was on my remote tour, Pat and the children experienced a number of exciting events! Reading the letters in order helped. Even so, I got the one that said Tami's arm was better before I received the one (numbered earlier but arriving later) that said Tami had fallen and broken her arm! Then there was the letter that told about Andy getting stuck in the garbage can and having the fire department come rescue him! Not really a garbage can, but in the apartment complex there were large 'in-the-ground' containers to deposit trash. Unlike large dumpsters, these were attractive, in-ground, with the top flush with the concrete sidewalk. They had a foot-operated pedal to open the lid, which would drop back down when released. Andy and some of his friends were playing hide-and-seek in the complex. He managed to get down in one of these (it was empty at the time) to hide. The only problem was that his broad shoulders wouldn't allow him to get back out and his little buddies weren't strong enough to help him. They came to report to his mother the situation but by then someone had called the fire department and they arrived to take the lid assembly off the 'hole' so that he could be rescued.

A major storm with tornado winds came through St. Louis and blew out the windows in the apartment Pat and the children shared. This ruined the drapes and the carpets. Worse than this, it broke the windshield in the automobile and pitted the paint job with the heavy hail that fell. Pat called USAA (our insurance of choice ever since my first entry on active duty in 1956) and reported the damage. They took care of the cost of the drapes and carpet and gave her the name of a place to have the windshield replaced and the car re-painted. This worked out well, however, the day she got the car back from the shop, a large wind came up and blew pea gravel from the flat roof of the apartment over the car and pitted the paint job once again! Although, she was tearful when she called the USAA representative, he reassured her that it was ok. They repainted the car.

Her letter to me relating these events reached me at King Salmon. I tried to get through with a space available call but was unable to do so. I did write her and reassure her that it was ok, though I was surprised that she'd had the car re-painted twice in one week!

The main site on my circuit was at King Salmon, Alaska. Located at the head of the Naknek River on the bay, the site included a forward deployed group of F-102 aircraft with crews. There were about 25 permanent party officers as well. In addition, some 200 enlisted personnel were assigned there for maintenance of the aircraft, the radar equipment and the Trope-scatter communication equipment. Before there were satellites for communication, the military had a large number of these units that 'bounced' their signals off the troposphere (or someone told me it was really the ionosphere that was used for the bounce) to be received by the huge antennas at the next location down the line. King Salmon, true to its name, also included a marvelous 'fish camp' that served many military personnel from around the command as well as from units in the lower 48 (as Alaskans refer to the 48 contiguous states). A great many headquarters folks (Washington, SAC, ADC and others) made 'inspection' trips to Alaska with a stop at King Salmon during the fishing season.

King Salmon was a great fishing spot when the salmon were running, Silvers, Kings, Chum, etc. My year with that as my main site gave me many opportunities for some great fishing! My first trip out on the Naknek River with one of the lieutenants at the site resulted in my catching two King Salmon; the total weight of the two was 58 and 1/2 pounds. The larger of the two took me almost an hour to get into the boat. With two of us in the boat, whoever got a 'strike' from a big King Salmon would holler out 'fire in the hole' and the other one would get the outboard motor started immediately. It was not possible to just reel in a large salmon. Instead, we would work him awhile, and then when he began to 'run' down stream, the motor tender would follow him with the fisherman keeping the line taut but not allowing it to break. When the big fish got tired and wanted to rest a while, it was time to reel him a little closer to the boat. Hence, I had the need to spend an hour working the nearly 40 pounder that I hooked that day. Once he was next to the boat, it was necessary to net him in order to get him into the boat. The following day, I paid for this episode with a very sore shoulder!

On one occasion, a senior general officer and his entire entourage of subordinate commanders came to the fish camp. I counted the stars on one shoulder of each general and came up with 56! I wrote a little essay about that trip that I entitled "Four Stars to the Boat". The idea was that a four star got a boat to himself. Two stars had to share with each other. One Stars could pair up with a three star or three one stars, etc. Anyone below general would have to settle for a half of a 55 gallon barrel and a paddle. Some of the young officers who read it thought I should send it somewhere for publication. My question always was, 'would it be worth as much as my retirement someday?' All agreed it would not! So it was never published!

My other site responsibilities included Ohlson Mountain. This unit was located on the mountain just out of Homer, Alaska. Hardly remote, you could drive through the Kenai Peninsula to Anchorage in less than a half day. There were about 85 men stationed here, including a dozen officers. Because the town of Homer was right down the hill, I was not required to visit this site but once a quarter. We had auxiliary civilian chaplains (one Protestant who was the local Methodist pastor and one Catholic priest) who covered the site with services each weekend and at least one day of visits per week to provide counseling or other support.

The rest of my site responsibility was to visit the Aleutian DEW (Distant Early Warning) line sites each month. The main site was in Cold Bay, Alaska. Here were six or seven officers and 25 or 30 enlisted personnel. It was the squadron headquarters for the remainder of the sites that stretched some 600 miles on either side of Cold Bay. They consisted of Port Heiden, Port Moller, Cape Sarachef, Driftwood Bay, and Nikolski. Port Heiden and Nikolski had nearby Aleut villages. The others were pretty much isolated. Cape Sarachef was unique, in that it was located about five miles up the hill from the 3000 foot gravel runway. A mile down the hill from the runway was a Coast Guard Station with one officer and 18 to 20 men. (I have used the term 'men' in describing the personnel at all of these locations since no women were assigned to remote stations in those days.)

There were eleven site chaplains in Alaska at that time. Two were permanently stationed at Shemya (on the West end of the Chain), one Catholic and one Protestant. The others, five Protestant and four Catholic, covered the other 26 sites throughout the state. Basically, they divided the sites into five zones - King Salmon, Ohlson Mountain and the DEW line (my circuit) North of the Range Outboard (Cape Lizburne, NorthEast Cape, Tin City (no city there!) and Kotzebue. North of the Range Inboard (Indian Mountain, Sparrevohn, Fort Yukon, and Galena.) South of the Range Outboard (Bethel, Cape Romanzof, Cape Newenham, and Unakleet) and South of the Range Inboard (Middleton Island, Fire Island, Tatalina, and). Each of the circuits had four sites to visit with the exception of my tour down the chain. It was the largest circuit in number of locations, however the total manpower of the sites was less than the other circuits that only included four locations. My Catholic counterpart was only required to visit the sites once a quarter since there were so few Catholics in these locations and in the case of both King Salmon and Ohlson Mountain we had a Catholic auxiliary civilian chaplain.)

The program for the nine site chaplains (excluding the two at Shemya who were fulltime for their year) was for them to visit their respective sites during the month and at the end of the month to arrive back in Anchorage at Elmendorf AFB for a Wednesday morning site chaplain staff meeting. Following that, they would collect their TDY (temporary duty) travel pay and pick up official travel orders for another month and be on their way for another circuit. Most of the men (there were no women chaplains anywhere in those days and certainly not on remote tours) would plan their schedule to arrive back on Monday or Tuesday, planning to depart on Thursday or Friday. Some of this was dependent upon the days flights were actually available from their remote locations to Anchorage. Although some travel was accomplished on military aircraft that happened to be going the direction a chaplain needed to travel, most of the travel was by Government Travel Request (TR) and the various civilian airlines in Alaska.

It was possible for me occasionally to fly to King Salmon after the monthly staff meeting on a military aircraft. There were frequent flights with C-123 cargo planes to King Salmon and occasionally there would be either an Air Force C-54 or C-121 going that direction. Otherwise, I would fly on Northern Consolidated Airlines or Pacific Northern Airlines. (The locals often referred to these as the Tri-Weakly Airlines.) NCA flew small twin engine flights to King Salmon. PNA flew a large DC-4 (Air Force C-54) and later a DC-6B. My flights East and West to the DEW sites were always on Reeve Aleutian Airline. Technically, they were not authorized to serve King Salmon from Anchorage (in the days when flight schedules were tightly regulated), however since I would be flying further on the chain, they could fly me to King Salmon as part of my monthly schedule. My flight from King Salmon out the chain and back would be by a TR that read "King Salmon to Cold Bay, Cold Bay to Nikolski, Nikolski to Cold Bay, Cold Bay to King Salmon. Transfers authorized." The airline approach was that I had not used up my ticket until I had visited all six of the DEW sites. (As best I remember, the cost of this ticket was $500.) I would fly from King Salmon to Port Heiden and deplane. The stewardess (before we called them flight attendants!) would give me a slip of paper that said "deplaned at Port Heiden en route to Cold Bay." When the plane came back in and I got aboard, the next stewardess would take that paper and issue me another which read, "deplaned Port Moller en route to Cold Bay". In this pattern I used my ticket up by the end of the month by visiting each of the sites.

On my first month's circuit I was introduced to the above pattern for traveling to my sites. I had flown to King Salmon on this occasion on an Air Force C-123. I had a good first weekend there with services on Sunday and plenty of opportunity to visit with troops and counsel several. I delivered my monthly character guidance lecture three times in order to reach all the men who were on shift work. Now it was time to fly down the chain to explore my new sites there. I had been briefed on the use of the TR to visit all the sites, however it was suggested that from King Salmon on the first trip out, I should skip Port Heiden and Port Moller and go directly to Cold Bay where the squadron commander for all of the six units (detachments officially) was located. I could still make trips back and forth until I had gotten to all the other five locations before the month was over.

Reeve Aleutian's schedule was printed on a mimeographed page. It listed all the places they were flying. Most of them had either a 'C' or a 'crossed out zero' next to them. The code was revealed at the bottom of the page. The 'C' signified sequences of stops variable. The 'crossed out zero' indicated arrival and departure times variable. My thought in reading this the first time was that here is an airline not sure where they are going nor when they will get there or depart! Basically, they left Anchorage on Monday morning at 0800 hours en route to Big Mountain (This was an FAA communication site) and then King Salmon. They were 'scheduled' to arrive at King Salmon at 1000 hours. I had my TR for travel as outlined in the previous paragraph. A sergeant from the motor pool at King Salmon said he would take me from the site around the runway to the civilian side where I could catch the Reeve flight. The military side of the runway included alert cells (hangars) where our forward deployed F-102's were located. When I arrived on the civilian side of the runway, he took me to the Northern Consolidated building, a nondescript Quonset hut! I had a B-4 bag (a large cumbersome soft sided suitcase that I would live out of all month as I traveled to the sites) and an A-4 bag that included some equipment, including literature, often a religious film and other items. The sergeant bade me good luck and left to return to the site. I went into the Quonset hut. A pleasant woman heard the door and came from the back of the hut (which it turns out housed her family's living quarters.)

She looked at me and asked, "Where you headed?"

"I'm catching Reeve's flight down the chain to Cold Bay", I replied. (Translation: How do I get my ticket and find out when the plane is coming?)

"Oh, they have nothing here. This is Northern Consolidated. They usually get here about 10 on Mondays and again on Thursdays." (Translation: They don't pay me.) With this comment, she turned around and went back into her living area and left me standing there.

I stood for a while and wondered what I should do. If Reeve had nothing there, how was I to get a ticket? How would I know when they were coming? I knew I had excess baggage but how would they know? I was pretty much confused. No cell phones in those days. No public phone that I could see on the counter or anywhere else. I stood for a moment or two and decided, after checking my watch, that I might as well sit down and await what would happen next.

About 0945, the woman reappeared. She said, "They should be along soon."

"How will I get my ticket for my Travel Request?" I asked.

"Oh, the stewardess will write it for you."

"How will she know my overweight baggage?" (Translation: How do my bags get on the plane?)

"Just tell her how much you think it weighs." (Translation: Carry them yourself. They don't pay me anything.) With this she disappeared once again. I could hear an automatic washer cranking up for the spin cycle and guessed she was going to take care of it.

About 1000, she came out once again. Pointing out the window, she told me, "I think that speck is them now."

Indeed, in a few moments, the plane (a war surplus C-47 - military version of the DC-3) appeared and landed, taxied right up to the edge of the runway where the Quonset was sitting. Only the left engine was shut down. The door (hinged at the bottom) was opened, dropping down and revealing the stairs. A young lady leaned out and beckoned to me. I grabbed my two heavy bags and made my way to the aircraft. When I crawled up the steps, she told me to just 'chuck the bags in there', pointing to a web belt cage in the corner across from the door. I started to show her my TR and she said, "Take a seat. We'll deal with that when we get in the air." With this she pulled the stairway/door up to locked position, belted herself in and the crew cranked up the left engine and we were off to the end of the runway and into the air!

We flew west until we came to Port Heiden. The aircraft landed at the short (3000 foot) gravel (mostly crushed lava rock) runway. Again, they only turned off the left engine (the side of the opening door/staircase) while they unloaded mail and some cargo, picked up mail and sometimes a passenger. (The reason for keeping one engine running, I discovered, was that they had no facilities to assist in starting an engine at these unmanned remote locations. By keeping the one engine running, they maintained some warmth in the aircraft and enough power to battery start the left engine when it was time to go. Over the year, I often helped in loading and unloading cargo. I know they thought I was being helpful, but I was really trying to stay warm!) At Port Heiden, I met the young captain who was the detachment commander. He and a couple of sergeants had come to the runway to meet the aircraft.

After we left Port Heiden, we flew to Port Moller where we re-enacted the same scene, even to meeting the site commander and some of the men from the site. From there we flew southwest across the area to Sand Point where natives from the nearby village met us. The approach to Sand Point was treacherous to observe the first time. The winds were so strong that it appeared from the right side of the aircraft that we would fly directly into the 200 foot bluff that ran along the North side of the runway, which was shorter than most. At the last moment, the pilot corrected the 'crab' against the wind and brought the aircraft around to the proper position to land. When we left there it was to cut across the peninsula to Cold Bay. Here we landed in another strong wind. I got used to these over the year I was visiting out the Chain. The wind was always strong! Several trips later, I was in the Reeve operations shack (they had one at Cold Bay in an old Quonset hut as they did at Umnak, on the same island as Nikolski. This one was in an old World War II hangar.) The Reeves operations manager was watching the wind machine gauge and suddenly let loose with a string of expletives. Finally, he said, "There goes the damn wind machine off the roof again. It does that every time it pings on 100 knots."

The runway at Umnak was 8000 feet long, a real treasure in the Aleutians. Fort Glenn had been at this location in World War II and there were still some of the old buildings there including the hangar where Reeve kept their aircraft overnight. (The trip officially ended at Nikolski, but they would fly back to Umnak for the night. On some occasions when they were picking me up at Nikolski, heading back up the chain, we would return to Umnak for the night and I would stay in one of the 'guest' rooms they had in the hangar there.) This part of the island was an area of large sheep herds and cattle herds. The owners leased the grazing rights from the US government. On more than one occasion, approaching the runway at Umnak, the crew would fly over the runway once to either scare away cattle on the runway or, at least, to insure it was clear to land.

On that first trip down the chain, I met the commanders at Port Heiden and Port Moller as I indicated when they met the planes. I discovered any aircraft arrival was a big deal. This was especially true of the commercial flights twice a week. For one thing, the mail came in on the aircraft. Furthermore, there was a stewardess on the flight - the only female these fellows would see during their year's remote! (This was even true of the sites where there was a nearby village, since the Aleut women never came to the plane.) After Sand Point, we headed back across the peninsula to Cold Bay. As we approached the runway, again I noted the 'crabbing' against the wind by the pilot. Then at the last moment, the plane came about and we touched down, leeward wheel first, then the other and then a burst of speed to head toward the end of the runway where the site commander and some of the men were waiting. As we taxied up to the 'shack' where Reeve had their operations, I noticed the seagulls on the top ridge. They would lift off the ridge, flap their wings a few desperate times and then sit back down where they had started! The wind effectively kept them from getting any headway.

Taxi complete, the crew shut down both engines. They had crew and equipment to re-start here at Cold Bay and would spend the night in the airline's buildings. The captain (civilian crew) came out of the cockpit area, looked out the window and said in a stutter, "N-N-Nice d-d-day, for C-C-Cold B-b-b-bay!" It shook me just a moment to discover that the crew captain on our flight stuttered rather badly! After I got to know him through the year I realized that this was typical of all his comments except when he was on the radio talking to the ground crew or tower! Then, his stammer disappeared! I met his daughter many years later in San Antonio, Texas and we laughed about his stutter. She said he had retired from flying commercially years later and taught flying in Seattle!

Monday and Thursday, Reeve flew from Anchorage to Cold Bay via the sites in between. Tuesdays and Fridays they flew from Cold Bay to Nikolski (doubling back to Umnak for the night). Wednesdays and Saturdays they would fly the entire route back to Anchorage. All of these flights were in one of the two C-47s they operated. They also covered some of the interior sites primarily with one of two C-46s they flew. (These were fitted with 'fuel bladders' and were used to fly in aviation gas and motor vehicle gas to sites that were not on a stream where it could be barged in.) On one occasion, I 'bummed' a ride with a Reeve C-46 from Indian Mountain to Anchorage. I say I bummed a ride because I didn't have a specific TR for a ticket and was awaiting a military aircraft to arrive. However, by then, in the headquarters job, I knew all the crews quite well and they volunteered that I could ride back to Anchorage with them. When we got to altitude, I noted from the jump seat between the pilot and co-pilot where I was sitting that the captain had lit a cigar! I looked at him and tapped his headphones. He turned them on and

I said in my mike, "Isn't that dangerous with possible fumes from the fuel bladder?" "Nah," he replied. "Besides we've got the chaplain aboard so we are close to heaven anyway." In addition they had a Grumman Goose (on floats) that they used to fly into some of the even more remote places where there was no runway.

On one of the early flights I met Bob Reeve, owner of the airline. He was a bush pilot from the 30's and had serviced most of the sites as they were being constructed. One of my prize possessions is an autographed copy of his book "Glacier Pilot" which depicts much of his early career landing aircraft on skis on glaciers as he took folks into remote areas of Alaska. His son and both his daughters worked for the airline, the girls serving as stewardesses on flights on the chain.

I got used to the rhythm of my monthly tours up and down the chain. From the monthly staff meeting at Elmendorf (where all the site chaplains kept a room in the bachelor officers quarters) I would fly out to King Salmon. Then after a weekend, I would start down the chain, spending the time between Reeve flights to that particular site giving character guidance lectures, conducting worship, counseling and visiting in the duty sections. When the Reeve flight came back, I would go to the next site. It would take me two weeks to make this circuit if all went well. But the weather controlled where I might go next and even if I would go. Driftwood Bay was the most difficult site to get in and out of, so sometimes I might be there for an entire week. My Catholic chaplain counterpart got stuck there once for two weeks. He said he enjoyed the time there, however only the young captain who was the site commander at that time was Catholic and he was divorced and somewhat isolated from the church in those days.

I established a program of volunteer 'chaplain's assistant' at each of the sites on the chain as well as at Ohlson Mountain and King Salmon. At Ohlson Mountain, the assistant's task was to support the auxiliary civilian chaplain who came from Homer throughout the week and on Sundays as well as providing me help when I visited once a quarter. At King Salmon, his task was to assist me in setting up the altar when I was there for services. In addition, I made available some religious films that he would schedule in the site theater in between regular movies. When I was not there he would lead a song and prayer service with a cassette taped message that I provided regularly. This latter task was also the responsibility of the assistant at the DEWline sites down the chain. When I visited the sites, I would record the cassettes to be used until my return. This worked rather well and some of the other site chaplains adopted the concept for their sites. Later, when I was the director of the program, I encouraged all of them to do so.

I knew that Reeve flew their 'big' aircraft (DC-4 later replaced by a DC-6b) from Anchorage to Cold Bay to St Paul Island in the Pribilofs and back to Anchorage one day each week. After several efforts to make that flight, I managed to schedule myself on the leg from Cold Bay to Anchorage via the Pribilofs. These islands in the middle of the Bering Sea are home to the world's largest colony of fur seals. Annually, a harvest of these animals for their pelts took place. (It was considered fiercely cruel and was fought by the environmentalists groups every year and may no longer occur.) My first effort at this flight resulted in 3 hours and 45 minutes Cold Bay to Cold Bay. We got out there and the fog was so bad we couldn't land and returned to Cold Bay. The successful trip I made happened to include Bob Reeve himself coming back from Cold Bay to Anchorage. At St. Paul, they loaded six huge fur seals in great wire crates onto the aircraft for transport to Anchorage and then to zoos in the lower 48. They were on one side of the plane and our seats were on the other side. Bob and I were the only passengers other than daughter Roberta as the stewardess. When we got aloft from St. Paul, she came to bring us our inflight meals, a very nice fried chicken box lunch that she had brought out from Anchorage. Bob couldn't eat his, because he said the stench of the seals was so great. All the way to Anchorage, the seals 'arfed' and smelled! Finally, Bob said to remind him the next time he was going to fly with this airline to check the passenger manifest! He didn't want to fly with any more stinking seals! (He allowed that I was a good passenger and he'd fly with me anytime.)

My fondest memento of my year flying with Reeve is the 'official' ticket that Roberta Reeve, flying as stewardess, gave me on my last flight back from Nikolski. It indicates that I am entitled to a one-way flight from King Salmon, Alaska, to Siberia to be paid in crew labor!

One more memory before I leave my year on the 'Chain'. With the exception of Cold Bay, there was only one officer on each of these sites, usually a young captain, although there was an Air Force Warrant Officer that commanded one site. The sites consisted of a large two story building with another two stories rising out of the middle of the building with a radome 'bubble' at the top of it. The ground floor included all the administrative offices, the motor pool, the kitchen, the combination 'mess' hall/lounge/club/ gathering place. The latter was used for all recreation including the ping pong table and the pool table. It also became a quasi NCO/Airmen/officer club in the evening. It is the place where commander's call took place. Also character guidance lectures and worship services. The second floor included all the living quarters. The commander's quarters were on this floor and included a private bath/shower whereas the rest of the troops had 'two-to-a-room' barracks accommodation and a shower down the hall.

There were no visiting officer's quarters, hence, I stayed with the site commander who had twin beds in his suite. I had no problem with this arrangement. The only drawback for me was that the site commander had no one to 'talk' with at the officer level except when the chaplain visited. Many of them would want to stay up quite late conversing. Sometimes it was about site business or personnel. More often it was personal. Now the site commander could sleep in the next morning if he chose, however, my job was to be up and with the troops, interviewing, counseling, giving a lecture, etc. After a couple of days there, I would depart for the next site. I'm convinced the site commander probably caught up on his sleep after I departed, but I was at another site with the same regimen! By the end of two weeks when I returned from the 'chain' to King Salmon, I was often exhausted! Fortunately, I could catch up by sleeping in one or more mornings if I needed to do so.

The sites were all in remote locations, of course and this meant they were surrounded by wildlife. Good fishing was available nearby at all of the sites on the chain. This was true of most of the sites throughout Alaska; however, the heavy snow and ice prevailed in some locations, whereas on the chain it was mostly cold wind and dampness. I've mentioned my fishing expedition at King Salmon. While at Cold Bay, I went with a couple of sergeants in a pickup truck to a nearby stream to fish for 'dolly varden' sea trout. At the mouth of the stream, they would come in from the ocean to spawn and then swim back out. It was marvelous fishing. In fact, along with the sergeants, I filed the barb off my hook so it would be easier to release them from the catch and back into the water. Even with this technique, we brought back to the site fifty or more fish for a big fish fry for the troops. On one occasion, we had worked our way upstream from where we parked the truck to find a place where the water was shallow enough to wade across to the other side for more advantageous casting. We were wearing hip boots (issued to the site for the fire fighters!). I had moved back downstream from the others so my casting would not hook one of them. Suddenly, out of the corner of my eye, I caught some movement! I looked and about 25 yards upstream from my location was a great brown bear (Alaskan brown bears are a cousin to the Grizzly and generally huge) that was on three legs with the other front paw raised in the air getting ready to strike a fish as it swam by! I determined this might be 'his' fishing hole, and so without thinking about the depth of the stream, I waded across to the other side near the pickup truck. The sergeants had great fun back at the site telling how I 'walked on the water' to get away from the bear!

On another occasion at Cold Bay, the bears became a problem. They would feed at the 'garbage' dump about a mile from the main site. One late afternoon a large bear decided the dump wasn't adequate and made his way up to the site building. Following the scent, he arrived at the lean-to on the back of the building adjacent to the kitchen where the garbage was kept until it was transported to the dump. The wooden door opened in on this lean-to (a construction deficiency in retrospect). The bear pushed his way into the space, but after getting his fill and hearing shouts from the kitchen doorway, tried to get out, but was frustrated by the door. The solution was to put an airman in the back of a covered pickup truck with a long 2x4 board. They backed up to the outside door of the shack and he used the 2x4 to push the door open while the men inside the kitchen shouted at the bear and banged pots and pans to frighten him into leaving. Meanwhile, the site commander had phoned the local game warden in a nearby village and requested permission to destroy the bear as a nuisance. (Killing wildlife without a license or when not in season was discouraged even in the remote locations.) When the bear emerged from the lean-to, there were three airman on the second floor roof with hunting weapons and they all fired at the bear numerous times, killing him. Following the game warden's instructions, the carcass was towed down to the garbage dump and burned (no one was allowed to have the huge bearskin since the death was for nuisance eradication and not with a valid hunting permit!) One of the men suggested the bear gained about 30 pounds from the bullets shot at him in the process! The theory included the possibility that the odor of the burnt carcass would discourage other bears from coming around.

CHAPTER TWENTY-THREE

As the end of my year on the chain wound down, one of my tasks back at Elmendorf was to put in for my next assignment. This meant filling out a form known as Form 90 (or more often called the dream sheet). In my rare conversation with Pat, we decided that I should ask for something either on the West Coast or the East Coast since these were areas we had not visited much. One month, following the monthly site chaplain meeting, Chaplain George Wilson (Colonel, command chaplain) asked me if I'd thought about the possibility of requesting a 'consecutive' accompanied tour to Elmendorf. I had not given any thought to that up until that day. It seemed as though one of the Protestant Chaplains on the base was due to rotate back to the lower 48 the same month I would be departing my site tour. It would be possible, if approved, for me to take 30 days leave, fly back to St. Louis and drive to Anchorage for an accompanied tour with my family living on base at Elmendorf AFB. The chaplain I would be replacing was currently the religious education chaplain on base. Because this was such a huge base the religious education program was very large and active. Both because of my seminary major and my experience at Lafayette Park Methodist Church, he thought I would be an ideal candidate to take over this program.

After a call to Pat, we decided this might be fun. She and the children would get to experience much of what I had experienced in terms of the beauty of the Alaskan wilderness. So I went down to Personnel and 'adjusted' my dream sheet requesting this consecutive accompanied tour to Elmendorf AFB in Anchorage. Within a couple of weeks, while I was on my next circuit down the chain, I received a call from Chaplain, Major, Roger Makepeace, the director of site activity, that my request had been approved and my next assignment would be at Elmendorf.

I was due to rotate out of Alaska on 1 March, but I arrived back at Elmendorf the week ahead of that so that I could get ready to take my leave and travel time and bring my family to Alaska. Through a friend, I caught a flight to Eielsen AFB in Fairbanks and then a ride with a KC-135 tanker crew back to the lower 48. It was a working mission for the crew and we flew South toward Seattle, picked up some fighters over Western Washington state and accomplished a couple of re-fueling missions. It was fun to lie in the pod in the refueler's spot and observe the whole process. After the mission was complete, the flight headed for Grand Forks AFB, North Dakota. Here I discovered there were no flights scheduled to Scott AFB, Illinois but I could catch the bus to Minneapolis and then a commercial flight to St. Louis. By the time I arrived at Lambert St Louis International Airport, I'd been traveling a couple of days and without shaving and in my Alaskan parka, looked pretty weird, I suspect. Pat and the children knew my arrival time (from a phone call I made in Minneapolis) and were awaiting me at the gate. I don't think they recognized me at first! But it was a joyous homecoming.

During my leave time at home, we were able to make all the arrangements for our household goods to be placed in storage except for what we could ship to Alaska. I had rented a small-furnished apartment near the base on a monthly basis, since I knew we would have base housing within about six weeks. One of our family jokes from this era involved my suggesting to Tami that first evening that she ought to get her 'jammies' on so I could tuck her into bed. She looked at me with squinted eyes and then turned to her mother and asked, "Mommy, do I have to do what that man tells me?" (This wasn't so out of place for her. She once told a kindergarten teacher she didn't have to do what she told her because she wasn't her mommy!)

In preparation for the nine-day drive from St. Louis to Anchorage, Alaska, I obtained maps, booklets (Alaska Highway magazine known as the 'Milepost' was invaluable), and other things that I thought would make the trip in March an easy journey. We would be on hard packed snow for over 1000 miles up through the upper reaches of Canada and on the Alaskan Highway. This was actually better than later when the roads were thawed and would be gravel! I installed seat belts in our Mercury automobile (none came with them in those days). I put new snow tires on the car and obtained a set of tire chains for emergency use (never needed them). I bought a heavy-duty tow strap in case we needed to be pulled out of a ditch! (We didn't. But I used it to pull a young Canadian soldier's car out of the ditch!) We stocked up on warm clothing for the children and the kind of snacks we might need for the trip.

Our journey took us from St. Louis to Minneapolis where we had a chance to visit old friends from our earlier days there. Then we drove to Grand Forks and North to Canada. When we crossed the border from North Dakota into Canada, it was already late in the afternoon. We had planned to get all the way to Regina that evening. At the border, I presented all the documents I thought I would need: automobile title, insurance, military orders, identification papers. It was dark already and cold and snowy. The border agent requested seeing inside my trunk! I hit the trunk release and the trunk sprung open, packed so full of our moving needs that it was like on a spring release. He ran his hands through and among things and then told me it was ok. I put my hands in to straighten the area he had ruffled up and closed the trunk. Then I discovered that in the process of doing this I had lost my car keys. The guard thought maybe they'd fallen on the ground. We spent several minutes looking around. Pat retrieved her extra set of keys and I pulled the car forward so we could look more thoroughly. No keys to be found. Now convinced they must be in the trunk somewhere, we used Pat's keys and departed for our motel in Regina.

When we arrived in Regina, we discovered they were in the midst of a power failure. The motel clerk apologized and after checking in, I got the things we needed from the car trunk and took them in. It was past time for dinner and we had a couple of hungry children and a couple of hungry adults! Using my flashlight, I got the last things out of the passenger compartment and slammed the door. I suddenly realized I had left the keys in the ignition! Now I was in Regina, Canada, with both sets of keys locked somewhere in the car! It was my first experience of breaking and entering! But, I managed to get a coat hangar through the weather stripping on the top of the door and hook the door handle and unlock it. (Both sets of keys were back in our care, one from the ignition and the other from the trunk.) Fortunately, this was the only disaster on our nine-day journey that was otherwise enhanced by the beauty of the wilderness. With the use of the Milepost magazine, we knew to travel about 300 miles each day and that would put us at a great stopping point each night.

One of our stops was in Watson Lake, Canada. We stayed in a nice motel and found a Chinese restaurant next door. Here we learned that all across the upper part of the United States and the lower part of Canada were Chinese communities. These resulted from men who had been brought to work on the building of the railroads (Canadian National or Great Northern). When they had 'worked' off the cost of the transport to the Americas, many of them settled in whatever place they were and opened Chinese restaurants or laundries! Soon they brought their families and made a community. In the restaurant we ate at in Watson Lake, one of the menu items was Bola Gai (perhaps not spelled correctly). It consisted of fried chicken chunks in a sauce that included pineapple chunks, served over rice. All our children loved it, and later Pat re-created the recipe and often made it for us.

We arrived in Anchorage in the middle of the afternoon on our ninth day. I parked in the parking lot by the headquarters and went in to the office where Chaplain Makepeace was located. I wasn't sure if I should sign back in from leave at the 5008th Support Squadron of the HQ, Alaskan Air Command and then sign out for transfer to the 5040th Headquarters Wing of the base, or if I had been transferred automatically during my leave and I should just go sign in at the 5040th. When I got to Chaplain Makepeace's office and posed the question to him, he asked if I had talked with Chaplain Wilson since my return. Of course, I had not, so I went across the hall to the command chaplain's office.

I reported in to Chaplain Wilson and he asked if I had received his letter, sent to me at my leave address. I had not. (I began to have some eerie feelings about my assignment. All I needed was for someone to tell me I wasn't supposed to come back to Alaska now that I was here with my family and my household goods en route!)

Chaplain Wilson was direct. "Your assignment has been changed. Chaplain Makepeace is moving to the Wing/Base office as the Senior Protestant Chaplain and you have inherited the kingdom."

"I've inherited what?" I inquired.

"You are the new Director of Site Activities and Professional Programs here in my office. The site chaplains will all work for you and you work for me. So you can just sign right back in to the 5008th Support Squadron because that's where all of us headquarters types are assigned."

I was somewhat shocked. Roger Makepeace was a senior major. He'd make a great senior Protestant chaplain on base. But, I was a captain as were all the site chaplains. I would be a captain supervising nine to eleven site chaplains who were captains also. I didn't think any of them outranked me by date of rank, but it was still a somewhat unusual situation. I thanked Chaplain Wilson for his confidence in me. He told me to take my time getting my family settled, since there was no hurry about my taking over the job. There'd be time for Roger to brief me on everything I needed to know.

(Meanwhile, down in the parking lot, one of my fellow site chaplains who was a great tease, saw the car and realized it must be Pat and the children. He'd never met any of them. He went to the car, introduced himself as a fellow site chaplain, and then told Pat how much he'd enjoyed reading her letters over the last year! He had never read even one of them, but he sure enjoyed her look!)

The apartment I had rented was close to the base in an area known as Bootlegger's Cove. It was a nice apartment and allowed Andy to begin school in the Government Hill Elementary School where he would attend when we moved into housing on base. This school was right outside the gate of the base and our duplex (when we moved in) was just a couple of blocks inside the gate. It was a good temporary arrangement.

Within a matter of several weeks, our unit on base on Citrus Avenue was available for us to move into. (Whoever named streets on an Alaskan Air Base - Citrus, Orange and Lemon must have had some sense of humor!) Andy and Tami were soon into a routine at the Government Hill Elementary School and Pat and I were into the various activities of the chapel on base as well as my task with the site program.

One of the reasons Chaplain Wilson explained to me that he wanted me in the job was so that I could spend time visiting all the sites. He felt that I was young enough and healthy enough to awaken very early any morning and catch a military flight (mostly C-123s initially and later C-130s) to a site, spend the day and come back with the aircraft. My predecessor didn't do this primarily because of his health situation. He had suffered a slight stroke at a previous assignment and, although declared fit for general service by a medical evaluation panel, was hesitant to stretch his condition. When site commanders were due for their Officer Effectiveness Reports (annually, whether that came in the middle of their one year on a site or at their completion of the year was dependent upon when they had been given an evaluation prior to reporting to remote duty) the Alaskan Air Command general would circulate a questionnaire among the various staff agencies to get a feeling for what he might write about a commander and what numerical value he might put in the evaluation. The general explained to Chaplain Wilson that he placed great value on the report from the chaplain's office primarily because we were the one agency that had people on every site traveling back and forth to Elmendorf on a regular basis and were apt to pick up any problems on a site.

Over the next couple of years, I wrote many of these evaluations and was told by the general's secretary that he often used my 'word' pictures without making a change. Of course, all the site chaplains had the same annual OER requirement and with so many of them on one year tours, I got a lot of experience in writing word picture evaluations on officers while in that job.

One Monday morning, Chaplain Wilson asked me if I missed preaching regularly. Of course, I said. He then said he'd been talking to the base chaplain's office (Protestant Chaplain Roger Makepeace) about them having an early service in the small chapel by the headquarters. Chaplain Makepeace indicated that his chaplain staff was all tied up with services and religious education activities in the early morning hour. Chaplain Wilson's proposal was that we begin that service and that he and I would provide the preaching. Within a couple of months, this process was established and from then on while I was in the command office, I preached at least every other Sunday in the early service in the small chapel.

On one of my staff visits to King Salmon, I was able to take Andy with me and we enjoyed a fishing trip. It was great fun to come back with fish that we could clean and cook in the officers' lounge for our own meal.

During my tenure as the Director of Site Activities and Professional Programs, I was involved in the planning of all the command-wide chaplain functions. This included annual preaching missions, chaplain retreats and conferences, visits from the Chief of Chaplains Office (either the Chief, Deputy and/or staff members), and a retreat for singles from throughout the area. In addition to the Alaskan Air Command responsibility, Chaplain Wilson was the command chaplain for the 'joint command' Alaskan Command that included Army, Navy, and Air Force activities. Many of the activities for chaplains were planned on this inter-service basis and I was responsible for them.

My position in the command office also meant I was a participant in any of the 'war' exercises that might be entered into, either by the Air Force or the joint service team. (Ironicalliy, only Chaplain Wilson was considered 'assigned' to the joint Alaskan Command staff and thereby entitled to the joint command ribbon.) This included deploying to a secure facility in the Kenai Peninsula for several days at a time. I became the responsible person in the command office for the review and updating of chaplain activities in the 'Alaskan Command War Plan'. (AKYWAP was the acronym.) If an attack were imminent, or if hostilities broke out somewhere, then this plan was the means whereby chaplain personnel would be deployed. (The scariest aspect of this was the possibility of needing to evacuate 15,000 dependents from their bases in Alaska to some more secure facility! Fortunately, we never needed to do this. Even during the Cuban missile crisis, the Kennedy Assassination and the Alaskan Earthquake, we never evacuated the entire dependent population. But we did have a plan for that if needed!)

One Monday morning I arrived in my office to be told that one of the airman we had assigned to us was under arrest and in jail in Anchorage! Originally, the only enlisted in the office were the senior enlisted man in the command chaplain's office and one young sergeant in my office. In addition, the command chaplain had a civilian secretary assigned. When my position was divided into two positions (site activities and professional programs) a second young enlisted man was assigned to the office. It was this second airman who was in jail. Actually, he was in jail with another airman from the base chapel section and two other airmen from the base. It seems as though they had been arrested for assault and battery, rape, and robbery! All of this was a result of an encounter with a 'known' prostitute in Anchorage. Evidently, she had agreed to go with these young men, all somewhat inebriated, and have sex with all of them for a stated price. Her later testimony was that she didn't mind them getting rough with her, but when they not only refused to pay her the sum she had agreed to but took money from her purse ... she called the police!

I won't go into all the details of this difficult situation. The other chapel airman from the base was accused of being the one who hit her. He wound up with a bad conduct discharge, a large fine, and some jail time. A similar fate was the lot of the other two airmen from the base. My airman denied having hit her. He denied having taken any money from her. Furthermore, he told me he was too drunk to have sex with her when his turn came! His parents obtained a lawyer for him on a retainer basis. Eventually, his charge was reduced to 'disturbing the piece' (sic) and he paid a small fine and was released. I think he learned a valuable lesson from the event!

The chaplain who succeeded me on the sites that I had covered (Ohlson Mountain, King Salmon, and the Aleutian DEW line) got into trouble at King Salmon on the first or second trip he made to the site. The site commander, whom I had known while serving there, called me and told me the chaplain had become drunk and disorderly in the officers' lounge and he'd ordered him to leave the site and not return. Would I please assign a different site chaplain to King Salmon? After a discussion with Chaplain Wilson, I counseled with the chaplain in question and made the decision to 'switch' circuits between the North of the Range Outboard and the King Salmon/Aleutian DEW line for Protestant coverage.

The following month the chaplain I relieved from King Salmon and moved to the North of the Range Outboard circuit called me to tell me that his mother was deathly ill in Tennessee, and he needed to take emergency leave. Without hesitation, I approved the leave time for 30 days and he departed. This left me with four sites that needed Protestant coverage. I plugged myself into the gap and made the trips. I needed to make regular staff visits to all the sites anyway and this was a way in which I could do that and provide the necessary coverage for character guidance, worship services, counseling and interviews.

A couple of months after that, I received a call from Chaplain Wilson on a Saturday morning. Could I come over to his quarters on base immediately? When I arrived, he was waiting on his front porch dressed in his topcoat (it was wintertime). He came down and got into my automobile. I asked where are we going? "Nowhere, but I wanted to talk where I was sure we wouldn't be overheard."

"What's up, Chief?" I inquired.

Then he told me that the OSI (Office of Special Investigation - the investigative arm of the Air Force) agent had visited him that morning early to tell him that they were in the process of deciding whether they should 'arrest' my site chaplain at King Salmon! It seems as though the teenage son of the owner of the King Salmon Inn (a civilian fish camp, inn, restaurant - in the village at Naknek - the town of King Salmon) had reported that this chaplain had some intimate sexual contact with him. Furthermore, the OSI had then investigated and discovered that this same chaplain, when serving North of the Range Outboard, had such contacts with a couple of young airmen who were also being investigated! In questioning the chaplain, he had admitted both events.

Chaplain Wilson told me he had informed the OSI that he would prefer they not arrest the chaplain, but allow us to dismiss him from the service under the provisions of the appropriate regulations. I counseled with the chaplain (who had a wife and children back in the lower 48) and he told me that he had never done anything like this before but that the loneliness of the site tour and the stress had created this problem. With Chaplain Wilson's approval and the 'go-ahead' from the Alaskan Air Command Commander, I proceeded with paperwork that allowed the chaplain to resign from the Air Force under honorable conditions for the good of the service. I typed all the paperwork myself in order to maintain maximum confidentiality.

I knew it would take at least a month to get the paperwork up through the headquarters to Washington and approved. I couldn't allow him to return to site coverage, but I was determined he wouldn't just sit in his Bachelor Officers' Quarters and do nothing. I knew from a previous conversation that the chaplain who had taken over the religious education program (that I thought I would be doing) was trying to get things organized in an old un-used mess hall that had been assigned to the chaplain's office for religious education. Among the tasks he was hoping to get accomplished was the structuring of the huge number of religious books that had been donated to the chapel. I called him and asked if he could use the assistance of one of my site chaplains for a few weeks in that regard.

"You bet. That would be great," he responded. "What will this cost me?"

"Nothing. I just want to be sure he's at work at the beginning of the duty day and stays throughout the day at whatever task you assign. And, I don't want him working directly with children or youth."

"Oh, wow," the chaplain said, "can I guess what this is all about?"

"You can guess, but I'll not confirm or reject or comment on your suggestions. OK?"

"OK. I think I understand."

Now it may be difficult to believe, but the following week, Chaplain Wilson called me into his office along with his Catholic Deputy Command Chaplain. He commended me on the fine job of paperwork I had done on this difficult case and then assigned me another. One of the Catholic chaplains assigned to the base had been investigated and it was discovered that he had a wife and two children living downtown in an apartment! Obviously, this was a no-no! Although the Catholic deputy thought he should be immediately reported to the necessary endorsing agency and pulled out of the service and sent somewhere for rehab, Chaplain Wilson and the senior Catholic chaplain on base felt that he should be allowed to depart the service in the same manner I had arranged for the site chaplain.

So I began typing the paperwork to make these arrangements. The senior Catholic chaplain on base had a friend who was in charge of a private school in Southern California and he arranged for him to be in contact with him for the possibility of a teaching career after he left the priesthood.

Now I'm thinking that I've had all the unusual training experiences I need in this job. But it wasn't over. The chaplain I had moved from King Salmon to North of the Range Outboard (and who had returned from emergency leave after being gone for a month) was now in the hospital under psychiatric care! The report said he had a fear of flying! Well, he spent a month or so on the chain; that would have been the time to fear flying. Furthermore, he was a former Air Force pilot, served in Korea before he got out and went to seminary! I went to visit him. Then I visited with his doctor. I got the same story in both cases, fear of flying. Then I spoke with an old friend who was the NCO in the psych ward. He told me that he couldn't tell me any information, (except that the chaplain was being 'dried out'!)

I was now back to covering sites on a regular basis because I had two of my five Protestant site chaplains (not counting the one at Shemya) who were dysfunctional! Prior to this latter chaplain's return from hospitalization, he got word that his father had a heart attack in Tennessee! I immediately suggested to Chaplain Wilson that we apply for a 90 day curtailment of his tour and send him on his way. His next assignment had been named already. Chaplain Wilson approved and we pushed the paperwork through as rapidly as possible. My comment to Chaplain Wilson at the time was something like, 'You really know how to train a young guy in a hurry, don't you?' He just grinned.

New site chaplains were arriving to replace those I'd had to dispatch one way or another. Then the argument began! No argument between my boss and me. Chaplain Wilson seemed very pleased with the duties I was performing and the way in which I performed them. However, it came to the attention of the Chief of Chaplain personnel section in Washington, DC, that I was a Captain, serving in a major slot, and supervising 11 captains. I never knew for sure but always suspected it may have been through the endorsing agency of the chaplain who succeeded me on the chain and with whom I had so many problems. First, his drunkenness at King Salmon, then his two 30 day emergency leaves (during a 12 month tour - certainly not his fault that his parents had health problems, but did put pressure on the program) and finally, his psychiatric care (for drying out from alcoholism) and his 90 day curtailment and return early to the lower 48. I gave him an appropriate rating which was mediocre at best. Chaplain Wilson actually marked him down a notch below where I had rated him, the only one to my knowledge he ever changed of my ratings. His endorsing agency was the same denomination as the man who was chief of personnel in the Chief's office.

(Parenthetically, this chaplain went to Maxwell AFB, Alabama from his tour in Alaska. Within a year, he was thrown out of the chaplaincy after he was involved with a teenager who became pregnant, ostensibly by him.)

Over several months, the chaplain personnel folks in Washington came up with reasons why I shouldn't be in that slot. They had majors for whom they did not have slots in which to assign them and, as a captain; I was occupying one of those slots. At one point, Chaplain Wilson got the Alaskan Air Command manpower office to give him an extra slot and determined he would separate the job of site chaplain director from professional programs. This would allow him to put me in the professional program slot and let the chief send in a major for the supervising site chaplain job. However, when the chief's office discovered that I would still be in a major slot, they determined to send in two majors to the command! Finally, one day when I was in Chaplain Wilson's office discussing some business, he took a call from the personnel chaplain in Washington. He put him on speakerphone and I listened to the argument (discussion?) that went back and forth. Chaplain Wilson rejected a couple of names they suggested they were going to send to the command jobs. He told the personnel man in one case, you send that one, and I'll put him somewhere else!

When he hung up, I spoke up, "Chaplain Wilson. Let me go down to the base and let them replace me with two majors here in the headquarters. I don't really need my name remembered this well In Washington?"

The last year I was in Alaska, this all came to a head. When they determined to send me to the base level and bring in two majors (Thomas and McDuffy) to replace me in the two positions my job had been split into, it was to assign me as the senior chaplain in the main chapel on base. Here, I spent my last year responsible for the largest chapel on base and preaching every Sunday in the 1100 (main) Protestant Service which the Armed Forces Radio Service decided to broadcast live to 56 locations throughout Alaska! It was great duty. The sergeant from AFRS liked to tease me by saying, "Chaplain, don't start the service till you see the red light on in my booth in the balcony. You can preach as long as you want, but we go to network news at 1200 hours!"

This last year and a half in Alaska was marked by two other remarkable events! One of these was the famous Alaskan Earthquake on Good Friday, 1964. The earth rumbled like it had not rumbled before in Alaska or all of North America. (The former was known for its frequent tremors.) At 5:36 p.m. on March 27, 1964, the largest earthquake ever recorded in North America, and the second largest in history, rattled coastal Alaska for close to 5 minutes. Though the epicenter of the Great Alaskan Earthquake was deep beneath Prince William Sound -- 75 miles east of Anchorage and 56 miles west of Valdez -- the magnitude 9.2 temblor (later revised to 9.6) rippled water as far away as Louisiana and even made parts of Florida and Texas jump a couple of inches.

I was not home! The Air Force, in those days, encouraged a three-day minimum preaching mission to be held at all the locations around the world. For the most part, local pastors were invited to come on base and preach three nights in a row. Maximum support was provided from the commanders for these missions, believing them to be good for morale and morals! (Might be something that needs to be done now!) Catholic as well as Protestant programs sponsored these events. When I was visiting the sites in the Upper Midwest, I employed local pastors near each site to preach on base for these missions for the Protestants. I had cultivated the friendship of a Franciscan mission priest in St. Paul, Minnesota and for three years, I would take him on the road with me for about three weeks to conduct such programs at all my sites. The first year I was in Minneapolis, I attended the division staff meeting as these missions were getting ready to kick off and announced them to the staff and requested that personnel be given ample opportunity to attend, even if it meant some shifting of duty responsibilities. I still remember the Division Commander, who was a brigadier general and devout Catholic and a remarkable man saying to the staff, "Now, listen here men. These are official functions and, G D it, I want good attendance."

In the Alaskan Air Command we followed the usual practice of employing local pastors or priests where available to conduct these missions. However, this was not possible for the remote sites throughout Alaska that were not located near a village or local church. My plan as the director of site activities was to send a site chaplain to a site different from his regular coverage for these missions. When I was organizing this activity in the late winter of 1963-64, I received a phone call from the commander at Shemya. It was none other than Colonel Hollon Bridges who had been the survival school commander when I was survival school chaplain at Stead AFB, NV. He insisted that he wanted me to come do the preaching mission there on the island 1500 miles West of Anchorage. I agreed to do this and we set the date as Holy Week, 1964. The plan was that I would fly out to Shemya in time to preach on Palm Sunday morning and again that evening. I would also preach on Monday and Tuesday evenings as well. Then I would fly back to Anchorage on the Reeve flight that came out on Wednesday and returned to Anchorage.

We had good services on Palm Sunday. We had great attendance on Monday evening and Tuesday evening as well. There were about 1000 men assigned in various missions on the island at that time. In addition, Hollon and I had a real re-union time together sharing our memories from days at the Survival School and catching each other up on family changes. Then came Wednesday. Reeve's 'big' plane broke down at Adak (where there was a large Naval Base) and they were awaiting parts for repair. When it became apparent that they would not arrive on Thursday either, the chaplain serving there full time asked if I had ever conducted a Maundy Thursday service. Of course I had many times. He had not. So we planned a Maundy Thursday service for that evening to include Holy Communion.

On Friday morning, we got word that Reeve would arrive probably on Saturday since they were now making repairs at Adak. Again, the question came, had I ever conducted a Good Friday service and the answer again was in the affirmative. As we were going into the chapel to begin this service, the sergeant in the chapel office told me there had been a quake in Anchorage. (There is a two-hour difference in time zones between Anchorage and Shemya.) I inquired as to whether it was a 'quake' or a 'tremor' that we had frequently. He didn't know.

When we came out of the service, I asked the sergeant if he had any further information about Anchorage. He said, "We have lost all phone service with Elmendorf, however we've been monitoring a short wave radio operator in Sacramento, California and he said Elmendorf is destroyed and Anchorage is in flames!"

"What?" I exclaimed. "My family is at Elmendorf. I better try to reach them."

"Sir," he reminded me, "We've have no phone contact with the Alaska switch which serves Elmendorf."

I walked into the chaplain's office and picked up the phone, as the sergeant stood by shaking his head at my unbelief! After dialing the number for the access code to the Alaska switch and getting a dial tone, I dialed my home phone number on base at Elmendorf. It rang only twice before Pat answered the phone! (She says she was calm and collected till she heard my voice and then she began to cry!)

"Are you all right?"

"Yes. We are fine." She described briefly the shaking of the house that occurred. There had been no fire and Elmendorf was certainly not destroyed. This quake was not only severe from an intensity level, but it lasted for five minutes! "They have come around with speakers on the Air Police cars and told us to fill our bathtubs with water, since they don't know how long the water system might function. We are to put 'C' rations (emergency food rations) and blankets in our automobiles to be prepared for evacuation, if necessary. Andy and Tami are over at the neighbors (who had teenagers) until I can get all this taken care of. When will you be home?"

"I really don't know. The Reeve flight is still at Adak. There is a Navy aircraft here and if they are coming back to Elmendorf, I'll try to catch a ride with them." I asked for the neighbor's number and hung up. I dialed the access code once more and the neighbor's number. They answered and I was able to talk with both Andy and Tami and encourage them to do whatever Mom told them to do. I would be home as soon as possible.

When I hung up, the sergeant said he was going to try to reach some of his close friends at Elmendorf as well. He dialed the access code without success. In fact, there were no further calls that got through to the Alaska Switch for the next three hours! Of course, I did get razzed about having my 'own connections'.

As I went back down the hall toward the commander's office, I could hear a conversation going on between Colonel Bridges and the Lieutenant Commander Navy pilot of the naval aircraft on the island. They had arrived earlier in the week with a traveling USO show. He was now informing Colonel Bridges that he had a TWX (short wave radio message) from his base in Kodiak, Alaska to return immediately to home base. His crew was preparing now for takeoff imminently. Colonel Bridges asked if he was taking the USO show back with him. He told him he would not do that. He only had orders to return to base. Remember, there were no women stationed on this island and Colonel Bridges told the young naval aviator that he was not leaving this show with several women on the island among 1000 men. Furthermore, exact information on the possibility of tsunami conditions at Shemya might make it necessary to evacuate key personnel from the island.

The young officer drew himself up as tall as he could and said, "Sir, as I understand the situation, I'm responsible to the senior naval aviator present and that's me. So, I'll have to get my crew ready for takeoff."

"Well," replied Colonel Bridges, who drew himself up to his well over six foot height,"as I understand the situation, you are on my island and you'll do as I say! I may need to fly some folks out of here for recovery purposes in Anchorage, emergency response folks." (No wonder the men on the island used to refer to their commander as "Hallelujah Bridges!") "You'll leave when I say you can leave, even if I have to put a bulldozer in front of your aircraft."

"I'll have to see about that," the naval officer said. Immediately he headed down the hall to the Communications department to send a TWX to his headquarters. He came back in about twenty minutes, looking somewhat subdued. "They've instructed me to stay over night to see if you need to evacuate key personnel or take some of them to Anchorage for first response teams. I'll take the USO 'girls' with me then." He turned and headed back to his quarters.

The following morning, the Navy crew, the USO show, and myself, loaded up and headed east. We had received instructions to stop in Cold Bay and pick up a public health nurse to take to Anchorage as well. It was a long flight and late afternoon by the time we arrived at Elmendorf AFB and nearly dark since it was still 'wintertime'. I could see immediately some of the extensive damage that had occurred, including the collapse of the control tower onto the passenger terminal itself. I found a working telephone and called Pat to let her know I was back on base, but that she wouldn't be able to drive to the terminal because of the damage. I gave her information on where to pick me up, and with my B-4 bag in hand, began the walk away from the flight line damage.

(An aside from Pat. She and the children were in the kitchen unpacking a gift I'd sent from a previous trip to Nome, Alaska. As the shaking began and the children, especially Tami, indicated their fears, Pat got them in the corner of the kitchen away from windows and the things that were flying out of cabinets and off of shelves and sat in front of them. She reported the rumbling sound was like a multitude of railway trains going directly under the house that seemed to tip back and forth beneath them. They could hear things falling throughout the house. After the five minutes of shaking was over, they got up and began to look around at the damage. Pat realized that she couldn't find our little dachshund (Huntz) and when called, he did not come. She and the children looked through the house for him. She eventually found him under our bed in the master bedroom. He wouldn't come out even then. She finally crawled under there and 'scooped' him out from under the bed. When she sat him down, he staggered away as though he was drunk. The cause of this became clear when she discovered the broken bottle of aftershave lotion (alcohol based) on the bathroom floor! She has said since, that had she had another bottle of it she might have been tempted to consume it herself.)

(Let me share just a couple of anecdotes that came out of the earthquake. There were countless stories and most of them have been published somewhere or other. These are only from the many I learned about. Bob Reeve, previously mentioned as founder and owner of Reeve Aleutian Airline, was in the Anchorage Westward Hotel (Now renamed the Hilton) top floor bar with a business associate when the building began to shake. Bob reported that he looked at his friend and asked, 'how many martinis have I had?' They immediately began to make their way out of the bar to the staircase for the 14 floor trip to the ground when Bob turned back with the comment, 'wait a minute. I have to get my hat!' He was famous for keeping paperwork in his hat, to be fished out by his secretary every morning when he came to the office!)

(Then, there was the Air Force officer who was in his apartment in town taking a shower when the building began to shake. He grabbed a towel and started out to get dressed, but his cat was so disturbed that it leaped on his shoulders and scratched him badly. Now bleeding down his back and trying to get out of the apartment he fell and injured his shoulder. Subsequently a rescue squad was transporting him down the stairwell on a stretcher (no elevator to use with the electricity off) and dropped him and he broke his leg! He later allowed as how he had wished he'd just stayed in the shower the whole time.)

(Then, my friend David Green, who owned Green Furrier Company in Anchorage, reported his story. He was across the street from his business in a gym/spa place getting a massage. David was in his 70's and this was his one relaxation at the end of most weeks. When the shaking began everyone quickly left the facility. He rolled off the massage table and wrapped the sheet around himself and headed for the outside. There a group of folks had created a circle for protection, with everyone holding hands to insure if the earth opened up and closed, none of them would be caught in the crevices. This was a widely practiced way for groups to avoid being swallowed up by the opening and closing of the earth during such severe quakes. Only when the quaking stopped did he realize that he had let go of the sheet to take hands in the circle and was now standing on Anchorage's main street in the freezing cold totally nude!)

The weeks following the quake were very busy ones in the command office as we were the center for much of the personal recovery programs on base that didn't include direct construction problems. Amazingly, the physical damage on base was not nearly as extensive as might have been expected. Perhaps the worst damage was to the seven-story hospital, located between Elmendorf AFB and Fort Richardson Army post. It consisted of two towers with connecting hallways. The two towers split in two and rose and fell as independent units. When I accompanied some of the inspection teams, it was possible to stand on the seventh floor and look down the chasm to the subbasement. Engineers stated that it did what it was supposed to do, ride independently but not fall down. It cost over a million dollars to repair it but the replacement cost was said to be seven million dollars. One of the nurses in obstetrics told me they evacuated the hospital following the quake with no injuries to patients or staff. They delivered their first baby across the street in the nurses' quarters about twenty minutes after the quake ended!

In our discussions in the command chaplain's office, we proposed the idea of having an Air Force wide offering to be received in all chapel services on one of the following Sundays and all the funds deposited with the Chief of Air Force Chaplains. This Alaska Disaster Relief Fund was eventually deposited in the bank at Elmendorf and the command chaplain's office was the office of responsibility for the distribution of the funds. It became a part of my task as a 'professional activity'. We received requests directly from some personnel (primarily enlisted) who had suffered great losses and from some agencies. We provided funds directly to two campgrounds that were used extensively by military personnel for youth activities and couples and men's retreats. One of these was in the Kenai Peninsula and was operated by a Catholic order. The other was at Kings Lake Camp, near Wasilla. Our military personnel used it to the extent of more than 50% of its availability. The rest of the time it was used by the YMCA, the Campfire Girls, the Alaska Crippled Childrens Association, and several local church groups. Because of our extensive use of the campground, we were represented on the board by Chaplain Wilson and myself. (I later was the President of the board.) King's Lake Camp had just begun a drive to raise funds for a new recreation building. Obviously, with the quake damage, this was now a non-starter. Through the Alaska Disaster Relief Fund we were able to get that back on track.

The design for the new recreation building called for a 56 by 76 foot structure. Its basic support would be poles set in the ground and the structure would literally hang on these poles. This was considered good technology because of both the shifting soil in the tundra and the possibility of quakes. I discovered that after the earthquake, many of the communication poles throughout Alaska were being replaced. The poles that were being taken out of use were still long enough for our needs with the recreation building. With the assistance of the Alaska Communication Region Commander we were able to acquire these poles, get them transported to the Camp and, as a training exercise, install them in the right places for the new building. This saved us a considerable amount of investment. The mayor of Anchorage donated a large sum of money to build a huge fireplace at one end of the building.

I believe this was the first time the Chief of Air Force Chaplains had conducted a service wide offering drive with the funds designated for a specific purpose. That became an annual event in Air Force Chapels and a great deal of money was raised and distributed through the Chief's office for worthwhile causes.

CHAPTER TWENTY-FOUR

The other event in our last year at Elmendorf was more delightful. Our son, Tom, was born. My overseas tour was scheduled to end on 1 March 1966; however, my parents would be celebrating their fiftieth anniversary in February of 1966 and wanted to have a renewal of their vows as a part of that event. Since I was the only clergy in the family, they thought it would be great if I could officiate at this service. A justice of the peace had married them in 1916 and so the plan was to hold this ceremony in their church. One of my mother's older brothers and my dad's only sister would stand up with them at the service and it would be followed with a reception in the church fellowship hall. In order to be there, I decided to request a curtailment of my tour to 1 February 1966. We knew that our child was expected about the middle of October and so this would work out well for us.

Then came the curtailment. For some reason, they decided to curtail my tour by 90 days instead of the 30 I had requested. I discovered much later it was because the person I was replacing was due to depart for Johnston Island in the Pacific sooner and they decided I would be needed at my new assignment. There were only two Protestant chaplains at Perrin AFB, Texas (near Sherman) and the senior man had some health problems as well. Now, instead of departing sometime in January, we had a port call (not by ship but aircraft) of 7 December. Combine this with a late arrival of our baby at the end of October instead of the middle and we were faced with the dilemma of having to travel with an infant under six weeks of age. Air Force regulations at the time required any infant under six weeks of age had to have a doctor's ok to travel. Fortunately, Tom was healthy and the doctors agreed to his travel.

We left Alaska on 7 December, flew to McChord AFB, Washington (Seattle area) where we picked up our automobile that had been already shipped South, and headed for Perrin AFB, Texas. Our route took us down the West coast to Edwards AFB, California. Here Tom was baptized by our friend Chaplain Makepeace (now stationed there as Wing Chaplain) in the Astronaut Chapel on base. We then traveled South East to El Paso, Texas and then up through Dallas to Sherman, Texas where we signed in from travel and almost immediately signed out on leave. By the time Tom was seven and a half weeks old, he and his siblings had traveled over seven thousand miles by air and auto. We had visited Knott's Berry Farm (plans to go to Disneyland were thwarted by the fact they were closed on Tuesdays during the winter months!) We also went across the border in El Paso to Juarez for a shopping trip along the way.

This early return allowed for our presence at my parents' fiftieth anniversary renewal of vows in St. Clair, Missouri. As events turned out, the chaplain I was scheduled to replace in Texas was in the hospital with a serious kidney problem when I arrived. As a result of this medical problem, his assignment to Johnston Island was cancelled and he and I overlapped by several months before he finally was transferred to an assignment in Southeast Asia (Thailand). I was later told by Chaplain Roy Terry (then Air Defense Command Chaplain, later chief of Air Force Chaplains) that he really wanted to bring me to the headquarters but at the base chapel level in Colorado (not on the staff) because they needed good preachers there, however, the need at Perrin with only the senior man present was too great. All of that changed when the man I was replacing stayed for many months.

Perrin was an Air Defense Command base, however, the mission was a training mission. They provided all the lead in training for delta wing aircraft, which included the F-102, F-106, B-58, and the F-104 (though the latter was not delta wing, its stub wings gave it similar flight characteristics). It was a relatively small base. The chapel was a World War II cantonment chapel facility, and we also utilized an old barracks building a block away for offices and classrooms. Base housing was 'Wherry' housing with three rather small bedrooms. Since we were not required to live on base and our children really needed their own bedrooms (boy and girl 3 years apart and a new baby) we elected to purchase a home in Sherman. This was a good decision and we thoroughly enjoyed our home there. (We paid $19,250 for the four bedroom, two bath, two car attached garage, fenced yard, cedar shake roof, all brick home! We lived in it for over two years and sold it for $20,000! We thought we'd really made out well!)

(Time to include the story of my parents' wedding anniversary! As they were planning this event, my mother thought I might need to see their marriage license in order to conduct a renewal of vows. I didn't need that, but she thought I did and she couldn't find it anywhere. So, she wrote to the office in St. Louis where they had been married to acquire a replica of their marriage license. My father was home the day the reply came in the mail. My mother was not home. He steamed open the letter and replaced it with a handwritten note stating, "Mrs. Jacobs, or Miss Moise, as the case may be, please give me more details since I'm unable to find any record that you have married." Of course, it didn't fool my mother since she was used to my dad's left-handed scrawl! But it made for a funny joke. The renewal service went well and the reception was fine. It was a great time together with family and friends.)

We enjoyed our home in Sherman and the children were established in a good school system. The chapel program was a strong one. The senior man discovered that with the advent of the Viet Nam situation, chaplains were notified that if they had any humanitarian reason that prevented them from being assigned to a remote tour in the war zone, it would have to be documented before they received the assignment or it would not be honored. Almost immediately, the senior man contacted personnel with evidence that his aging mother in Sacramento, California needed his presence nearby since he was the only living relative. His request for humanitarian reassignment was honored and he was transferred to one of the bases in Sacramento where he completed his twenty years for retirement.

When I took over as the temporary senior chaplain, I discovered the sergeant in the office was maintaining a 'separate slush' fund from the authorized petty cash fund in the Protestant Chaplain Fund area. This had been a practice for some time, I guess, but was strictly against regulations. Furthermore, the Catholic chaplain didn't trust the safe, so had a habit of putting the offerings in a bank bag and hiding them behind books in his office. The safe was not bolted to the floor as required by regulations, although a work order had been executed requesting this be done. I explained to the Catholic Chaplain that I could easily defend his loss of funds because someone had carried off the very heavy floor safe because it was not bolted down. I could not defend his loss of funds if someone stole his bookcase and got his bank bag! He reluctantly agreed to comply with the rules. I also had the 'slush' funds deposited in the bank and instituted strict controls on the chaplain fund situation, including the use of petty cash as authorized in the regulations.

A few weeks later, I had another encounter with this young chaplain. Vatican II had occurred and changed many of the rules for celebrating mass. I walked into the chapel to see the engineers there with the Catholic chaplain discussing how they were going to 'remodel' the chapel for his purposes! The altar railing would be removed completely. The lectern would remain, but there would be a platform in the center behind the altar with a raised chair on it from which he could preside! When I questioned this activity without any discussion with the other chaplains, he told me it was necessary for these things to be done.

I asked the engineers to depart and then sat down and explained that some other groups used the chapel as well and they still used the altar railing. Furthermore, I wasn't sure that he fully understood the requirements of his own faith now since Vatican II, but that we would have to make some compromises in order that the chapel was still appropriate for all denominations to use. He wasn't happy about this but agreed finally to comply!

Within a matter of months of our arrival in Sherman, I attended a Methodist Chaplains retreat in Austin, Texas. Dr. Joe Quillian, dean of Perkins School of Theology (SMU) was the main speaker. Joe had been a WWII Navy chaplain and understood the chaplaincy quite well. In one of our informal discussions he discovered I was going to be in Sherman, Texas. He encouraged me to come by SMU on my way back to Sherman and check out the possibility of my working on a second seminary degree while at Perrin.

This resulted in my enrolling at Perkins and over the next eighteen months, I was able to complete all the course requirements and write my dissertation and defend it before a faculty panel. As a result, I received my STM (Masters in Sacred Theology) in June 1967. The day I met the three professors for the oral defense of my dissertation, they discussed my paper at length with me and then excused me while they had further discussion and made a decision. I sat in the hallway for about 30 minutes before my advisor came out and looked surprised at my presence. "Oh my, we passed you twenty minutes ago. I guess we forgot to come out and tell you all was well."

(A note about seminary degrees: Originally, seminary degrees were considered professional education and after four years of undergraduate work, a seminarian spent three more years in graduate work. For this he was awarded a professional degree, a Bachelor of

Divinity. So most pastors in mainline Protestant denominations had a BA and a BD for their seven years. Then in the mid to late sixties, seminaries began to realign their degree programs to parallel other professions. Physicians, lawyers, educators who spent four years of undergraduate work then received either a masters at the end of one year beyond the undergraduate work or a doctorate if they stayed for two more years. Medical people received doctor of medicine (MD) or doctor of dental surgery (DDS) or doctor of veterinary medicine (DVM). Lawyers usually received a doctor of Jurisprudence (JD) and educators often received a masters of arts (MA) and then a doctor of philosophy (PhD) or doctor of education (EdD). As seminaries began this process of change, many notified their graduates to send in their BD degree and they would be issued a Masters in Divinity (MDiv). Eden chose to offer this 'swap' if you spent 3 weeks in a summer course at the seminary. Meanwhile, the changes continued so that the STM degree became an STD or a DMin (Doctor of Sacred Theology or Doctor of Ministry). I did not return to Eden for the 'swap' because by then I had received the STM from SMU! Furthermore, I was subsequently awarded an honorary Doctor of Divinity from my undergraduate school, Central Methodist University.)

After a few months as the senior chaplain (temporarily since I was still a captain and the slot called for a lieutenant colonel!) a replacement arrived and took over as the senior man. He was a congenial chaplain, though I developed little respect for his work ethics. He spent much of his mornings in his office going over his portfolio (he had inherited a large amount of money from an uncle) and the rest of the morning at the base-exchange cafeteria drinking coffee and playing the pinball machine! He told me that since I was already leading the religious education program, the men's program, the young adult program and preaching half of the time, he would leave things as they were. He would be responsible for the women's program and preach the other half of the services. There were two services each Sunday morning. There was no evening service, although I worked with the Protestant Youth of the Chapel each Sunday evening and also started a Protestant Adult League (PAL) for single young adults - military or dependent - that met Sunday evenings. Many Sundays we would attend the movie on base and then have a group discussion of the movie along with refreshments.

We were not immune to difficulties from time to time. One that caught my attention was the visit of the OSI agent (remember Office of Special Investigation) one Monday morning. It seems that one of our airmen had been apprehended in Denison, Texas - North of the base - dressed as a woman and harassing some other women in a Laundromat. More paperwork became necessary to allow this young man to be discharged from the military service!

After I had been at Perrin Air Force Base, Texas (Sherman) for over eighteen months, I realized that my last overseas tour at Elmendorf was considered an 'accompanied' tour'. I had been promoted to major during this period as well. In those days, many chaplains received a remote tour, then a stateside tour and then an overseas accompanied tour and then back in the states. Then they were eligible for another remote tour. Since my remote tour in Alaska had been followed by the consecutive accompanied tour, I suspected that I was due for another remote assignment. The military situation in Southeast Asia was in a rather major build up. Thinking that I probably would be sent remote to one of those bases, I called the staff chaplain (our next higher headquarters at the time was the 14th Air Force at Gunter AFB, Alabama) and asked how I might go about volunteering for a remote assignment. My thinking was that we were buying our house in Sherman, the children were in a good school situation, and if I were going remote this would be a good place for them to remain while I was overseas for a year.

The staff chaplain informed me that he didn't think this was a good idea. His logic was that the Chief of Chaplains personnel folks knew where I was located; they knew my FSSD (Foreign Service Selection Date) and likely had me programmed eventually for a remote tour. If I volunteered, they would have to work me into the current schedule of assignments that had already been determined. This would mean some other assignments would have to be changed in order to make this possible. It was better, he thought, to just wait out my turn. I agreed that this probably made sense.

A couple of months later, I received a phone call from the staff chaplain at 14th Air Force! He asked me, "Bill, are you sitting down?"

"Yes, sir. I'm sitting down." I figured this was the advance notice of my overseas remote tour that would come through the personnel office eventually. Pat had come out to the base that day to shop at the commissary and was in the office as I spoke to him.

"Well," he continued, "how does Hickam in September sound?"

Hickam AFB is in Honolulu, Hawaii! "Are you pulling my leg, sir?"

"No. You are scheduled to go to Hickam in September."

All I could say was "Wow" before I said goodbye and hung up. We were going to Hawaii! We shipped our second car (a VW Bug) from California at our expense and kept the Mercury to travel in on leave and to the West coast where it was also shipped to Hawaii. This worked out well, since our VW was there when we arrived and therefore available for us to get around in until the Mercury arrived.

CHAPTER TWENTY-FIVE

Information we received indicated that base housing at Hickam was greatly limited because of the buildup in Southeast Asia. As a result, we could expect approximately a year to eighteen months before gaining base housing. With the sale of our house in Sherman, we decided it would make most sense to purchase a house in Honolulu rather than to rent for that length of time. All advice we received indicated that it was possible that we might even make a profit by purchasing rather than renting as well.

When we arrived in Hawaii we were put up in TLA (temporary lodging accommodations) off base. This was an apartment not too far from the base, and although not too expensive, it was also not too desirable from the standpoint of the facilities and some of the more permanent neighbors! I knew a Methodist pastor in Honolulu and he put us in touch with a realtor that he believed we could trust. He met us and took us to lunch and then set about helping us to understand the Honolulu realty market! He told us the first day he was not going to show us anything in which we would have an interest. We thought that a bit strange until he explained that most folks coming from the mainland (remember in Alaska it was the lower 48? In Hawaii, it is the mainland) were shocked by the high prices of things in Hawaii, so it was better to get that shock over with first!

The next day he would show us places we could afford and in which we might have an interest. This proved to be a very beneficial arrangement. On that second day we found a brand new house on the mountain overlooking Pearl Harbor. It was three bedroom, two bath, two car carport, single wall construction (this means that the board you are looking at that is painted on the outside, is the same one inch board you are looking at that is stained on the inside - no insulation) with cathedral ceiling (this means that the ceiling that is finished inside is the inside of the roof on the outside!) There was no heating system or air conditioning system. The windows were jalousie (small panes of glass that rotate like shutters). The price was $37,000. It was probable that we would not qualify for a mortgage at the rate of down payment and remaining balance required. However, in Hawaii it was common to purchase such a home with a contract for sale. That is, you paid a small down payment and you paid so much each month, against the eventual possibility of increasing your payments or selling the house. Once we understood this system, we entered into a contract for sale on this house. Oh yes. We didn't own the land under the house, but it was on a 99-year lease from the Bishop estate! This also was common in Hawaii at that time. The house was approximately four or five miles from the base. It was on a ridge about three blocks from the top of the mountain. There were no houses behind it, since the chasm fell off rapidly into a valley below. The edge of our property blended into the wilderness below where there were wild guava fruit trees and huge monkeypod trees. (The guava attracted wild feral hogs and the monkeypod attracted our oldest son, Andy and his buddies who built tree houses in more than one of them and connected them with cables to send things back and forth.)

(Some fourteen years later we re-visited Hawaii and drove up on the mountain to see the house. Neighbors we had known still lived across the street and told us the house was worth over half a million dollars then. The land had been purchased by the present owners for $15,000 from the Bishop estate that had begun to sell off the leased land under homes. Much of the house looked the same as when we left it. The landscaping had not been changed. In fact, when we visited the current occupants, they still had the same shag carpeting we had installed originally! We sold the house for $45,000 when we moved on base two years from our first arrival. By then I had been promoted to Lieutenant Colonel.)

Andy was enrolled in the Aiea Middle School and Tami in the Alva Scott Elementary School, both of which were toward the bottom of the mountain. Tom, of course, was a stay at home-helper to his Mom. The neighborhood in which our new house was located was about 90% Japanese descendants. They were all great neighbors. Some were part Hawaiian or part Philippine. A party in the neighborhood was always interesting because there would be a multitude of sandals/shoes on the front stoop since hardly anyone wore shoes indoors that had been worn outdoors! There were a couple of little boys near Tom's age that became good playmates.

The first day of school was a near disaster for Tami. When she met her mother who'd walked partway down the hill, she was in tears. She told her, "Momma. All day I felt like a giant white refrigerator!" Tami is not tall now and wasn't for her age then, however the other children in the class were mostly dark hair, dark eyes, dark complexion in comparison to her blonde hair and blue eyes and were short by our standards!

Andy had a somewhat different experience. As a newcomer he was warned that the following week was going to be 'kill haoli' day. Haoli was a word used mainly in Hawaii to describe a white person. Depending on how you say it, the word can mean either an insult or just a fact. Among the local kids in Aiea, it was used to try to intimidate newcomers! Needless to say, no such day took place!

Andy was always a bright youngster, with a habit he probably inherited from his Dad to not work too hard! By midterm of his first year, he was having problems in Algebra, mostly because he didn't turn in his homework. His teacher called me to tell me about his problem. So, I sat down with Andy and assisted him in doing the homework, mostly to insure he actually did it. The teacher told me that it didn't matter if he flunked algebra because he still was learning more than if he was in general math. I disagreed with this, pointing out that this was his only high school education and every grade counted, especially if he decided to go to college. His algebra teacher didn't speak very plain English and this got me thinking. I wondered how he was doing in his other classes. In this way, I discovered that he was not taking his clarinet to band class. I knew he practiced it at home and left the house with it in the morning. He had been excused from music class sometime after Thanksgiving because he had bitten his tongue and it became infected, hence he couldn't play the clarinet. But after Christmas vacation this was healed and he should have been back with his clarinet. I asked the teacher what did he do during band if he didn't bring his clarinet. The teacher said, "Oh, he play the drums."

"He plays the drums? Why does he play the drums?"

"Because he's better at the drums than the kid s'pose to play drums."

Well, we had a good discussion about band that day. But I also began to think that the Aiea high school was not helping Andy in his real needs of education. We had friends who had a son at Punahou School in Honolulu. This school was founded originally by the missionaries for educating their own children and had evolved into the most desirable private school on the island. We made arrangements for Andy to be tested to see if he qualified to attend Punahou and when this proved true, he transferred to Punahou and completed the first two years of his high school there.

With this experience, we determined that the following year when Tami finished the Alva Scott Sixth grade, it would be wise to seek admission for her at Punahou as well. She went there the last year we were in Hawaii. (The tuition at Punahou for the two of them was greater than later when they both were in college at once! But it was worth it for the quality education they received.)

After we had been there two years, we felt that the economy was stalling somewhat and it was suggested we might put the house up for sale and move on base. The house sold quickly and we had a three-bedroom unit on base available to us to move. But, as in the great scheme of things, I was not home! For many years I had been interested in working with those who had alcohol problems. When I was serving in St. Louis with Alfred Watkins, we had several old veterans in the neighborhood that lived in boarding houses and some of these had alcohol problems. I prayed with several of them on many occasions, without really doing much for their problem.

When I was visiting radar sites out of Minneapolis, again I was confronted with airmen on remote locations that dealt with their loneliness and fears through the use of alcohol, which was all too available and inexpensive. During this time I became acquainted with Wally Christiansen who was very involved with the Alcoholics Anonymous program in the city. The chapter of AA there was the second one organized in the United States. In my various conversations with Wally, he invited me to their facility downtown Minneapolis. He thought it might be helpful to my understanding if I attended the sessions that beginners in AA attended. He told me their plan was for the alcoholic to attend a training session on Monday night and then a squad meeting that Friday. Then the next week, the training was on Tuesday and squad meeting on Friday. Then Wednesday and Friday and then Thursday and Friday. If the person made it sober through that month long training program, he/she had a month of sobriety already.

I explained that I couldn't do that because of my need to travel to my various sites around the upper Midwest. He asked if I thought I could take an entire week to attend. I could come Monday, Tuesday, Wednesday, and Thursday to the training sessions and then visit a squad meeting on Friday. This way I would get the experience and since I didn't need to maintain any sobriety anyway, it would be a good experience. I agreed to do this and so I reported on a Monday evening to 401 Nicollet Avenue near downtown Minneapolis. When I came in, there was a woman at a table who greeted me and asked me a question that I didn't quite understand. She repeated the question. While I was trying to figure out what she meant, Wally came over to the table and whispered in her ear; 'he's the pastor I was telling you about. He's a chaplain at the Air Base. Just list him as a guest.' Then I figured out what she was asking; "Was I a periodic or a chronic?" Well, of course, I was neither.

I completed the week's program, spending some time with a squad of recovering alcoholics. Later, I was privileged to attend their two-week residency program as well. (My commander was willing to list this as 'permissive TDY', meaning at no expense to the government but not accountable as leave time.) At that, I received everything the rest of the participants received, except for the vitamin B shots they got. This is a common deficiency among long-term alcoholics. I was involved in the years in Alaska in similar AA work, especially on the sites. In this context I continued to work with those who had substance addictions when I arrived in Hawaii. I soon became aware that we were experiencing a large number of addiction problems among our young military personnel as well as teenage dependents. Everything that could be imagined in terms of hallucinogenic drugs seemed to be available in Hawaii, much of it coming from the West coast. In addition, there was a considerable amount of drugs filtering back from Southeast Asia, where the opiates and other substances were widely available.

In some of the literature to which I was subscribing for my own continued education in these matters, I read about an effort on a national level for the expansion of training for working with addiction problems. The first Federally sponsored and funded Drug and Alcohol Abuse Education program was scheduled for January - February 1970 to be held at Adelphi University on Long Island, NY. I made the suggestion to our hospital commander that I thought some of the medical folks should get this training, however he told me this was a social problem and not a medical problem and he couldn't justify any of his doctors being gone for an entire month for such a program.

I recommended to our Command Chaplain that this needed some push from a higher level, perhaps the Chief of Chaplain office. Shortly thereafter, I heard that the Air Force had applied to the Federal program for training slots in this program and been allotted four spaces. One was allocated to the Air Force Academy, one to the Air Training Command and one to the Air Force Chaplain School. The fourth was allotted to the Pacific Air Force and I was tapped to attend the program.

In January 1970, I flew from Honolulu to New York City. When I arrived, I used the telephone number that had been given to me to call Adelphi University in order to arrange transportation from the airport to the campus. When I called, the answer I received from the other end was, "Boiler Room!"

"I beg your pardon. I'm trying to reach Adelphi University."

"This is the boiler room."

"No, this is the number I was given to call. Dr. Jerry Edwards sent me this number to call to arrange for transportation to the campus for a month long seminar I'm attending."

"I don't know nuttin' bout seminars. This is the boiler room." And he hung up!

This left me with the only option - take a taxi (or shuttle if one was available, but there was none) to the University campus on Long Island and hope I would be able to recoup it on my travel voucher later. It was a lengthy and expensive trip, but I arrived on campus without knowing where to go anyway. I had the taxi take me to the administrative building. From there I was directed to the gymnasium across campus. I lifted my B-4 bag and walked across campus with the stares following me. I was in uniform! Of course, this was a requirement of travel on official orders in those days. It was not a comfortable walk! When I arrived at the gymnasium, several assistants to Dr. Edwards, the director of the program, greeted me.

The next thirty days were a mixture of group processing techniques, drug and alcohol culture, addiction difficulties, psychopharmaceutical information, and field trips to free clinics and similar locations. Each evening I taped a cassette of my feelings about the day to include something of the activities experienced. I mailed these at the end of each week to my friend and co-worker Chaplain Floyd Chambers at Hickam AFB so that he could vicariously know something of what I was experiencing and could brief others on the event. This proved helpful, especially later when Floyd took over some of my work after my transfer from Hickam.

(It was during this period of my absence from Honolulu that Pat sold the house and moved on base to the unit we had been provided. She did leave me a forwarding address so that I could find the family when I returned! It was this two-story unit we were living in later when on a Sunday evening, Andy arrived home from youth group only to discover he had forgotten his door key. Pat and I had gone following evening services with the single young adults to a local restaurant for a late night snack. Tami and Tom were already in bed. Andy tried to rouse them with the doorbell without success. Then he tried tossing some pebbles at Tami's bedroom window, again without success. So he climbed up on the small roof over the front porch where he could knock on her window. Unfortunately for him, a passerby saw this, didn't recognize him and notified the Security Police who came immediately and shined their bright light on him! He had some explaining to do about who he was and why he was on the roof! Tami was awakened and identified him and let him in.)

Most of the four weeks in Adelphi were spent in interactive exercises or field trips. The straight lectures were only in areas of knowledge and data, e.g. effects of various psychedelic and other drugs. The field trips included experiencing something of the drug culture in and around New York City. In one of these visits, those who desired to do it were allowed to smoke marijuana under a controlled situation. (I did not do so for several reasons!) But I monitored some who did. As a result, I was able to accurately report on the behavior of a couple of the participants as they went through the stages of getting 'high' and then coming down. These I reported in my taped accounts. Many of the participants were from educational institutions, educators, counselors, and administrators. The only military personnel were the four of us from the Air Force. From the Air Training Command, Captain George Eychner. From the Air Force Academy, Captain Jim Speight. From the Air Force Chaplain School, Chaplain Bob Shannon. And from the Pacific Air Forces, myself. None of the other service branches were represented at this first Federal Seminar in Drug Abuse and Education. I firmly believe this put the Air Force a step ahead in combatting these difficulties in those early years.

We were all challenged to devise plans for how we would use this information when we returned to our places of endeavor. We also developed an appreciation for measuring the success of our work, through pre-testing and post-testing participants. I focused in on what I thought I could 'sell' back at Hickam, namely, a three to five day workshop. My target group of participants would be First Sergeants, squadron commanders, security police, doctors, counselors, legal officers, personnel officers and chaplains. My plan was to provide training for these with plans that what I called the multiplier effect would reach out to the personnel they either supervised or with whom they came into contact. I also came up with what I later called the 'carbon paper' effect, in which awareness develops as each trainee becomes a trainer but the results are not as powerful as the original training. As a result, after a while, there will need to be additional training for those who have received their training 'down the line' from the original workshops. I had several in-depth discussions with Dr. Jerry Edwards, the director of the program, concerning this approach. He agreed that this approach would make sense in the military climate. I had discussions with the other three Air Force officers there as well concerning this possibility.

When the four weeks were over, I flew back to Hawaii, inspired and determined to bring about some change in the way addictions were being handled. We were seeing increased numbers of men coming back from Southeast Asia with developing, or developed, addictions, mostly marijuana, but also many with heavier drugs. (Later, when I was directing the program at Lackland AFB, we discovered the rate of drug use on the part of returnees from Southeast Asia was very similar to that of new enlistees arriving from the streets of the USA!)

I gave a complete report of the four-week seminar to the chaplain staff at Hickam and subsequently to the Wing Commander and his staff. Then I proposed the kind of workshops I wanted to institute. The responses were positive in almost every case. The PACAF Commander suggested I try to keep the workshop to three days instead of five. He felt that most duty sections would be more apt to allow personnel to attend three days than an entire week. So I set about organizing the first of these three-day workshops. I developed pre-tests and post-tests and six-week later follow-up tests. I ran these by the folks in the comptroller's office who had access to computers and personnel who were trained in statistics and could provide scientific analysis of our results. I also sent information to the other three Air Force officers who had been at the Adelphi seminar concerning what we were doing.

After the second seminar, there was an inquiry from the Hawaii State School Board (all of the school system was under one administration since territorial days) about the workshops and whether they could send a couple of their counselors to attend one of them. We agreed to permit this. Eventually, this led to my being appointed to the newly constituted Hawaii Governor's Drug Council and invitations to present seminars of various durations to school sponsored programs. Most of these were in Honolulu, although I did travel to the island of Kauai for a workshop with teachers.

We were aware that many folks had questions about drugs and the problems that ensued with their abuse, but didn't know where to get answers. In the case of young airmen, they didn't want to ask anyone for fear they would be identified and discharged, if not prosecuted. Parents also needed information in terms of their teenage children but didn't know where to turn. I proposed and was able to get approved a special telephone in my office where anyone could call and ask for information or arrange private counseling without fear of being in trouble. I wanted to call it the 'drugline' and have the phone number be d-r-u-g. Unfortunately, the communications folks were not able to do that, the closest they could give me was d-r-a-g! So it became the dragline for anonymous info on drug problems. This led to many opportunities for counseling with those who were having problems or with parents who were concerned. In quite a number of cases, it was a parent who found something they believed to be illegal drugs and wanted verification before they confronted a son or daughter and perhaps sought counseling. I was able to identify most drugs with no difficulty, but occasionally I wasn't certain. I had a great working relationship with the Office of Special Investigation. The major assigned there was father to one of Andy's good friends. I could contact him and he would bring a test kit with him to the chapel and make the necessary identification. He didn't want me to ever bring anything into his office because theoretically he would have to make a 'case' about it then. In this fashion we were able to help a good many folks, not only from Hickam but from the other military communities who heard about our program and had none on their own facilities.

I set up a program for families where there was a concern for a drug problem. We called it the Family Reintegration Education Experience (FREE) and it was quite successful in helping families of teenagers deal with the problems.

One situation that became quite involved concerned an Army Colonel. He and his family lived on Hickam Air Force Base, however his assignment was to the Pacific Command (joint service command located at Camp Smith on the mountain nearby). He called me one day and then came to my office. He brought with him a small box that his son had received in the mail that very day. The Colonel had come home for lunch, which he usually did not do. The package had come from an unknown address in California and raised his curiosity because the outside included the ascription, "Happy Birthday". Since it was not near his son's birthday, he became curious. The box rattled. He opened it and found a large number of little tablets that he decided must be some kind of drugs. The note inside listed "100 tabs. Your cost, one dollar each. Sell for three dollars each. Send us your remittance immediately."

I examined the tabs and then licked one just a little. I was nearly certain they were LSD, which I'd had the opportunity to lick while at the Adelphi seminar. They had a rather distinctive flavor. The Colonel left them with me and I called my friend from the OSI. He came by the office and confirmed my suspicion. We laughed that day, because he said he knew one of these days he was going to read about a major fish kill caused by the stuff I flushed away at the chapel toilets. After he left, I realized I had an appointment at the Wing Headquarters to attend a committee that was considering renovations in the chapel facilities. (FUB or Facilities Utilization Boards are a part of life at most military installations.) I grabbed my briefcase and jumped in the car and drove across the base to the headquarters. Only when I was double stepping up to the second floor conference room did I remember that I still had the box with the 100 tabs of LSD in my briefcase! I surely hoped that I would not be inspected nor have to show anything in my briefcase to anyone that day!

A broad aside: The fifteen year old son of the Colonel I mentioned in the previous paragraph had plans to sell the LSD tabs and keep the profit so that when his Dad was transferred to the pentagon (immanently) he would use these funds as a stake to stay in Hawaii and live on the beach! As it worked out, he ran away from home a few days before they were due to depart. Although his dad reported him as a missing person, the Honolulu police told him frankly that they couldn't tell a runaway from anyone else living on the beach but that if he were apprehended for some reason they would contact him.

Several weeks later, I received a call from the Colonel, now in Washington, D.C. The boy had been found and detained. He was downtown in the juvenile holding area. The Colonel wanted me to visit with him and then let him know how he could get him sent on to Washington. I made the visit. The boy seemed genuinely contrite and anxious to be re-united with his family (or at least to get out of detention!) Subsequently, his Dad made arrangements for a one-way ticket from Honolulu to Washington, D.C. on a non-stop flight (commercial). The police would bring him to the airport where I would meet them and see that he boarded his flight. His dad would meet the flight at the other end.

The day arrived and I went to the airport to meet with the police. They had turned him over to an airport police officer and he was in the office there. When the flight was called, the officer wanted to know if I wanted to take him to the gate. I told him I would feel better if he kept a tight grip on him and accompanied him to the gate. We were half way to the gate, when the boy wrestled his way loose from the officer and took off running. (The officer was heavy and slow!) I took off after the boy and chased him through the terminal. He ran down the up escalator and into the parking garage. There he disappeared among the thousands of autos. I called for him for a while but finally realized this was a lost cause. So, reluctantly, I called his Dad to tell him what had happened. But I assured him the boy would turn up again and I would let him know.

Sure enough, about a week later, I saw the boy in the housing area with another teenager. I was certain he had not seen me. I went home and called the security police at the gate and told them that I was pretty sure he would be coming out the gate with this other lad in his pickup truck and he should be detained. It played out as I thought it would. He was detained. He was returned to the detention center. His dad was called once again. This time, I insisted the police officer not only accompany him to the gate, but that he be handcuffed to the officer until we had him belted in his aircraft seat! We did this and I notified his Dad that he was on his way. His

Dad called me the next day to tell me he had arrived on time and to thank me. I never heard again about the boy or his Dad. He remains among the myriad of 'counselees' with whom I was involved in my Air Force career that I wonder about.

My next proposal, after inquiry from the PACAF commander's office, was for workshops for personnel throughout the command. My initial response was to set up workshops at Hickam and bring people in from throughout the Pacific. The Commander decided it was more economical for me to put together a team and take the workshops abroad. This led to an extensive trip around the Pacific. I had a young lawyer (captain) and doctor (captain) and an airman on the team. (I had been promoted to Lieutenant Colonel sometime along the way.) They had all been through a workshop. The airman had been through a workshop after he had entered into counseling with me concerning his own addiction. He had never been apprehended for this and so his record was clean and he had beaten his experimentation.

We covered the command in January-February of 1971 with workshops in Thailand, Viet Nam, the Philippines, Japan and Korea. Among those attending the workshop in Thailand was a rated officer, Lieutenant Colonel Gilbert Kaats. He had been an instructor at the Air Force academy and had a doctorate in psychology. Because of the need of rated personnel, he was ordered back to the cockpit and assigned duty in Thailand, with a promise (tentative?) that after his year remote tour he could return to his position at the Air Force Academy. As it worked out, that position was not available to him and he was assigned to the Air Training Command, in Technical Training. This was the same office where Captain George Eychner was assigned. These two men provided considerable support that played a significant role later in the development of the program.

In May of 1971, the Air Training Command determined to hold a world-wide drug abuse conference at Lackland Air Force Base, in San Antonio, Texas. This was developed as a result of Captain Eychner's attendance at the Adelphi seminar. Two slots at this conference were allotted to the Pacific Air Command and the command personnel officer and myself were tapped to attend. At the conference, there was representation from all the major commands. Several had plans they hoped to put into effect if they could get funding from Headquarters, United States Air Force. Only PACAF had a program in being; the one we had begun at Hickam and expanded throughout the command. Furthermore, we had statistics from our pre and post and follow-up testing to show the effectiveness of what we were doing.

I was selected to chair the sub-committee on curriculum at the conference. We discussed how to train folks from throughout the Air Force to go back and develop programs like ours in their areas. We focused on a four week curriculum that somewhat paralleled what Adelphi had presented, however with changes that would make it more appropriate for military personnel and their mission.

Captain Eychner and Lieutenant Colonel Kaats were observers at this conference. Lieutenant General George Simler was the commander of the Air Training Command at the time and convened the conference and attended the final summary session, along with Colonel Peterson, director of technical training and several others from the staff.

I arrived back in Hawaii and within two weeks, received orders for temporary duty at Headquarters, Air Training Command at Randolph Air Force Base, in San Antonio to write the curriculum for this course. Although I had never written curriculum prior to this, with the guidance of Captain Eychner and others who were familiar with the requirements of military training (desired learning outcome approach) I spent two weeks in late June and early July polishing this material. I presented my summary to General Simler and his staff at the end of this time and returned to Hickam. George Eychner took me to the airport and suggested to me that this report was going to result in the establishment of a course or school within a technical training group at Lackland Air Force Base. He asked me if I thought I could direct such a program. I reminded him that I was not a training officer, but a chaplain.

Back in Hawaii, I continued the work I had been doing with workshops and was the senior chaplain at the housing chapel in what was called Hickam Village. Our facilities consisted of an older cantonment chapel and an old barracks building for classrooms. After moving to this chapel (designated as Chapel 3) I did away with the old desk in my small office and equipped the office with several wood/canvas 'directors' chairs. I had a small credenza or parson's table against the wall and a large brass coffee table in the middle of the room. It was very comfortable, especially for young airmen who came for counseling. A Japanese Sake bottle for coffee and some cute mugs made the office feel more comfortable for most. This also was the office where the 'dragline' phone was located.

Within a couple of weeks, I had a visit from the base commander who just happened to be passing by. (You couldn't pass by this chapel, because of its location, you had to be coming there!) He apologized for my not having a desk and offered to get one for me from the retro-shipped supplies coming back from Southeast Asia! I allowed as how I didn't really need a desk. My typing was done by the enlisted man and I had a telephone on the narrow table against the wall. Mostly, I sat and counseled when I was in the office.

Two days later, the command chaplain just 'happened to be coming by' and stopped in to see me. He offered to get me a new desk if I needed one! Whimsically, I told him I didn't need a desk. I didn't work, I prayed! The airman heard this and it became an office joke among the chapel staff!

Among the joys of the chaplaincy was the opportunity to be involved in the once-in-a-lifetime experiences of families. This certainly included baptisms and weddings. With baptisms, most were of infants. Of course, not all denominations perform infant baptisms, but many do, and Methodists certainly participate in this solemn ceremony in which a child is dedicated to God, given a Christian name, and parents agree to raise the child in the Christian faith and teach the child the proper ways of becoming a full child of God in every way. Infant baptism isn't really something we do so much as it celebrates what Christ has already done for each and everyone of us in his atoning death on the cross. Our part is to recognize this and accept it for ourselves. Over the years, I baptized many infants. I pray that in each and every case, the parents who took the vows to raise the child in the faith, were faithful in their duties and that the child became an active Christian when confirmed in their faith somewhere in puberty. I also participated in many programs of confirmation training for youth, usually in the sixth or seventh grade. If they were Methodists, I would send their information to a 'home' church somewhere, or transmit it to the Methodist Commission on Chaplains where it would reside until they requested a home church transfer. If they were non-Methodists, I would attempt to 'hook' them up with a chaplain of their denomination or a civilian church after they completed their training.

Ah, yes, the weddings! I've not kept track numerically of the weddings I've performed over the years. It has been gratifying often to hear from couples whose weddings I conducted many years before and know that they have continued to build upon the Christian relationship that was established at their wedding. Among these from whom I have heard years later are cases where I've then been involved in baptizing children born to the union later on as well. Because of my transient ministry around the world, these events have often been separated by many miles. I performed a wedding in Alaska for a young F-102 pilot who married the daughter of the Command Dental Surgeon. Several years later, when we were sent to Perrin Air Force Base in Sherman, Texas we rented their house while he was in the fourteen week program at Squadron Officers School and we were awaiting the completion of one we'd bought just up the street. Then, I baptized three of their children over the years ahead. And, to finish off that story, we attended their 40th wedding anniversary party just across town in San Antonio.

One young airman that came to visit me in Hawaii wanted to marry the daughter of an Air Force Colonel. They were a wonderful young couple. I did warn him in our counseling session that he was taking on a heady responsibility - supporting a Colonel's daughter in the manner to which she was accustomed. They were very much in love and the wedding was beautiful. You can fast forward over forty years later and imagine my surprise when they showed up at Air Force Village where I was pastoring to visit the retired Colonel and his wife! Still very much in love, they had come to help out their parents as her mother's health deteriorated. They continued coming regularly through her death and then, when the colonel's health resulted in his moving to the Alzheimer unit at the village, they took up a residence in the nearby community, alternating their time between San Antonio and their West Virginia home.

A telephone call brought my attention to the nearby residence of a couple I had married fifty years previously when pastoring in Houston, Missouri. We coordinated our schedules so that I could meet them in Fredericksburg, Texas to celebrate their renewal of vows on their fiftieth anniversary! There were many similar situations through the years and they brought joyful memories of service in the larger circuit of ministry in many places around the world.

When I was pastoring in Flower Mound, Texas (to be covered in detail later in this document) I had many youth in my confirmation classes. Many of them came back to me in adulthood to perform their weddings and in one case I have subsequently baptized two of their little girls. Recently, one of them posted a picture of his confirmation class! Several others have tagged their own photos in this picture on Facebook!

Our religious education program at Hickam was divided between the main chapel and the Hickam Village Chapel (Three). In Hickam Village near chapel three we used an old barracks building that I considered quite unsafe. There were places on the second floor where you could actually poke a hole in the flooring quite easily because of the termite damage. We had been trying to get permission to use the on-base elementary school building in that area for an hour on Sunday morning, but with no success. Somewhere between the school authorities and the civil engineers we were turned away. One day, I was in the old barracks building with some of the teachers who were planning their work for the following Sunday. The four-by-four uprights in the classroom seemed somewhat unsteady to me. I took out my pocketknife and pushed it into the wood. It gave way easily and the inside was hollow. Later that day I called the base commander and asked him if he had a few minutes would he stop by the Chapel Three education building. He came and I showed him the four-by-four. He tried the experiment himself. Then he jumped up and down a little and pronounced the building as dangerous and condemned. Within a month we had access to the on-base school building for our Sunday School and shortly after that they razed the old World War II building we had been using!

While attending a chaplain's retreat in the Philippines at Camp John Hay at Baguio, I received a phone call telling me there was a drug abuse conference at the University of California in Berkeley and the Air Force wanted me to attend. The time restraints resulted in my flying from Baguio to Clark Air Base (near Manila) and immediately to Honolulu, Hawaii, where Pat met me with the necessary clothing change. I was rushed through the DV (distinguished visitor) lounge, immigration, and back on an airplane going to Travis Air Force Base, outside of San Francisco. From there I took a taxi to the University. From the Administrative building there, I was directed to leave my B-4 bag with the secretary and walk across the campus to the conference center where this meeting was just beginning. I was in uniform! Traveling across the Berkeley campus in that era in military uniform treated me to the catcalls and, even one 'spit' in my direction that many Viet Nam Veterans had to endure.

When I slipped into the slanted theater seating in the conference center, I was a 'standout' in terms of clothing. The others in attendance were from free clinics and drug programs around the nation. The young man I sat next to looked at me and asked if I was a soldier.

"No, I'm an Air Force chaplain."

"What's that?"

"It's like a pastor in the military."

"Oh, then you haven't been bombing innocent kids in Viet Nam?"

"No, I haven't."

"What's your rank?"

"I'm a chaplain."

"But don't you have a rank?

"Well, yes. I'm a major."

"Is that high or low, or what?"

"It is lower than a general and higher than a private."

"Okay."

At this conference, I met Dr. Herbert Freudenberger, a clinical psychologist of New York City. He was the founder of one of the 'free' clinics for treatment of drug addiction in the city. We developed a close friendship during that conference and he continued to be a good friend and advisor for many years. I later brought him to San Antonio as a consultant to the Air Force program.

The conference was worthwhile and I returned to Hawaii with additional zest for the work I was doing.

Then one day in August 1971, I received a call from the command chaplain's office requesting I drop in sometime that day. Actually, chaplains were entitled to a 'comp' day during the week to make up for their work on weekends and when doing duty chaplain on a 24 hours basis. This was my day off and I really had intended to go sailing. (After deciding to sell our house in a somewhat soft real estate market and move on base for our final year in Hawaii, Secretary of Defense Robert McNamara announced that all overseas tours would be extended from three to four years in duration in order to save funds - PCS - permanent change of station. Now looking at spending two years in the smaller on base quarters, I set about fulfilling a lifetime dream of owning a sailboat. We purchased a

Columbia 22 foot keel sail boat that we kept in a slip at Keehi Lagoon in town.)

Reluctantly, I reported to the command chaplain's office. When I arrived the senior enlisted man in the office told me that the Chaplain was on the phone but he knew that one of the things he wanted me to look at was a letter from CINC PACOM (Commander in Chief - Pacific Command - the joint service command for the entire Pacific theater - then commanded by Admiral McCain - whose son was Navy Captain John McCain at that time a POW of the North Vietnamese). It concerned a command wide policy on drug abuse that was vague and misleading, in my opinion. I told the sergeant what I thought of it and made suggestions that the Command Chaplain could forward back to the CINC (Commander in Chief, Air Force or Pacific Air Force Commander) for a recommended change. (This was subsequently done and the change implemented.)

I had just finished writing these proposed changes when the command chaplain opened his door and ushered me into his office. He told me that he had been working with manpower to get an extra slot in his office for me to occupy and work full time in the drug/alcohol education business so that I would not have the responsibility of directing the program at Chapel 3, where I preached twice each Sunday and with the assistance of one other chaplain directed the religious education program and youth activities for the entire base.

However, he continued, he had just been on the phone with Washington, DC and Chaplain, Major General, Roy Terry, the Chief of Chaplains. In this conversation, he discovered that Chaplain Terry had 'waived' assignment authority over me so that General Simler, Air Training Command, could direct me to duty at Lackland Air Force Base, Texas to establish the Drug/Alcohol Abuse Education and Counseling Course. (Chaplain assignments were the prerogative of the Chief's personnel system and not the usual personnel assignments.) Furthermore, personnel were working on my orders and I should go immediately to check with them because the direction was coming by TWX (telegraph message) that this should be a move ASAP (as soon as possible). Needless to say, I was shocked by this sudden news. I went directly to personnel and they had just received the TWX. I was relieved of duty at Hickam AFB and directed duty assignment to Lackland Air Force Base, to establish the Department of Drug/Alcohol Abuse Education and Counseling, with a reporting date as soon as possible.

I called Pat and told her the news! We were glad the house had been sold. However, we had a second car to sell and a sailboat to sell! Nine days later we departed Hawaii! In that time we took our Mercury automobile to Barbers Point Naval Station to be put aboard a Naval Vessel in order to get it to San Francisco by the time we would arrive there. This was necessary because there was a civilian dock strike in San Francisco so the car could not be shipped in the normal fashion. We sold the Volkswagen with the stipulation that we would keep driving it until our departure date. We sold the sailboat for enough to recoup what we'd paid for it plus enough to cover the slip fees we'd paid since acquiring it.

Personnel asked me how my family and I wanted to travel. I guessed the clerk meant choosing a military flight or a civilian contract flight (which was my preference). However, she asked if I was interested in surface travel. (Aboard ship.) When I inquired further about this she told me that the Defense Department was required to purchase a certain number of spaces aboard the American Far East Lines between Honolulu and San Francisco every year and if I was interested she would check availability! After checking, she informed me that she could get a cabin for Pat and myself, and another cabin for Andy and Tom to share. If Tami were willing to share a cabin with a Marine Colonel's daughter, then she'd be able to book us on the USS Monterey to San Francisco! I assured her that Tami would be happy to share that cabin! In this way, our sudden departure from Hawaii was capped by a five-day cruise back to the Mainland. It was a welcome rest time after what had been a somewhat arduous schedule for about a year plus the hurry-up getting cleared to depart.

After arriving in San Francisco, picking up our automobile, we traveled across country for a brief leave in St. Louis and then back to San Antonio, Texas. Housing on base was not a near possibility and since we'd sold our house in Hawaii, we needed for tax purposes to re-invest in another home. Friends from our Perrin AFB, Texas days had a family member in the real estate business and he assisted us in finding the right neighborhood and the right building and we proceeded to purchase a new home still under construction. During the time it was being completed we lived in an apartment not too far from the base. By the time school began, we had an address so that both Andy and Tami could enroll in the schools they would attend after our move was complete. Tom had been in all day kindergarten in Hawaii, however, Texas didn't have such at that time and because of his birthday, he was a few days short of being old enough to enter first grade. He stayed home until January of 1972 and then went to a church sponsored pre-school for the remainder of that year. While we were still in the apartment, Tom received his first sex education! He came running to his mother and said, "Quick. I need a string." When asked why he needed a string, he exclaimed, "Because there are two dogs out in the yard and they are stuck together and I need a string to pull them apart."

PETS

It seems appropriate here to mention the pets we have enjoyed through the years. Pat and I had not been married very long when we acquired from the Humane Society in St. Louis a little black dog. Supposedly, he was half Scotch Terrier and half Kerry Blue something or other! Because he was such a rascal from the beginning, Pat decided to name him after her grandfather from Arkansas! So Alonzo came to live with us in the parsonage on Tyler Street. He would on occasion get loose! He would run down the street with

Pat chasing him. If she slowed down, he would await her action and then run some more!

From one of his nefarious ancestors he inherited hair that hung over his eyes. When Pat and I both were gone to a conference on one occasion, we left him with her mother, Ruth or Granny. When we returned we discovered she had trimmed the hair over his eyes, because, "why the poor thing couldn't see where he was going." We explained that evidently in one of his ancestral breeds this hair grew to protect their eyes from the underbrush! I mentioned his rascality. We had a lovely baked chicken for a meal one evening. I've forgotten if we had guests, which is likely. But after the meal when Pat went to clean up in the kitchen, the chicken was gone and the dog was nowhere to be found! A careful exploration of the three-story house eventually led to a bathroom on the second floor where the carcass, carefully cleaned of edible meat, had been deposited against the wall behind the commode! Alonzo went back to the Humane Society to find a new home when we left St. Louis for the Washington, D. C. area.

I was guilty of bringing pets home. One beautiful English Setter named Princess lived with us briefly before finding a home at my folk's farm. Then in Minneapolis, I found the most loving black Labrador for little cost and brought him home. "Duke" was a great outdoor animal. I built him a doghouse in the backyard. He loved to run and play in the fenced yard. And, if Andy, three years old, was out to play as well it made for a great game. Duke would run around the yard about three times and on the last lap, hit Andy broadside and put him on the ground where he would cover him with sloppy kisses. Again, our move from Minneapolis back to St. Louis with no definite location arranged caused us to give Duke away to friends.

We developed an affinity for Dachshunds. The little 'hot dogs' are loving, loyal and easy to train. But don't tell that to Huntz, the first one we adopted in Alaska! We only had him for about a year, but in that time he managed to chew Tami's coat from the back door coat rack and chew on most everything else in sight. Furthermore, in spite of our best efforts, we were never totally successful in 'house-breaking' him. Only when we knew we were leaving Alaska and giving him to friends who lived in the country did Andy tell us that his friends who had previously owned Huntz kept papers spread on the living room carpet! Aha! Previously, I have mentioned that Huntz claim to fame was earned when the great Alaskan Quake took place.

When we lived in Sherman, Texas, we got the 'bug' to have another dog. We found friends who had a dachshund with pups and we acquired one of the little females. (We thought she'd be easier to train than Huntz especially since we would have her as a puppy. That turned out to be true.) Because she was such a long skinny little thing when we got her our kids decided she looked like a pretzel when she curled up and so that became her name. She was a marvelous little dog, very smart to catch on to house training and nearly anything else.

I had heard from several folks, including a veterinarian, females do much better if they are permitted to have one litter of pups before being spayed. We arranged for Pretzel to be bred so that she could have a litter before being spayed. When she was due to give birth, I had to fly to Amarillo Air Force Base for a conference. She had been restless all night, in her bed and then by our bedside. We were fairly certain this would be the day of delivery. I was in the conference room at the chapel at Amarillo planning the forthcoming Spiritual Life conference in New Mexico when the chapel sergeant came into the room. He asked for Chaplain Jacobs. I raised my hand indicating my presence.

He began tentatively, "I'm not sure what this means, sir. But your sergeant from Perrin just called. He said your wife had called the office and asked him to pass on the message that you are a dad? Two boys and a girl and one is black." You can imagine the guffaw that ensued until I explained that Pretzel our dachshund was the mom! Pat had been watching the dog carefully and she had given birth to two of the puppies. She examined her, felt her tummy and thought she probably was finished. She was quite shocked when she returned a half hour later to discover this little black puppy in there as well! (It turned out that the male that had bred Pretzel had black-and-tan in his ancestry!)

However, when it came time to go to Hawaii, we discovered that Hawaii had a quarantine law that required dogs from the mainland to be in a kennel for six months to insure they were not bringing disease (especially rabies) into the state. None of us felt that was a good thing for Pretzel to suffer and thinking we might be on base where animals were under strict regulations as well, we gave Pretzel away to friends. The children made us promise that when we returned to the mainland, we could have another dachshund.

We weren't back in San Antonio after our Hawaii tour but a few days when Andy and Tami began scouring the newspaper for information about available puppies. This led to our purchase of a pedigreed dachshund puppy that the children named Daisy. She lived with us for nearly fifteen years thereafter. Even-tempered, loving and easy to train, Daisy was a part of the family. We arranged breeding for Daisy. We had a friend who had a registered male dachshund and with a little encouragement (after what Pat insisted had to be a legal ceremony of marriage) the two conceived. When the pups were born, there were six of them! They were as cute as they could be. The owner of the male received choice of litter for breeding rights, and then we eventually sold the rest of them. I think the children would have kept them all if allowed to do so.

Daisy traveled with us to Oklahoma City and later to Germany. While there she developed a typical Dachshund back problem and later a heart condition. The scariest experience we ever had with a pet came one night in Bitburg, Germany. Daisy had developed what appeared to be a little cyst on one ear. The veterinarian who initially looked at it thought it was quite harmless. I guess it would have been, except that a couple of years later, she managed to scratch it. The bleeding that ensued was enormous - and all on the white shag rug in the living room! It appeared we might have been in the hog butchering business that night. There was no longer a veterinarian assigned at the base and we had not had a need for shots or treatment for the dog since the military vet had rotated back to the states. But, I knew a neighbor had used a local German veterinarian in a nearby village and called and got his phone number. Ascertaining that he was available, Pat and I left with the dog. Pat was holding a towel on the ear and trying to get the bleeding stopped. Tom was left behind to begin the cleanup process. (Amazingly, his work and Pat's subsequent follow up managed to restore the carpet.)

When we arrived at the vet's office, he brought us immediately into the examining room and we placed Daisy up on the table. She was very frightened and getting weaker by the moment. The vet asked me a question in German and I couldn't understand his words. He repeated the question. I still didn't understand (although my German was pretty good by then). He then asked in English the same question, "Is she a woman or a man?" I would have thought he could tell quickly by reaching beneath her belly, but he had not done so, instead concentrating on ending the bleeding. This was completed and then he gave her a shot of blood extender because she had lost so much blood. Needless to say, Tom was very distraught by the time we got back to our quarters on base. But, Daisy did recover from the ordeal. She continued to have back problems and would have to be carried up and down steps in our on-base quarters.

Nearly fifteen and somewhat hard of hearing and with a little blindness, Daisy finally expired when we lived in Lewisville. Tom, our youngest, had grown up with Daisy and felt obligated to call his sister and brother and let them know of the loss. When he spoke to Andy, this older brother wanted to console him, and his words came out as "Well, Tom. Just look at it this way. Daisy went to sleep and woke up dead." Well said, I think.

CHAPTER TWENTY-SIX

I reported to the 3575th Technical Training Group at Lackland Air Force Base, Texas on 19 August 1971. Although the unit had been told about the program from Air Training Command Headquarters, nothing had been done about where the courses would be held or where my office would be located. Furthermore, the commander of the Group at that time informed me the day I reported to the unit that he had no idea what or why this was being done. "I don't understand any need for this business. When I was a C-123 commander in Southeast Asia, I said the answer to the drug problem is to shoot the bastards when they're caught."

Later, in a consultation with General George Simler, he told me he understood that I believed there were no drug or alcohol problems, only people who used drugs and alcohol to handle their problems. I agreed that this was approximately my view. "Then," General Simler said, "I'm going to give you the rest of the people problems, race relations and human relations training." As a result, what began as the Department of Drug and Alcohol Abuse Education and Training (TDSA in acronym form) became the Department of Social Actions

Training (TSL in acronym form). When this shift became known in the Training Group Commander's purview, he told me he didn't understand this problem either. His words were, "We didn't have any problems with our niggers when I was growing up in Gadsden, Alabama." These attitudes gave me some indication of the problems I would have in establishing this new program for the Air Force. (Ironically, this Colonel was awarded posthumously the meritorious service medal for his job as Technical School Commander to include the establishment of the Social Actions program. This was announced at his memorial service after his death from lung cancer. My ribs are still sore from the 'ribbing' I got during that service from one of the other course directors who sat next to me!)

Temporarily, I was housed at a desk in the Training Group Headquarters Curriculum department. This was made up of mostly civilian employees who had been there for many years and knew what couldn't be done! And I was reminded of this at every turn of the road! Fortunately, I had this DD 95 (Department of Defense action memo) that General Simler had signed in which he notified me that he wanted this to be a hard hitting, fast moving, well supported program. If I needed anything just ask him and it would be provided. I confess to having copies of this made numerous times in the first months and placing a copy on the top of my request for some support item.

My next office was the old 'radome' on Lackland. This had been the operational end of an air defense radar system some years before and had been empty for a long time. Two stories high with a bubble on top. In fact, it wasn't completely empty. We had to dispose of the skunk and snake population when we moved in. Between August 19th when I arrived and September first I spent much of my time at Air Training Command headquarters at Randolph Air Force Base, which is across town from Lackland. The Division of Technical Training there gave me the support I needed to access personnel from the entire Air Force and get them orders to report to Lackland as soon as possible. This division under the department of military training was very helpful. The deputy commander for Air Training Command for Technical Training was under the leadership initially of Major General Carson, and shortly thereafter, Major General Felix M. Rogers. In the department were Colonel Harry Peterson, LtCol Gilbert Kaats, and Captain George Eychner. Here the matter of previous personal contact with the latter two officers proved invaluable.

By the first of September I had assembled a staff of fifteen military personnel (mixture of officer and enlisted) and six civilians. One of the civilians was my own secretary. Three were departmental secretaries to work in curriculum, resources, and mobile assistance. The fifth (who actually reported somewhat later) was in charge of a resource development branch. The sixth was Ben Randall. Ben was in another department of the Technical School at that time but became an invaluable member of the program in developing curriculum and getting them into the shape they needed to be to 'pass muster' with those who approved curriculum items.

After cleaning out the radome, we transformed it into offices and in the main area (which had been the operational area with seating for forty or more where they could monitor the blips on the big screen in the radar surveillance days) we created a classroom. On October 6, 1971 we received our first class of 40 students in the first ever-military course in Drug and Alcohol Abuse Education and Counseling. The students, about half enlisted and half young officers came from throughout the United States Air Force. We had been told numerous times that it couldn't be done this quickly, however, we did it!

Within a matter of weeks, an unused mess (dining) hall on Lackland was identified as the future home of our department. The upstairs offices at this huge building were being used by the Marksmanship Department within the Tech School but the downstairs was unoccupied. We worked with the civil engineering department to modify over 100,000 square feet of this space into offices and seminar rooms as well as one large classroom that could seat about 90 students. This room also had a one-way glass observation space at the rear where the events could be monitored without disturbing the class. We were able to 'sell' the idea of a stage and a rear screen projection at the front of the room as well. The resource branch included a large space for developing a library of materials for research in the areas of drug/alcohol and later, race and human relations training. The curriculum branch occupied space for several desks. We developed a Mobile Assistance Team of six officers and six enlisted who were prepared to take classes and monitoring activities worldwide as needed. The administration section included a private office for myself, and an office for my secretary and my executive officer (a senior master sergeant, Jim Mullen who became invaluable in his support.) In addition, there was a break room and rest rooms. The seminar rooms, or as we referred to them as 'group process' rooms were designed to handle about a dozen students in an informal setting, with movable furniture. We had to do battle with the Operations department within the Tech School for this change and several others, as they tried to force us into the mold of typical technical training as they understood it. In each case, we won partly with the support of the friends we had at Air Training Command Technical Training division.

One thing we introduced that created problems for us with the training group staff involved an innovative technique that I called 'feedback stations'. This consisted of mounting large sheets of butcher paper on the wall of each of the restrooms with crayon markers hanging nearby. We encouraged our students to write on the wall. I maintained that we got better feedback from these anonymous efforts on the part of the students than we got from the 'official' end-of-course surveys and evaluation sheets. It seemed to me that many students answered those evaluations with what they thought we wanted to hear. On the other hand, they wrote outrageous things on the wall in the restrooms. One that brought attention involved the recent Defense Department mandate for random urinalysis throughout the services. Commenting on this, one student referred to this process by stating the 'gold flow' is a real pisser.

I don't know who reported this to the Tech School Commander, certainly none of my staff. Perhaps one of the operations staff who frequented our building checking to see if we were complying with regulations in terms of curriculum and management. In any event, I received word through my executive Sergeant Mullen one day that I was to report to the Tech School Commander that afternoon to discuss 'course conduct and objectives' and especially the permission for 'vile' language being used! The Sergeant was told that it specifically involved our 'feedback stations'. I called Air Training Command Technical Training Office to let LtCol Kaats know about this issue. He called me back and told me to report at 1500 hours (3 p.m.) as requested.

When I arrived, I was surprised to find not only Lt Col Kaats and Captain Eychner already in the office, but also General Felix M. (Mike) Rogers the deputy commander for ATC for technical training. Immediately, the Tech School Commander brought up the issue of the 'feedback'. I explained the reasons we used this technique and the value we felt it carried in giving us feedback. When the commander began to tell me why I was no longer to do this, General Rogers interrupted. "The Social Actions training program had to be placed somewhere and Lackland was the location that had physical space. We put them under the Tech School because that was the logical place. However, Jacobs is responsible directly to me for course content and conduct, not to the Tech School at Lackland."

Colonel Greenhill looked at me and then looked back at General Rogers. "You mean, I don't have anything to say about how Jacobs runs this program?"

"That's it!" said General Rogers.

Then he asked me if I had anything else to say. I looked at the colonel and then I said quietly, "You know, sir. We change the butcher paper on the wall of our latrines nearly every day because we want to keep the language clean and we want to know how the course is going. If you go down the hall to the restrooms here in the headquarters, you'll find that you have worst things on the wall and it will have to be painted over! You might want to consider butcher paper." Several of those present chuckled, but not Colonel Greenhill.

As we left the building, General Rogers turned to me and said, "Don't worry about your OER (Officer Effectiveness Report) chaplain. I intend for you to be directly under General Malloy here at the Lackland Wing."

The following day, I received a form telling me that my rating officer was General Robert Malloy, Center Commander, Lackland Air Force Base. I suppose General Rogers wanted to be sure that the OER wasn't used to punish me for being 'out of line' with the tech school approach. As a result of this, General Malloy asked that I attend his weekly staff meetings in addition to my attending the Tech School weekly staff meetings. (General Rogers' next assignment was as the Commander of the Air University including the year I was a student in the Air War College, a part of that institution at Maxwell Air Force Base (Montgomery) Alabama. Then, he moved on to be the commander of the Air Force Logistics Command, as I moved from the one year school assignment to wing chaplain at Tinker Air Force Base, Oklahoma, which was under the AFLC structure.)

The special assignment outside of my career field as a chaplain was supposed to be a two-year duty assignment. However, halfway through the first year, I was notified that General Simler didn't feel I'd be done by then and so I was to be extended for two additional years. This didn't occur, however, as halfway through the third year, I was notified of my selection to be a student the following year at the Air War College mentioned above. Every quarter, I would receive a form from the Military Personnel Center at Randolph Air Force Base, awarding me an AFSC (Air Force Specialty Code which defines your career field and the level in it at which you serve) of 0016. This code was for field grade (Major or above) commanders. I would endorse it back to the MPC telling them that I was declining this code because my primary career was 8916 (field grade chaplain) and I didn't desire to be given a secondary code of 0016. My concern was that if that was on my record, the MPC would want to assign me to yet another command task and I intended to return to the chaplaincy when this special assignment was over. After this occurred several quarters in a row, I received a phone call from a Colonel at the personnel center at Randolph AFB telling me that I was messing up their computer system! When I explained the matter to him, he agreed that he could fix that. I didn't get additional paperwork options to be a 0016!

During the three years I was assigned as Director, Air Force Social Actions Training, I was involved in many activities. Certainly, my primary concern was adequate leadership and supervision of the department. This included knowing what was developed and instituted in the entire social actions area in our course structure as well as throughout the Air Force. On a daily basis, I monitored various courses throughout the day, handled the correspondence that was directed to the department from throughout the Air Force, and participated in discussions at both Air Training Command and Air Force levels concerning these programs. From the beginning, I encouraged the idea that this program should not be permanent but should result in appropriate training in these social areas throughout all aspects of Air Force training and education. Even when they established a separate AFSC (Air Force Specialty Code) for those assigned in the career field, I supported the concept that this should be temporary (meaning over several years but not decades). This eventually occurred and the programs were incorporated into all phases of training.

I lectured in the local programs initially, however, as the administrative effort and wider demands were placed on me, and as more of my staff was trained, my lecturing time in the local classes diminished. During this time, I also was invited to lecture in other programs around the military and civilian communities. Among these was a regular lecture to the 'new commanders' course at Maxwell Air Force Base, Alabama in a cycle that ran about every eight weeks. The purpose of this lecture was to bring them up to date on what the Air Force was attempting to achieve in the areas of Social Actions. Generally, I was able to schedule this in coordination with a trip to Patrick Air Force Base, Florida where I was invited to lecture to the Defense Race Relations Institute in each cycle of that program. This program was mandated by congress and established as THE program in Race Relations for all the service branches. Although they did a commendable job of teaching Minority history (primarily black or African American as the term changed), they did not incorporate the kind of teaching techniques that satisfied our needs in the Air Force. We subsequently developed a four-week 'practicum' for our Air Force personnel after they had completed the course at DRRI. We made this a requirement before they could be used in classroom situations in the Air Force.

Invitations came also to lecture to Army medical students at the training program at Brooke Army Medical Center at Fort Sam Houston in San Antonio and the Navy programs in California. Frequent invitations also were received from various colleges and universities, especially in the San Antonio area. It was as a result of one of these lectures that I became acquainted with a number of local counselors, and one of these later invited me to serve in a co-therapist position with her clients who had drug or alcohol addictions as well as young clients, categories with whom she'd had little experience. During the year I was a student at the War College, I returned to San Antonio on a regular basis to continue work with her clients.

During this time, Dr. C. Eugene Hix, professor at Central Methodist University requested information (then Central College - my bachelor degree undergraduate alma mater) concerning the work I was doing. Dr. Hix had been my advisor at Central and we had maintained close contact. In the winter of 1972-73, Dr. Hix told me that the College Board of Curators had voted to award me the honorary degree of Doctor of Divinity at the next Commencement in the spring if I was available to attend. Needless to say, I was greatly honored by this offer and arranged my schedule so that I could be there. (I know that honorary degrees are sometime disparaged by those who do not have them! I often joked that some faculty members thought my bachelor's degree was honorary! My record at that level indicates otherwise. I was a very good student. I believe I am the only military chaplain thus honored by my alma mater. On the commencement day at which I was honored there were three other honorary degrees awarded. One was to a very popular and successful United Methodist District Superintendent in the conference where the college is located. One was given to an alumnus who had become president of a large insurance company. The other was awarded to the president of a corporation in St. Louis that had been very generous to the college. He was later elected to the Board of Curators of the college.)

I was in the middle of one of the lectures that I was still giving to the entire basic Social Actions class when Sergeant Mullen came into the classroom to hand me a note. This was most unusual for him to interrupt a class. The note was to inform me that General Simler and his aide had just been killed in an aircraft accident on takeoff at Randolph Air Force Base. They were en route to Scott Air Force Base, Illinois where the general was to be given the command of the Military Airlift Command and promoted to four stars. I was shocked at the information and too overwhelmed to continue the lecture and dismissed the class immediately. I believe that General Simler's forward looking understanding and support of the social actions program led to its establishment and acceptance in the Air Force. And I firmly believe, the United States Air Force was spared some of the problems in addictions and race unrest that afflicted the other services during this tumultuous period because of this program.

Military schooling for officers normally follows a certain pattern. As a company grade (Lieutenant or Captain) it is expected that an officer will complete Squadron Officers School. This might be completed in residence (fourteen weeks at that time) at Maxwell Air Force Base or through correspondence. The year I was on my remote tour in Alaska, I completed SOS and all the other correspondence courses offered in the chaplain area. The next level of military training is the Command and Staff College at Air University at Maxwell AFB. This was a nine-month program in residence or, again by correspondence, or seminar. The senior course is the Air War College, designed for Lieutenant Colonels and Colonels. It was a ten-month course at Maxwell Air Force Base, involving a permanent change of station to include the move of one's family. It could also be taken by correspondence or seminar. They offered it by seminar at Lackland Air Force Base and I was invited to participate several times, but because I travelled so much while directing the social actions program, I always declined! (There were also junior, intermediate and senior courses in most career fields as well. I had been through the basic chaplain course upon my first tour of duty. I later went to the senior chaplain course at Maxwell, however, I never did attend the intermediate course.)

Now, I was directed for assignment to the Air War College in residence. Frankly, I didn't want to go. One primary reason was that Tami was to begin her senior year in high school and I didn't want to uproot her. The Air War College is a program in residence (permanent change of station). Secondly, I had been 'out' of the chaplaincy for three years in the directing of the Social Actions Courses, and I wanted to return to my ministry calling. I made numerous trips to Washington during this time to brief the Deputy Chief of Staff for Personnel concerning the Social Actions programs. (Sometimes this was General Robert Dixon, and sometimes his deputy General John Roberts. I also briefed one or the other of them when they came to San Antonio either to Lackland or to Randolph AFB. I also briefed General John Ryan who was the Chief of Staff of the Air Force on one occasion. After General Rogers left for Air University, I briefed General Bill McBride on several occasions. He became Vice Chief of Staff of the Air Force in his last active duty assignment. We met again when he and his wife Kathryn moved into Air Force Village 2 about the same time we did.) Since I was about to go to the pentagon for one of these periodic briefings, I took the opportunity to visit with the Chief of Air Force Chaplains, Major General, Roy Terry to tell him of my hope to be relieved of going to the War College.

I explained to him the reasons I didn't want that to happen. I really wanted to stay in San Antonio for our daughter's sake and, if this was not the case, then to be reassigned to a chaplain slot in San Antonio. I explained that I didn't need the training for staff work. I'd had staff duty at Alaskan Air Command. Furthermore, as director of the Social Actions program, I had approximately 75 persons (mostly military) under my supervision and had directed up to nine courses with as many as 300 to 400 students in classes at any one time. (We had a basic course in Social Actions for Social Actions officers and enlisted; a basic course in Equal Opportunity and Treatment; a basic course in Drug and Alcohol Abuse Education and Counseling; basic course in human relations; advanced courses in each of these areas; and developed a practicum course to follow the Defense Race Relations Course for those who would be teaching the mandatory race relations course throughout the Air Force.) The training for senior officers at the Air War College could be better given to someone who'd not had these kinds of experiences already. Hence, I didn't need to go.

Chaplain Terry explained to me that he didn't nominate someone to go to the War College for what they needed but for the needs of the Air Force. "You will be chaplain to your class there, 300 Lieutenant Colonels and Colonels, who are the future leaders of the Air Force. You'll be of more ministry to them than the chaplains assigned to base can possibly be. Furthermore, your participation there at that level will give these other officers a close up feeling of knowing and working with a senior chaplain. You will represent the best in the chaplaincy for them."

Then he proceeded to tell me about the surgery he was getting ready to have on his knee, caused by an early basketball injury while in college. I listened carefully, and prepared to go to the Air War College!

Pat stayed in San Antonio in the house we had purchased and Tami went on into her senior year of high school. I moved into the Bachelor Officers Quarters at Maxwell Air Force Base while attending the War College. I enjoyed the opportunities that the training provided, although I missed being with my family. As I mentioned previously, I had been 'moonlighting' as a counselor in town in San Antonio with a marriage counselor. I had met her through some of the speaking engagements I'd been involved with during my time in the Social Actions program. She had no experience in drug/alcohol or addiction problems and contacted me to see if I would be willing to co-counsel such cases with her for a fee. I did so many times during the last couple of years I was at Lackland. When she discovered that I was leaving to go to Montgomery, Alabama, she asked if I would be coming back and forth since my family was staying in San Antonio. I told her that would depend on how expensive it might be. (I was thinking of maybe coming some on military flights that might be available.) She offered to arrange cases in which she wanted my assistance in a group on a weekend schedule. In this way, she could use my assistance, pay me for my time, and this would pay for my commercial flights back and forth. This worked out very well and I got home about every four to six weeks on a weekend.

I threw myself into participation in the War College classes, seminars and discussions with the best I knew. I enjoyed the lectures we received, often from persons of significant experience in government and world affairs. Of course, my experience as a chaplain gave me some advantage over other students when making oral presentations to a seminar group. After all, speaking is a valuable part of being a chaplain! After I had been there for a while, I developed close relationships with several of my fellow students and at the request of one of them I began teaching a Bible class on Tuesday noon lunch break. It began with only three or four who would bring a brown bag lunch and we would study together. Soon it expanded until I was filling up the seminar room we were using and had to move to a larger location.

This led to an expansion of this idea into having a prayer breakfast at the officers' club on one morning each week. Different individuals would give testimony to their faith. This also grew into a large number of students from the War College. Several staff members also attended and in fact, the commandant, General Hartinger came on several occasions.

Among those who began attending my class and the breakfast was an exchange student from the Israeli Air Force, a Colonel Ivrahim Ben Nun. He and I had numerous discussions away from the class concerning biblical prophecy. He had met the author and speaker on prophecy, Hal Lindsey. One of our discussions included the possibility of inviting him to come speak at the Air War College. After consultation with General Hartinger, Ben (as we all called him) and I got on the telephone with Hal Lindsey in California. He jumped at the chance to come speak to our class. Some class members arranged his air transportation from California to Alabama and back, using airline points they possessed.

It was decided in our discussions with the general, that this would have to be a voluntary activity. We would begin it on one of the afternoons when nothing was scheduled in the main auditorium so there would be adequate space for all who wanted to attend. It would be open to Air War College students, staff and family members. On the day he spoke, the program began at 3 o'clock with the plan that he would follow the usual schedule, speak for an hour and then take questions for another hour. The auditorium was completely full! The observation room in the back was also full. Lindsey spoke for an hour and then the 'Q&A' took place. We finally had to 'shut it down' at 5:30 so that the janitorial staff could do their job in cleaning things up for the following day's activities. (Colonel Ben Nun later became the Chief of Staff of the Israeli Air Force. On one of my trips to Israel, I was able to locate him and visit briefly by telephone. He had retired from their Air Force and become the CEO of Mazda, Israel.)

I don't know that anyone was brought into a closer relationship with God that day, however, I know it became acceptable in the class to discuss religious matters and spiritual approaches to the problems that senior officers might face in their later commands. In light of recent events, I'm not sure any of this would be possible today. I finished the course at the Air War College as one of the ten per cent declared 'distinguished graduates'. I flew home following the graduation program that morning in order to be in San Antonio for Tami's high school graduation that evening! (I had driven my little MG midget home the weekend before and flown back, which made this possible.)

One of the site commanders during my time in Alaska now lived with his wife in nearby Prattville, Alabama. They invited me to come have dinner with them on several occasions and this resulted in my being invited to preach both in their church and several others nearby.

In my first interview with my faculty advisor, I was asked if I intended to pursue a master's degree program during my year. Most students chose to do this, earning a master's in either public administration or some similar area. This could be done through several universities or colleges that had on-base programs. Attending classes in non-duty time, the war college student would choose as his/her project during the year something that would tie in with the dissertation or thesis that would satisfy the degree requirements. Since I already had three earned degrees and one honorary doctorate, I wasn't sure I wanted to pursue this matter. My faculty advisor, Colonel Ken Haff had studied my record and knew that I had just recently been directing the Social Actions schooling. In fact, he had observed one of the lectures I gave periodically to the senior officers course at Maxwell while I was directing the social actions courses. These were designed for senior officers who were about to take a command position to be up-to-date on the various activities in the

Air Force. In our discussion, he suggested that if I were not going to pursue a degree, would I consider teaching an elective in the second semester as my project. I inquired as to what he thought I might teach and he suggested that my background with Transactional Analysis would make an ideal course. I could teach TA for Commanders, helping these future commanders to understand the kinds of interpersonal relationships that either promote or hamper good communication and leadership as commanders. (Reference works by Eric Berne, the founder of TA or that of Tom Harris entitled "I'm Ok, You're OK". Another valuable resource for me in those days was the book by Robert and Mary Goulding, "The Power is in the Patient". I had the opportunity while directing the Social Actions program to spend 30 days living with the Gouldings in California and studying their counseling and teaching techniques.)

I agreed that this would be an interesting project and set about putting together the necessary curriculum outline that would help the faculty approve or reject this as my project. It was approved and I was greatly surprised when over forty of my fellow students signed up to take my course as their second semester elective. It was a very gratifying part of my year at the War College.

About half way through the academic year at the War College, I was on my way to class one morning when several folks stopped me and said congratulations. I discovered the reason for this when I arrived at the War College building and found a large number of my classmates gathered about a bulletin board. With the assistance of several, I made my way through the crowd to the posting and there discovered that I had been selected for promotion to full Colonel. It may seem silly, but I had not realized that the promotion board was meeting and the results would be released!

About this time, most of my fellow students were on the telephone in the hallway talking with friends, former associates and personnel folks about their follow on assignments from the War College. Knowing that I would be assigned as a chaplain somewhere, and likely in the states as a senior chaplain now that I was a Colonel,

I didn't worry about any of this. I did have a phone call from the personnel officer in the chief of chaplain's office telling me that I would likely go to a staff job at a major command somewhere. I explained that I really would prefer returning to a base chapel job. Again, I had been out of the chaplaincy now for four years (three years at the Social Actions School and one year at the War College) and I wanted to be back in the pulpit and visiting with the troops.

The new Chief of Chaplains came to Maxwell to attend the graduation of one of the classes at the Chaplains School there and I had the opportunity to have lunch with him. I told Chaplain, Major General, Henry Mead about my desire to return to a base chapel job. He asked if I were serious about this. Evidently, most chaplains reaching full colonel and graduating from the War College wanted to be 'Command chaplains'. I told him I was very serious. Within a week, I received a call from the personnel officer in the chief's office and asked if I would like to go to Tinker Air Force Base, Oklahoma City as the center chaplain. (This was the equivalent of being the wing chaplain but in the Logistics Command there were several Maintenance Depot Centers and this was one of them. I would be both the Base chaplain and the Center chaplain at Tinker.) I quickly agreed to the assignment and in due course received the official information. When I graduated and then flew home for Tami's graduation, Pat had already shipped our furniture and we left the next day from San Antonio to move to Oklahoma City. (After I had received the assignment, she and I met in Dallas and flew on to Oklahoma City and arranged to purchase a new house. She stayed another day and fully decorated it with the builder. Again, housing on base for senior officers was limited and we had determined to sell our house in San Antonio and purchase one in Oklahoma City. For the second time in our marriage, Pat sold a house while I was elsewhere!)

CHAPTER TWENTY-SEVEN

T ami went with us for the summer before entering Central Methodist University in Missouri the following fall. Andy remained in San Antonio until the following January when he returned to complete his college education, partly at CMU and finally at Missouri University. Later, when we got an assignment to Germany (Bitburg Air Base) Tami delayed her senior year in order to travel with us to Europe. This provided her a year of travel throughout Western Europe in order to visit most of the major art museums. Since art was her major, this was a real opportunity for her. At the end of the year, she returned to Central Methodist to complete her degree.

Andy had completed a year at CMU, then transferred to Texas A&M in College Station. After a year there, he resumed his studies for one semester at the University of Texas in Austin. But, not knowing for sure what he wanted to study, he returned home and worked in several jobs for the next year, including driving cement trucks, working on an offshore oilrig as a 'mud-logger' and similar activities. Then he returned to Central and finally received a degree in Agricultural Economics at Missouri University. Here, he wrote a senior honors paper on the net cost of fuel from grain, which led to his being offered a position with Senator Eagleton's office in D.C. where he wrote the tech specs for the gasohol bill.

Although Pat had some misgivings about moving to Oklahoma City, by the time we had been there for a few months, she fell in love with the city. (Her concerns were about the 'tornado alley' of which we'd all heard. And, indeed, the day we arrived, a tornado touched down on the runway at the base as we were having dinner in a restaurant across the highway.) She quickly found a place to volunteer at Children's Hospital and in visiting the County Home (a tax supported skilled nursing home for indigents) that was located near the base. (At the latter she became known as the banana lady since she brought with her fresh fruit each week that the residents greatly prized. When we left Oklahoma for our overseas tour, ladies from the Protestant Women of the Chapel at Tinker Air Force Base presented her with a little necklace that had a lovely little ceramic banana on it.)

The base chapel included a separate religious education building (unusual for most Air Bases). When I first arrived, I visited with the Center Commander, Major General James Randolph. His first question to me concerned my knowledge of Logistics Maintenance Centers. I told him I had looked over the hill from Lackland Air Force Base to Kelly Air Force Base (which adjoined Lackland and was a center similar to Tinker) and thought it a strange animal since most folks there were civilian workers. He laughed and told me that Tinker was another one just like it!

My first week at the base chapel, I realized that there were many maintenance and cleaning tasks that were being left undone. In reviewing past inspections from higher headquarters, I discovered the last one had been marginal. Some closets were stuffed with 'old' stuff and were quite dirty as a result. I asked my NCOIC (Non-Commissioned Officer in charge) to get a clipboard and a pencil and follow me around. As we walked the facilities, I pointed out various things that needed cleaning or repair or disposal. He filled many pages on his yellow tablet. Then, I explained to him that he should use this as a working list for things to do in the days ahead.

On Monday of the following week, I asked him to get his clipboard and his yellow page list and follow me around. Some things had been accomplished, but many had not. So each time we found something that was still not cared for, we put a checkmark against it. When we finished, he asked me, "Are we going to do this every Monday morning?"

"No, we are not," I replied. "But you are going to do it as often as necessary till we get things in shape. And, by the way, if I have to do this, then I should get part of your pay, because this is your job." He made good progress in the days ahead and later in the year when we received another inspection from the command chaplain's office, we rated an excellent!

My second in command out of the six chaplains was my senior Catholic chaplain as well. He was the only Catholic chaplain assigned, although we also had an auxiliary civilian priest to call on when needed. I thought I was getting along quite well with all the chaplains at the beginning. Then, I began to sense some distance between 'Father John' and myself. So one day, I stopped in his office and asked if we could visit a bit. He agreed that would be fine. I asked him if I had offended him in some way or not provided what he needed for support, since I sensed that we had developed a tension that had not been there previously.

John looked at me, and said, "It's ok for you, of course. You got YOUR Eagle!"

I realized that John, a Lieutenant Colonel, had not been promoted to full colonel. I asked him if he had been eligible in that last cycle for promotion to 0-6 (full colonel). He allowed how he was on the same eligibility list that I had been on.

"John," I said calmly, "I didn't get YOUR eagle. There were only five chaplains promoted to Colonel in this last cycle. Two of the five were Catholic priests. Since the Catholic chaplains constituted only

26% (at that time) of the chaplain corps, and they got 40% of the promotions, I didn't get yours."

He looked at me for a moment or two and then said, "Yes. I guess that's right."

We had an excellent relationship from that time onward during our time together at Tinker. He did make Colonel on the next cycle. I like to think the rating I gave him helped that happen.

My Protestant chaplain staff was somewhat unusual. Two were majors who had been passed over for Lieutenant Colonel on two occasions each and therefore were waiting out their twenty years for retirement, since they were within less than three years of this goal. More about them later. A young chaplain who was a captain had been passed over twice to major and the rules at that time gave him seven months until release from service after the second failure to win promotion. I didn't know the details of his service that might have led to this situation, an unusual one since most chaplains were promoted to major as soon as eligible on the basis of what was called, 'fully qualified'. (Promotion at that time to Lieutenant Colonel and full Colonel were based on 'best qualified' on a quota basis. For instance, the year I was promoted to full Colonel, the promotions were best qualified at 20% of those first eligible. This meant all Lieutenant Colonels were considered if they had been in grade a minimum of three years, but only 20% of those eligible for the first time would be promoted. Those who had been previously non-selected were considered also and might take up one or more of the 20% quota. In actuality, it was most unusual for someone to be promoted once they were non-selected.)

There were two Protestant services in the chapel on Sunday morning and two Catholic services. These alternated: 8:00 - Catholic service. 0930 - Protestant service and Sunday school. 1100 - Protestant Service. 1215 - Catholic service. On the first Sunday that I was at Tinker I slipped into the back of the chapel and observed the first Catholic service and then attended the two Protestant Services. I discovered the bulletin listed a Sunday evening service as well. So

Pat and I came back for the Sunday evening service. The young captain previously mentioned conducted it. There were about 8 or 9 folks there, including us. There was no real order of worship. He began with a couple of Gospel hymns and then a prayer. His sermon was not well organized and seemed mostly ad lib. After this he invited folks to come to the front for prayer. He prayed for each one who requested prayer and then offered 'proxy' healing prayers for friends and relatives of those present. In this regard, he would lay his hand on someone's shoulder or head and pray that through this someone elsewhere would receive healing of the Holy Spirit. Afterwards, I thanked him for the service.

The following Sunday evening, Pat and I thought we would go back and attend his service again to see if he conducted it in the same manner. I had preached both of the morning services that day. When we arrived a little ahead of the appointed time that evening, the chapel was dark and still locked up. I thought I must have missed something, since there was no announcement in the bulletin about the evening service being cancelled. The next day, I asked him about the service not being held. "Oh," he said, "we've been having so few that I moved it to my house." I began to realize part of the reason he had not been promoted. Over the remaining months before his separation, I discovered many other reasons.

I had always followed a procedure of sitting down with each chaplain when I was assigned senior responsibilities. I learned to do this in their office so they would not be intimidated by being in the boss's office. Generally, my approach was to ask them what they did in the program. Then I would ask them to tell me what of these things they would rather give up and what other things would they prefer to be doing. I often had to tell them not to read their job description to me, since I knew how to read. I wanted to know in their words what they were doing.

When I sat down with the two chaplains, majors, I mentioned, I found out some interesting things. The first one informed me that he did as little as he could since he got passed over. He had seven

months till retirement and he could do that standing on his head!
His attitude was one of depressing and disgusting laziness. I was
taken back, needless to say. I listened anyway. When he finished,
I reminded him that he was being paid as a major and I expected
him to earn his pay right up till the day he left. As far as standing
on his head was concerned, I thought that might be difficult with
my foot up his rear end! (I will admit that this was neither kind nor
appropriate although he deserved it!)

On the other hand, my interview with the other major was quite
different. He had been an enlisted man originally, then was a civilian
missionary after seminary and finally had returned as a chaplain.
Most people saw him as a somewhat 'old, disgruntled' character! I
could readily understand why some supervising chaplains might
have given him a rating that would not get him promoted.

The Viet Nam War was winding down and many refugees were
coming to the United States, especially from among those who had
been loyal to the South Vietnamese government or its military.
This was also true of some who had cooperated with the Americans
during the war. I spoke with the chaplains identified previously
about our possibly sponsoring a refugee family through the chapel
program. My Catholic chaplain contacted his sources and began
the process of sponsoring a Catholic family through the Catholic
parish. I asked Frank (the former enlisted now chaplain mentioned)
to find out how we would go about identifying a family to sponsor
and what would we need in financial resources and other means of
supporting such a family.

A week later, Frank came to me with 20 reasons why we should
NOT sponsor a family of Vietnamese! I listened to him carefully
and then explained that I was sorry I had not been clear about the
project. I didn't want to know why we SHOULD NOT do it. I
wanted to know how we would do it. Would he please go back
to the drawing board and next week bring me the information I
needed. The following week, Frank came back with a complete
packet. He had identified a family and knew all the answers. In

fact, we followed his plan completely and it was highly successful. I sent his plan forward through command channels to the Chief of Chaplain's Office and it was subsequently sent out to all bases as an operational plan for anyone seeking to do this. (I wasn't sure when Frank first told me the names of the men involved in our sponsorship were Tuong and Huang. It sounded like a Chinese acrobatic team, I told him.)

The family he had identified was separated. The father (Tuong) and a friend (Huang) were both former Royal Vietnamese naval officers. They were at Camp Chaffee, Arkansas. The friend's family was still in Viet Nam. (He paid a large ransom several years later to get them out of Viet Nam where the communist government had taken over.) Tuong's wife, her mother and seven children were in a refugee camp in California (at the former Parks Air Force Base). This made a unit of eleven people. Frank had determined how much it would cost to arrange housing for them. He had a list of potential job opportunities for the men. He determined what the school situation would be for the children as well. He also found out how much in the way of funding we could expect from the Federal government to assist in their relocation. He had done a masterful job.

We put everyone into motion for this project to take place with Frank taking the lead. His committee found a nice house we could rent for a good price that would be large enough for the entire group. He located possible employers for the two men and even one possibility for the mother if she desired to work. The fact that both of the men spoke fair English was of great help in arranging their employment. The day the men arrived from Camp Chaffee and then we went to the airport to meet the family coming in from California was one of the highlights of our time at Tinker. Our entire committee loaded in the 'blue goose' (Air Force Blue School bus) and went to the airport. We had Tuong and Huang with us. There was great rejoicing and teary-eyed reunion at the airport. Then we proceeded to the house we had rented for the family in Midwest City near the base.

As the family and the chapel committee stood in the living room, we joined in one big circle and had a prayer of thanksgiving for the re-uniting of this family and for the opportunity that brought them into our lives. It was another teary-eyed experience. I only need to add that the family settled into the community. The men both progressed nicely in their jobs. The grandma looked after the house and the wife went to work and within a year she was a foreman at the candy factory where she worked. Tuong eventually because a postal service employee. Huang was able to send for his family and bring them to Oklahoma as well. All the children did well in school and many went on to college and at least one became a medical doctor.

CHAPTER TWENTY-EIGHT

Our tour at Tinker lasted two years. General Randolph retired and was replaced by General Carl Schneider who has remained a good friend through the years of retirement. Both of these commanders were strong supporters of the chapel programs in every way possible, both by their attendance and their encouragement whenever it was needed.

The house that Pat built - that is, in one day she managed to work with the builder in making some modifications to the original plans and choose everything from the outside brick to the inside colors and fixtures - became one of our favorite places in which to live.

Then came the day when the next assignment arrived. I was to become the Wing Chaplain at the 36th Tactical Fighter Wing at Bitburg, Germany. We had always hoped to receive an assignment to Europe but we weren't thrilled with the idea of leaving two of our children in the states in college. As I mentioned previously, Tami went with us for the first year and then returned to complete her college education. Andy came over for an entire month just before

Tami was coming back to the states and the two of them were able to travel and see London, Paris and many other places.

We moved into the quarters that were being vacated by my predecessor on base. I believe previous wing chaplains had occupied this same three-bedroom unit in one of the quad apartments over several transitions. It was a good location, less than a block from the family chapel (although my office was in the small chapel on main base behind the headquarters - a kilometer across a farmer's field from the family housing area.) We were within walking distance of the commissary, the Base Exchange and Theater and the schools.

When I arrived I discovered that a classmate from the Air War College (H. Norman Campbell) was the Director of Operations and lived at the other end of the quad. Most of the senior officers were in the building we were in or in the one that faced it. At the head of the quad, a duplex housed the Base commander and the Deputy Wing Commander. Next door was the only single family unit on base which was the Wing Commander's quarters. (Later, Norm Campbell became the Deputy Wing Commander and the last year we were there, he was promoted to Brigadier General and became the Wing commander. Many years later I had the high privilege and honor of presiding at the memorial service for Norm - then a retired Major General - at Fort Myers Chapel and burial at Arlington National Cemetery.)

Bitburg Air Base, through the years, had a reputation for getting the latest fighter aircraft first in Europe. In addition, most commanders arrived there as Colonel and departed as Brigadier General. A number of bases had the reputation of being 'star-makers' over the years. I was told that one reason for giving the latest 'birds' to Bitburg lay in it being the furthest from the possible conflict between the West and Russia. Therefore, the base would have the maximum time to launch its aircraft in defense of the Western Allied forces. And, since they had the latest aircraft, they would have the best armament as well.

The base originally had been built as a Luftwaffe base. Most of these facilities had been destroyed in World War II and been replaced by newer facilities. One of the things that had not been replaced was the infrastructure. The United States Air Force was in a continuing program gradually of replacing utilities throughout the base. During my tour, they finally replaced (at considerable cost) the underground communications cables and related equipment. Prior to this major project, when we had serious rainfall problems, it was not unusual to lose some of the communications between the alert cells (where the F-15s were on line to launch within minutes in the event of war) and the tower that would launch the aircraft. Only short wave radio would be available in such times. The old circuits would short out and were referred to as 'Hitler's Revenge'!

After I had been stationed about a year at Bitburg, I received a call from the Command Chaplain for Europe (USAFE). He told me the deputy command chaplain was returning to the States and he needed a new deputy and wondered if I would be interested in moving to Ramstein for the position. I asked what was the job as deputy. I would be the command chaplain when the command chaplain was not present and likely succeed him when he returned the following year. Otherwise, I would be the chaplain member of the command inspection team traveling throughout Europe to inspect bases. I asked if the move was voluntary or involuntary. He indicated that since it was 'in-theater' it would have to be voluntary. I told him that I thought I currently had the best job in Europe. Along with six other colonels we met in the general's office every Wednesday morning and decided how to run the base. Furthermore, the commander and I had been classmates in the Air War College. Why would I want to move to Ramstein and be one of a hundred colonels on base? He stated that he understood my answer was no? Right! I responded. I remained at Bitburg.

The housing on base was built by the French after the war, in whose zone Bitburg originally was located. (After the end of World War II, the conquered areas were divided between the four allies - the Western area was made up of the British zone (North) the French (West) and the US (South). The eastern zone was Russia's area of control, which they had pretty much occupied at the end of the war anyway. Berlin remained a joint occupancy in those days, but even here it was divided into four zones. By the time I was stationed in Bitburg, the French had pulled out of Germany (and forced the United States out of bases in France as well). As a result of the establishment of democracy in the Western area, the new German Republic had united the three Western zones and for practical purposes it was one area, although there were still bases of the British in the North and most of the rest of the bases were US. Of course, East Germany was a Communist nation on its own with considerable Russian involvement. The Berlin wall separated the East from the West in the city.

Bitburg and Trier (nearby) were involved in a military-civilian cooperative council that met once each quarter to promote better relations between the two societies. The location of the meeting alternated between the two groups who hosted the events. On one of these meetings the civilians hosted all of us at a marvelous winery in the Trier area. Great German food and the wines of the winery nearby made for a wonderful evening. On other occasions there would be entertainment appropriate to the hosting group. With considerable coordination, the Bitburg Air Base group was able to arrange to host one of the quarterly meetings in Berlin! This meant arranging for military air transportation from Bitburg to the Tempelhof Airport in West Berlin. Bus transportation then took us to quarters that had been arranged at the base. The following day, we had bus transportation to take us on a tour that included going through 'checkpoint' Charlie into East Berlin. We were not allowed off the bus there because of the East Berlin/Russian regulations, but we got a great bus tour of the city.

Every morning British, French and American convoys of military vehicles (staff cars mostly) would line up and go through 'checkpoint Charlie' just to exercise the right of passage that had been guaranteed in the treaties signed at the end of World War II. Likewise, the Russians would form a convoy and come the opposite direction and make the rounds through the British, French, and American zones of Berlin. Of course, when the wall came down and the East was freed from Soviet occupation this all became unnecessary. When Pat and I were back in Europe on one of our later tours, we had the opportunity to visit the united Berlin. Checkpoint Charlie was still there, but was now occupied by a 'team of folks in uniform who posed with tourists' for a price.

CHAPTER TWENTY-NINE

Our three year tour at Bitburg Air Base was an enjoyable one. It allowed us to travel throughout Western Europe and over to the United Kingdom. Tom was in middle school during this time and enjoyed the travel as well. The Base chapel had a youth choir that rehearsed and presented a musical every year, usually travelling throughout the area. On one of those occasions, Tom was able to travel with the choir when they went to bases and locations in Germany, the Netherlands, Belgium, Luxembourg and France. Another trip took the choir to England to present their musical at several American bases.

In 1979, I put together a tour to Jordan, Egypt and Israel for 38 of our folks at the base. Originally, Pat and I were going to lead the tour. However, it turned out that Andy and Tami (both back in the states) were going to graduate from College within a three-week period. I couldn't be gone for that length of time and it was right in the middle of the tour to the Middle East. Pat came back to the states for the two graduations and Tom took her place on the tour. This gave him an opportunity of a lifetime to visit the pyramids, the King Tut tomb, all the important places in Israel where Jesus taught and healed, bled and died. In addition, we visited Petra and its rock city in Jordan.

We had a staff of very congenial and hard working folks at the chapel and great command support during our three years in Bitburg. Overlapping most of our tour was Father Peter Flood. Peter eventually became a full Colonel in the Air Force and had a distinguished career as a priest and officer. He had worked for a phone company while in College and developed a great many skills related to electronics and wiring! This fit nicely with my desire to build another 'HO' model railroad. I first built a small one when we lived in Silver Spring, Maryland prior to entry into the Air Force. In that case, we were in a small apartment, so I designed my layout to be 2 1/2 foot wide by 6 foot long. It was hinged in the center so that I could fold it in half and slide it under the bed.

I think my interest in model railroading may have stemmed from my childhood. We had a Lionel (O27) train set when I was growing up. The layout was on a standard size 4x8 sheet of plywood. It was stored in the attic most of the year and only set up in the corner of the living room at Christmas time with the Christmas tree occupying the rear corner of the board. A tunnel beneath the tree went through the 'mountain' that was the tree stand. But, when the tree came down, it was time to put the railroad set away for another year. As a child, along with my brothers, we begged to keep the tree up one more week so that we could continue playing with the train. I remember distinctly my mother laying down the law one year. The tree was already without most of its needles (always a real tree in those days and they shed their needles constantly). Finally, she said, "The tree comes down tomorrow. It will be Valentines Day next week and it's long since past time to put that thing away."

When I arrived in Bitburg I was informed that there was a room in the basement of the four-story building that was available to me as either extra storage or hobby space. My predecessor had collected German clocks that he picked up at low cost around Europe and used this area to work on some of them. (In fact, after his retirement

in Colorado I heard he opened a clock shop!) The building had been
built with the intention of having maids' quarters in the basement.
There were three rooms in a row and then a large bathroom. This
plan was repeated several times across the basement. Evidently, this
extra space had always been allocated to the full colonels living in
the building. I was shown the bathroom directly below our first floor
quarters and told it was mine to use. It was actually a little larger
than the other rooms and had cabinets along one wall. In measuring,
I decided it would be easy to put a small railroad layout on top of the
bathtub in the room. And, because it was the bathroom with this
extra storage space and a toilet and lavatory, it was ideal. There was
water for whatever needs I might have in cleaning up after working
on things. Here I could build a layout that would be 3 1/2 feet wide
by 8 feet long. Furthermore, I decided that rather than building it
in 'HO' scale, I would opt for the newer and smaller 'N' scale. The
tracks were half as wide as 'HO' and so I could get far more layout
in the same space.

There was a dandy hobby shop in the village of Bitburg that
carried a supply of everything I needed in 'N' scale. Furthermore, I
had learned years ago that the communications people always had
odds and ends of wire that worked great with model railroading!
Peter took an interest in the project primarily from the technical
standpoint. By the time we finished rigging the railroad, it was
possible to run two trains at the same time for about twenty minutes
without having to touch anything. Peter acquired a 'stepping switch'
designed for telephone work and with magnetic reed switches and
little magnets on the trains, they would run around the track
automatically changing switch directions, turning on and off power
in appropriate blocks of the track and generally maintain the entire
process.

One concern was that as the senior chaplain there was always the
possibility that I might receive a phone call at any time. Peter found
a solution to that as well. He ran telephone wires from the apartment
down through the conduits he commandeered to a telephone in the

hobby room. It was designed in such a fashion that if I had a call, Pat could push a button and I could raise up the phone downstairs and answer it just like a normal phone extension would function. And, in the midst of all this, Peter and I had a good time working together on it.

Support for the chapel program included a secretary who was a local German woman. Gisela had worked on the base for many years and was a fixture in the chapel office. She not only provided continuity in the office workload, but served as interpreter when we needed that service. She had never married and still lived with her parents in a nearby Trier suburb in Konz-Trier. While we were there, she celebrated her 50th birthday and the chapel staff took her out to dinner in a local gasthaus. We arranged everything for the party including a birthday cake that thrilled her as she told us she had never had a birthday cake before!

I mentioned that she did some interpreting for us as well. This usually went ok, however, I did have her call for some reservations with an overnight ship to the United Kingdom that turned out with an interesting twist. Roger and Lee Makepeace (he was my predecessor in the Director of Site Activities office in Alaska and later came to Hawaii while we were there and directed the religious education program as a civilian) were on their round-the-world retirement trip. Their plans included flying into Frankfurt where we would meet them. We planned to take the overnight Ferryboat from Bremerhaven to York, England, including our automobile for travel throughout the United Kingdom. We didn't feel it was necessary to arrange for cabins for just an overnight trip, however, Roger indicated that his research showed it was possible to reserve reclining deck chairs in which one might rest or even nap on the trip across the channel. I asked Gisela if she could call the company and make those reservations for me since I didn't trust my German that well. She did so and left me a note to the effect that she had made our reservations for four 'declining deck chairs'!

Gisela had never owned an automobile and decided it was time that she acquire one and learn to drive. In Germany, she was required to take a course and a test. (I think she took the course twice before passing it.) Her brother was an automotive engineer with the German government and had suggested she should buy a used car and preferably a simple one. So she bought a DAF 40. This was a small car that had an automatic belt driven transmission. You put the gear stick forward if you wanted to go forward and you pulled it backward if you wanted to go backwards!

She was concerned about driving in traffic since she'd not done this before. One of the problems she faced was that her parents' apartment sat right next to the highway from Konz-Trier into Trier. From there she could take the highway to Bitburg. Parking for the apartment was at a right angle to the highway and she was greatly concerned about backing into the traffic in the mornings. Peter had been encouraging her in the driving area and so he had given her instructions on how to do this. He reminded her that she merely had to turn the steering wheel in the direction she wanted to go whether she was going forwards or backwards.

The following morning she arrived in a bit of a huff! She spoke to Peter rather harshly, "Vater Flood. Und Sie ein priester. Lying to me!"

Needless to say, Peter was shocked at this accusation. Then he elicited some explanation from her. It turned out that she was parked facing toward the apartment building. When she came out to depart, she wanted to go to Trier to her right. So she turned the steering wheel to the right. She backed out and found herself going the other direction! This led a couple of days later to my discovering Peter and Gisela crawling on the floor of the administrative office. Peter had borrowed from a parishioner a small toy car that had a working steering wheel with front wheels that turned like a real automobile. He was showing Gisela how to maneuver her automobile from the apartment in such a way as to go to Trier! We've had many a laugh over that experience.

Then came the winter storms, which came often in the Eifel Mountains of Germany. This one came in the night and the roads were treacherous. So as soon as I thought it would not be too early, I placed a phone call to Gisela's home to let her know that I thought it wise for her to just stay home and not be on the treacherous highway. Her mother answered the phone to tell me that Gisela had left quite a bit earlier in order to arrive at the base in spite of the bad weather. It was about 20 miles from Trier to the base. I went on to my office at the regular time expecting Gisela to be there already. She was not. And in fact, she arrived a couple of hours later than I would have expected her. When she came in she announced with great exhilaration that she had been the hero! The highway from Trier to Bitburg was mountainous and twisting. I could just imagine her stopping by the side of the road and rescuing someone who was stranded because of the icy conditions. However, I was wrong. Instead, she said, "I was the hero. I led everyone out from Trier all the way safely." Considering the time she had left Trier and the time she arrived at the base, I could just imagine how many folks she frustrated as she 'led them' out to the base - likely driving so slow that most trailing her lost their religion before they arrived!

Father Flood and I were asked to sit for an interview with a local newspaper reporter from nearby Trier. Lydie Hengen arranged this event and was present to assist in any language difficulties. She was Luxembourgish and served as a civilian employee working the areas of protocol and translation difficulties. She was fluent in English, French, German and Luxembourgish. As we began the interview and exchanged questions and answers in German, the reporter asked how we were able to speak the language so well. Peter responded with the information that, "Mein Oberst hat in universitat studiert, und Ich haben eine fraulein." (My Colonel has in the university studied and I have a girl friend.) Lydie quickly intervened with, "Nein, nein, Vater hat eine betranke." (No, no, Father has a lady acquaintance.") The first term implied that the priest had a real girl friend. Lydie certainly didn't want that information published in a local newspaper in what was a heavily Roman Catholic area of Germany.) Peter and I have laughed about that and many more funny incidents we enjoyed over the years. I will leave most of them for him to report in 'his' memoirs!

Our three years in Bitburg were capped with the loss of two of our F-15 aircraft in the final weeks. In fact, I was in the process of planning the memorial service for a young captain who had been lost in the accident of one of these aircraft when the sergeant came to my office to tell me that the commander was on his way to pick me up since we'd lost another aircraft. I couldn't help but remember that my first tour of duty in Minneapolis had begun with several aircraft accidents and now my final tour was marked similarly.

On my magic form 90 (remember the dream sheet) I had requested assignment back in the states as a wing chaplain somewhere in Texas. I had 26 years for retirement purposes and I figured this was my last assignment before retirement. My plan was to retire in Texas. Then came the day when the personnel officer in the Chief's office called me to tell me he had me slated to go to Minot, North Dakota. (Every Air Force person had heard and probably repeated the phrase - 'why not, Minot'!) I told him that I had gone to every assignment I had been given, but for my last assignment, I didn't want to go to Minot. My reasons were simple. Pat had discovered when we were in Alaska that she suffered from Reynaud's syndrome. This is a condition of the blood flow to the extremities that creates considerable problems. In extreme cold her hands would turn yellow, become very cold and ache. Doctors had told her to avoid getting them cold. While we were still in Alaska, I installed an inside heater in the car since we had to park outside our quarters. This kept the car warm enough that she could get in and not have a freezing condition on her hands before the car heater began its work. She also learned to wear heavy gloves or mittens when outdoors. She might even have an episode of this on a quite cold and damp day even though it was not freezing. I explained this to the chaplain personnel officer. He told me I would have to get it documented by medical authorities!

I hung up the phone and called the Base Hospital commander. He said not to worry, he'd write a very strong letter that would prevent them from sending me to Minot. By the time I got off the phone, the personnel chaplain in Washington was back on the phone telling me I didn't have to go to Minot and I didn't have to send in any paperwork. Chaplain Carr (the Chief of Chaplains at the time) had said to make an adjustment. Over the next few days, I was called and offered an assignment at Shaw Air Force Base in the Carolinas, or later to Kirtland Air Force Base in New Mexico. By then, Pat and I had prayed about the next step in our lives and decided that if I was going to serve a civilian church, it was time to begin that ministry. I went to the local personnel office and filed paperwork requesting my retirement at the end of my tour in Germany. Further, I requested that my return to the states be in May so that I would be available for an appointment at a Methodist Annual Conference. (This would mean taking my final couple of months accrued leave as terminal leave.) This was approved and we began plans for the next stage of life in Texas.

I wrote the bishop in Missouri (where my conference membership was located as I entered active duty) to inform him of my pending retirement, but to indicate that I hoped to transfer to one of the Texas Conferences for assignment. Bishop Bob Goodrich had been the pastor of First Methodist in Dallas before his election to the episcopacy and was now retiring himself and returning to Texas. I also communicated with the bishop in North Texas and with a couple of pastors I knew from that area, including one who had become the district superintendent of the Sherman - McKinney district. The latter wrote me that he had a small church in Bonham, Texas that would be available and a good place to start in the conference. The superintendent in the Fort Worth area also wrote me to say that he had a church that included serving a retirement community near Granbury that would be a good place to begin.

Then, my phone rang at 3 in the morning. It was Dr. Jim Palmer (who evidently had not considered the time differential) calling from Floral Heights United Methodist Church in Wichita Falls. He was looking for a senior associate pastor and he'd been told of my availability. We spoke for a while and then I told him of these other offers and that I thought I ought to honor one of them. I was told that the superintendent in the Sherman district was the one who had suggested me to him. With this, he offered to write me of the details. When they arrived, I responded by agreeing to this arrangement. This led to our arrival in Dallas for the annual conference on the opening Sunday evening in May of 1980. When the service ended, we looked around and found the Palmers looking around! We had a late night snack together that evening and a few days later at the end of the conference, I was transferred into the North Texas conference and appointed to serve as the associate pastor at Floral Heights United Methodist Church, a position I filled for nearly three years.

Early in my orientation, Jim Palmer suggested that one of the things needed at the congregation was an infusion of new and younger members. The median age of the congregation was in the sixties! He challenged me to develop a visitation program and outreach that would result in this possibility. He suggested he wanted me to take in more new members than he buried - and he had six funerals that first week! I worked at developing a relationship with many of the members in the congregation and began reaching out to anyone who visited the church with a welcome letter and then a pre-arranged by appointment visit. This paid off handsomely and during the three years I was there, the church did increase in membership even though many of the old timers were promoted to glory. Jim and I developed a great relationship.

In the summer of 1980, Wichita Falls experienced one of its hottest temperatures on record. It reached 112 one day, and then next the high was 119! As I indicated, the median age of the large congregation was 68 and so hospital visits were a daily responsibility between us. Most of our folks were either in Bethania or in Wichita General. These hospitals were about six blocks from the church with about four blocks between them. The air conditioner in the automobile would almost begin to cool down by the time I arrived at the first hospital. It wouldn't quite make it to cool between hospitals nor on the way back to the church. On the day the temperature reached 119, I took off my tie and sport jacket upon returning to the church and went into Jim's office. I said, "Jim, if you are going to fire me this would be a good day! I am not going to continue wearing a coat and tie with the temperature like this!" (Remember, I had just returned from living in the Eifel Mountains of Germany at Bitburg where the temperature rarely got above 70 on the hottest of days!)

Jim looked at me and grinned. "I think that's a good idea. Not to fire you, but for us not to wear coat and tie when it's this hot." From then on he joined me in the short sleeve - open collar wardrobe during the hot weather.

Our families were somewhat similar in structure. They had two daughters and one son and we had two sons and one daughter. In both cases, only the youngest (a son) was still at home. Their son, Bert, and our son, Tom were of the same age and became good friends. They went to high school together and both played football. They were both very active in the Methodist youth Fellowship at the church. Their friendship continued through the years, even though they chose different college experiences and different careers; Bert becoming a pastor and Tom an engineer/executive in the home construction business.

Jim and Ellen (his wife, a registered nurse and later a professor of neo-natal care at University of Texas at Arlington) were most gracious in their welcoming us to the community. There was no parsonage set apart for the associate pastor but we would receive a housing allowance. This worked fine for us since we had sold our home In Midwest City, Oklahoma upon our departure for Germany and needed, for tax purposes, to reinvest in another home. We found a lovely new home in a nice area, but it was not quite ready for occupancy. The Palmers invited us to stay with them in their large parsonage. This worked out very well. The Palmers had an African American woman named Irene who came once a week to take care of housekeeping chores. Since I was very busy every day getting involved in the work of the church, Pat often did whatever housework she saw that needed to be done during the day. (In fact, Bert referred to her as the white Irene, a term she used one day when the housekeeper showed up to clean. Pat introduced herself to Irene as the white Irene!)

Jim Palmer was generous in sharing the preaching responsibilities as well as other leadership positions within the church. I worked with the youth program extensively, taking them on mission field trips several times. One of these trips went to Juarez, Mexico where we were scheduled to work in a Methodist medical mission program. Knowing their needs in advance, one of the men of the church designed and pre-built several cabinets for the new clinic they hoped to have. Another church member, who owned a tool and equipment rental agency, made available a gasoline powered concrete mixer for us to take with us so that we could lay the foundation and build the adobe walls for the new facility. We discussed the difficulty we might have in getting this across the border. He gave me two invoices for the unit. One of these showed it as a rental unit and when used at the border would mean I had to bring it back with me. The other paperwork was a title to the unit. If we didn't have to register it at the border, then we could leave it there with the missionaries to be used whenever they needed it and it would be theirs.

The pre-built cabinets were loaded on a pickup truck. Another pickup truck held the tarp-covered mixer. We had a couple of vans in addition to a large bus rented by one of the church members to transport our youth and the chaperones. We knew we couldn't take the bus across the border, but had arrangements with the Lydia Patterson Methodist School in El Paso, whose bus had international insurance, to take up the cross border task once we arrived. I had all the personnel listed in a roster and paperwork for the vehicles, as well as the two separate invoices for the mixer. When we arrived at the border crossing, it was late in the afternoon. We had no problem departing the American side of the border. On the Mexican side, the border guards wanted to see the paperwork for everything. I had it organized in military fashion for them to peruse. Of course, he wanted to know what was under the large tarp on the back of the pickup truck. When we revealed it, he began telling us we would have to go downtown to register all of this, including the individuals. I speak no Spanish, so I replied in English that I understood this would not be necessary and showed him the paperwork, including information about the mission station we were going to serve in the barrios (poverty housing area) on the edge of Juarez.

After considerable language attempts, one of which found me speaking German to him, a young boy nearby came over and offered to interpret! He explained it to the guard, who continued to say we had to go downtown. I asked to speak to the supervisor, a request the young boy relayed to the guard. The supervisor was sent for and came and looked over all the paperwork. I had a feeling from what I'd been told in advance that the guards might well be looking for some bribe money and I was determined I would not do that. Then the supervisor began looking at his watch and talking to the guards who looked at their watches. I realized it must be near shift change time and they didn't want to work overtime, so I waited them out until they finally exclaimed, "Oh!" and waved me through. We left the mixer with the missionaries at the end of our workweek.

The mixer played another part in the week. The local missionaries had tried to encourage some help from the men in the barrios but without much luck. A couple of men did show up the second day. When they saw the mixer (which they called a cemento blender) they wanted to mix all the ingredients (sand, gravel, cement mix) on the ground first and then shovel it into the mixer. I assured them this was unnecessary and that we could just put it all in the mixer with the right amount of water and it would work fine. We poured the foundation and the floor for the new building that day. The following day we began laying the adobe blocks that would be the walls. I had never worked with adobe before, but had laid concrete blocks and bricks, so I applied the same process. The only change

I discovered was the adobe will dissolve if you get them too wet! Although we'd been told that men in the area were invited but had not shown up to help, within an hour of starting the adobe work, several men from the neighborhood showed up and gradually, we backed off and let them finish the project. It was a great experience for our youth and a fine addition to the barrios community.

CHAPTER THIRTY

One Sunday in early 1983, Jim Palmer was gone on a missionary trip to Haiti and I was in charge of both of the morning services. A visitor that day to the service was the Reverend Phil Mercer. Phil had been the pastor at First United Methodist Church in Lewisville when the Trietsch family offered to give some land from their 'chicken farm' to start a new church in neighboring Flower Mound, Texas. (Later Phil told me that he had remarked to a retired judge whom he knew and was sitting by, that he was disappointed that there was a 'guest preacher' instead of Dr. Palmer. The judge told him - as relayed to me - that he'd probably hear a better sermon!) After the service, Phil introduced himself to me. I knew his name but had not met him. He asked if he could come by and visit with me the next morning in the study. I agreed this would be fine. He came by and we had a good time getting acquainted. Phil was now in charge of new church development for the conference.

The following week I received a telephone call from the Wichita Falls district superintendent, Earl Kifer. Earl said he didn't want this to be public information as yet, but that the bishop wanted me to start a new church in Flower Mound. Up until that time, I had no knowledge of the community and, in fact, asked where it was. Between Lewisville and Carrolton and Coppell. Earl said that I would be getting a call from Dr. Gordon Casad, the superintendent of the Dallas-Denton District that included this area who wanted to talk to me about this appointment. Earl said they had wanted to start this project at minimum salary, however he had insisted it had to be better than that and include a parsonage allowance.

As informed, I received the call from Gordon Casad. He wanted to know if Pat and I could meet him in Dallas to discuss this possibility. We agreed to come down on a Saturday and meet him at a local restaurant. Again, we were asked not to discuss it with anyone else. After the meeting and a good lunch, we went to Flower Mound where we visited with Erwin and Velma Trietsch, the folks who were giving five acres for a new church, to be located on Morriss Road in Flower Mound. (When they first proposed making this donation to Phil Mercer, they had offered an acre or two, but Phil told them that there would need to be at least five acres and they agreed to that.) When Gordon, Pat and I, Erwin and Velma Trietsch met in their humble living room on the farm, we prayed together about the new church.

(When the issue of my move first was raised, Pat and I and Tom had a discussion about the matter. Tom was due to enter his senior year in high school the following fall. Here we were faced again with what happens to children when military or ministers get moved about. We came back from Hawaii expecting Andy to have two more years of high school, however, he had so many credits from having been in Punahou Private Academy that he graduated at the end of his Junior year. Then, when I was sent to the Air War College, Pat remained in San Antonio so that Tami would not be uprooted her senior year. Now we faced it again. Tom was very understanding saying that he had moved schools all his life and one more wouldn't hurt him. As it worked out, he and Pat stayed in Wichita Falls until the school year was out and he had completed his junior year. Then, he let me know that one weekend he would not come with Pat to Flower Mound because he had an appointment with the dean of the School of Engineering at Texas Technical University in Lubbock, Texas to determine if he could enter the following fall. It turned out that he needed two credits and he took them that summer by correspondence from the University of Nebraska Extension Course program and received his high school diploma in that manner, going on to Texas Tech the fall of 1983.)

I asked Gordon, if the appointment was for sure, then I would like permission to inform Jim Palmer about it myself rather than for him to hear about it in some other way. Gordon agreed and told me I could do that anytime that following week before the general announcement of the appointment was made. I thought long and hard about how to do that. I wanted to tell Jim that my choice was not to leave Floral Heights where we'd been made so welcome, but instead to accept the challenge of the new church start up situation. As it happened, on Tuesday morning Jim asked if I could follow him to the car dealership to leave Ellen's car off for service and then bring him back to the church. This seemed an ideal time for me to discuss this with Jim away from the church and any interruption. On the way back from the car dealership, I told him about the contacts I'd had and the appointment that was forthcoming. I reassured him that I would always be grateful for his welcome and the great time in ministry we'd had at Floral Heights as I readjusted to civilian ministry. He was very quiet for a while, and then said, 'Bill, I knew we should have offered to buy you a car from the church this year.' I replied, 'Jim, this is not about a car or money. In fact, I'm taking an annual pay cut of fifteen thousand dollars to take this appointment!' If I looked carefully at the changes in ministry through the years, I would discover that I often took a cut in pay to move to another circuit of ministry. This was true when I left the civilian world to go on active duty the first time and then was true when I left the military after three years and returned to civilian ministry!

When the announcement of the appointment was made, it was that the new church should begin on 1 March so that we would be in the upswing as Easter approached. Arrangements were made for us to meet at the Timbercreek Elementary School for Sunday services initially. Gordon Casad made arrangements for us to have a meeting at First UMC in Lewisville in February before I would be coming to Flower Mound. Although we had heard that the current pastor there was opposed to a new church in the area, the conference had decided it was time to do it. (Evidently, the pastor thought a new church in the area would dilute financial support at First church. He had persuaded them the year before not to begin this endeavor as yet. Interestingly, he did not bring his chair of evangelism to this meeting, but his finance chair, who looked around to see what financial dent might occur from this.) About 35 people attended the meeting at First Church. Gordon called on the local pastor to begin with a devotional and then I was introduced and called on to talk about the new church. I did so and asked for those who thought because of their residence they might be interested in being a part of the new church to raise their hands. Most of them did so. I then asked those who were certain they wanted to be a part of getting things started to remain after the meeting to discuss a steering committee meeting. About fifteen remained.

This steering committee met on Tuesday the 1st of March in one of the homes. We planned to hold services in the school the following Sunday. (I learned much later that the General Board of Church Extension of the United Methodist Church believed that to start a new church, the new pastor should meet with small groups in their homes for about 3 to 6 months before holding the first general worship service. I didn't know any better, so I plunged right in.) Others of the folks anxious to be on the steering committee included Steve and Margaret Griffin, still friends today. (Since beginning this story, Margaret has passed away.) Steve was Vice President of a local bank. When I told him that my last Sunday at Floral Heights had resulted in over $3000.00 given to me to help start the new church, he encouraged me to come by the bank and open an account.

Among those who remained for this first meeting were Vic and Gwen Ayres who offered support then and have remained good friends to this day. They owned and operated the Avion Sales and Service RV dealership in Lewisville. Among support they supplied initially was a place for the church to function for office space in the extra sales office in their facility. When they discovered that I would likely purchase a home in the area but that it would not be available immediately, they offered one of their trailers with complete 'hook-up' in which I could live until the house was ready. They offered to get a telephone installed in that trailer for me as well. We knew the school did not have enough folding chairs for us to use, since we would be holding services in their 'cafetorium' that was equipped with folding table/bench units. Vic offered to purchase 100 folding chairs on his business account from a local company with which he had contacts. The church could reimburse him the cost when it was up and running.

I went to the local post office in Lewisville to acquire a postal box for the church only to discover I had to be on a waiting list because they were short of boxes due to the growth in the area. I went to the bank to open an account for the church. The clerk involved with new accounts wanted a lot of information I couldn't give her. She asked the name of the church. I replied we didn't exist as yet but it would be the Trietsch Memorial United Methodist Church. She asked for an address. I had to tell her we were waiting for a postal box. She asked for my address and I had to tell her that I was staying in a trailer on the Avion Sales and Service lot and was waiting for a phone to be installed!

She looked at me and said, "Now, let me get this right. You want to open an account for a church that doesn't yet exist. You don't have an address or currently a phone number and you are living in a trailer on the back of the RV sales lot? Is that right?"

"Yes. That's right," I replied.

"Reverend Jacobs, I'm not sure I can open an account like that."

"Well, Mr. Griffin said I could do this and that's the reason I've come."

"If Mr. Griffin said so, then I'm sure it will be ok," she said, as Steve Griffin spotted me from his office and came to welcome me and reassure her that it was alright.

We knew we would need some materials to get the church started, hymnals among other things, and Sunday School material. So I visited the Cokesbury Bookstore (the local outlet of the United Methodist Publishing House.) I knew the manager of the store in Dallas, since her husband was a pastor in the conference. I explained to her that I was beginning the new church in Flower Mound and wanted to open an account and acquire some materials. We went through the same drill on the name of the church, its address, my address, the phone number, etc. She told me she could get a free starter set of Sunday School materials from the publishing house (which was a standard procedure). As to hymnals, she wondered how many I might need to start a new church, 25 or 50. "No," I said, "I think we will need 100 of them to get started." (Remember, this is before the days of using 'words on the big screen in worship'.) She looked in the back and then told me they were actually on sale right now. So I purchased 200 copies and loaded them in my car, opening a charge account to pay for them!

Before I left Floral Heights UMC in Wichita Falls, I had devised a very simple, one page flyer about the new church. When I arrived in Flower Mound, moving into the trailer in Lewisville, I began my work. It was a Tuesday and we met that evening as a steering committee. The next few days, I walked the streets from Timbercreek Elementary School at least four blocks in every direction and knocked on every door. If no one answered, I left a copy of the flyer in the door. If anyone answered, I introduced myself as the new Methodist pastor and explained that we would eventually be located on Morriss Road just North of the Marcus High School. Meanwhile we were beginning services the following Sunday (first

Sunday in March, 1983) at the Timbercreek Elementary School. If they had no church home I wanted to invite them to come and worship with us.

The following Sunday morning, Vic Ayres brought the 100 chairs on storage racks to the school. Several of the men who had been on the steering committee showed up and we moved the bench/tables out of the way and set up the chairs for worship. Using my old Air Force chaplain kit with cross and candles, we set up a temporary altar. When the appointed hour arrived, we had 125 people show up for worship services! This was the lowest attendance we ever experienced! The cafetorium was equipped with a piano and we had located Diana Coy and asked if she would play the piano for our worship service. She later became the first choir director for the church. We made arrangements that day for Sunday school to begin the following Sunday with an adult class (which I taught the first few weeks) and six classes for children in the various age groups. Our classes initially met in sections around the cafetorium divided by the uprighted folding table/bench units.

Later, when it became obvious that the noise of all these classes in one room was not acceptable, we began meeting in sections of the hallway around the building. The school board had determined that we could NOT use the classrooms for fear something would be misplaced and teachers upset. Furthermore, we were given use of the building only between 9:00 a.m. and 12:00 p.m. This meant that folks had to arrive at 9 to set up things that started at 9:30 and concluded so that we were out of the building by 12. The second Sunday we met we determined to have a potluck luncheon following services and we did this, but held it outside on the sidewalk with borrowed tables and chairs. Although this restriction on the use of the facility was hampering, it probably caused us to move forward more quickly in building our own first facility.

By the first Sunday in May we felt we were prepared to have an official day of charter for the church. We invited Dr. Casad to preach the service that day and at the end of the service invited those who wanted to declare charter membership to come forward and sign the book. There were 116 charter members officially received into the Trietsch Memorial United Methodist Church that day. This was sixty days from the time of our first service. The outdoor potluck dinners continued once a month throughout the summer and into the fall. Always there was some concern about what would we do if the weather was inclement, but we never had to face that situation.

By that fall we were looking at how soon would we be able to build our first unit on the property on Morriss Road. We were outgrowing the cafetorium for morning worship and our classes in the hallways were not satisfactory. We had established a building fund to get started on the process of raising funds. The Conference had set aside funds to pay my salary and housing allowance for the first year. By the third month, we were depositing those funds into the bank because our income was great enough to cover the salary and housing allowance that had been established. After school was out, Pat and Tom moved into the house we had built in Lewisville. Prior to their coming down, our youth group wanted to have a 'sleep over' party and since our house was sparsely furnished, it seemed like a great place. With more than adequate adult counselors, the youth came out in large numbers. One of the boys, Jerry Jones volunteered to bring a TV movie for them all to watch. I didn't think to question what he was bringing, except that he promised me it was not a naughty film. What he brought was the "Texas Chainsaw Murders"! Some of the kids chose to go on to sleep rather than watch the horror film! By the way, Jerry is now a Methodist pastor. One of the neighbors called the police that evening, concerned about the large number of youth in this yet 'unoccupied' residence. I assured them when they arrived that I was the owner, the new pastor and the youth were fine.

A committee was formed to map out the direction we might go with our building program and Vic Ayres was chosen to chair that committee. One of the early decisions they made was to employ an architect who would design the first unit and provide a master plan for the entire property. The committee looked at several possibilities and eventually invited three to make presentations to the committee. At this point the firm of Ron Hobbs was chosen. He was given instructions as to what we had in mind. When he brought his master plan forward, it appeared that to make it really work well, we ought to move it to the back of the property. To make this possible, Erwin and Velma Trietsch offered to give the church an additional five acres directly behind that which had already been given. The master plan called for three buildings to be erected on this property eventually, with the first one to be an all purpose facility with offices, some classrooms, a kitchen and an auditorium that would seat close to 300 persons.

When we received our first estimate of the cost of this first unit, we decided we needed to put together a bond program to finance it. We first contacted the Methodist Foundation in Austin, Texas to see if they could provide us some assistance in this regard. Their responsibility includes receiving funds from churches and individuals to invest in church loans. However, they informed us that they didn't do anything with new churches until they were three years old. We explained that we couldn't wait that long to build something. About this time, I received a call from Steve and Margaret Griffin to see if they could come by to visit me at the parsonage. When they arrived, Steve told me the Lord had really blessed them in the year past and they wanted to share those blessings with the church. He presented me with a large check ($250,000) that really put us over the top with our plans. It meant that we needed about $650,000.00 to finish out the master planning and first unit. When we presented again to the foundation our plans they were quite impressed with the progress and growth we were showing and agreed to buy the first third of our bond program last. This meant they wanted the third that would mature the earliest (ours would be on a fifteen year program) but they would take them after we had sold the other two thirds. Our board agreed to this proposition.

Floral Heights United Methodist Church in Wichita Falls invited me to come to their church board dinner meeting and present what we were doing with the bond program and our future building plans. I sold $87,000.00 worth of bonds in that one evening. Later, Emma White, widow of W. Earl White of White Home Auto Stores contacted me and bought an additional $25,000.00 worth of bonds. When they matured several years later, she donated them to the church. It was this kind of support that moved our program along so that the Methodist Foundation didn't have to buy any of our bonds.

CHAPTER THIRTY-ONE

T here were three basic legs upon which the growth and development of the new church was built: Scripture, personal spiritual growth and Christian service. From the beginning we were determined to be a church based in Scripture and a church that reached out in mission rather than focused inwardly. One of the first outreach attempts was to determine what our obligation to the annual conference apportionment program would be. (Apportionments are the way in which the United Methodist Church allocates to local churches their share of the overall administration, missionary and other support causes of the general church.) The conference had a policy of not expecting a congregation to participate in these apportionments the first year. However, the conference treasurer was able to calculate for us what our share would have been had we not been under this excusal policy. Our board voted unanimously to pay it anyway. In the church's more than thirty years history, it has never missed paying its apportionment and many years has participated in a second giving program that helped churches that were unable to meet their obligation.

One of the ways the church assisted the membership in developing a deeper understanding of scripture was through the use of the Discipleship program of Bible study. The church was one of the earliest users of this program and often had a number of classes meeting simultaneously. To further develop spiritual growth in the congregation, encouragement was given for participants in the Walk to Emmaus weekends. I attended the very first one held in Dallas and Pat attended the first women's walk. Subsequently, I served on many teams and for several years was the

Spiritual Director of the Dallas area program that spawned groups in North and East Texas. Many of the Trietsch members went on to help in establishment of the Kairos prison ministries as well. (Kairos is a program similar to the Emmaus Walk program but for inmates in prison. I also served as the first spiritual director of the area Chrysalis program - Emmaus weekend for youth.)

I began teaching a Bible class within the first few weeks of the church's existence. We had an adult class on Sunday, however some of our folks who taught children's classes indicated they couldn't attend that class because they were busy at the same time teaching. Furthermore, although I began teaching the Sunday adult class, soon I passed that responsibility on to someone else so that I was free to teach the Confirmation class during the Sunday morning hour. All seventh graders were enrolled in that class initially and it continued from the beginning of the school year in the fall until Pentecost in the spring when their confirmation took place. Even after we had our first building I taught this class in my office. It was a crowded spot when we got up to having 25 or more in the class.

Meanwhile, I initiated a class during the week on Wednesday evening. Linwood and Sue Arthur volunteered space at their home for this class to meet. We met in their living room, which was open to the dining area through a large archway. They decided that I should sit in the far corner from the dining area so the overflow could be beyond the arch and still see me and hear me as I taught. The class grew to where we had a full room and more every week. I was somewhat dismayed by their large cat that sat in the middle of the room and stared at me throughout the class session. I wasn't sure whether the cat was religious or just curious. After several weeks, I remarked about this strange position of the cat. Then, I found out that the chair I was sitting in to teach was the cat's favorite spot to sit! I was invading his space and I think he resented it.

I introduced the Journeymen program that I had developed many years before. When I first developed the program it was for use at Stead Air Force Base in Nevada. In addition to the Combat Crew Survival Training program, the Air Force training for helicopter pilots was at that base. Generally the chopper students and their dependents were there for only six months. Entry times into the program were staggered as well so there were always folks coming and going. I thought the best way to reach them would be in short term programs. So the Journeymen program began with a four-week commitment. At the end of this period of time, if they were still going to be on base, they could commit for an additional four weeks. Then after that, they could commit for eight weeks beyond that. After that, those who had completed the program were encouraged to begin a group of their own using the same materials I had written. Since I knew that many would get the material and read their way through the entire series and I wanted their meditations each week to be fresh and new, I only distributed the meditation material each week for the following week.

Later, when I was ministering on the remote sites on the Aleutian Chain, I used the program again, but gave out the materials for a month at a time since that's how often I would be back to meet with the group. I organized each site with a lay representative to lead the group in my absence (and also to assist me when I was on site conducting services). The program was designed for about 12 members meeting once a week. The schedule included 15 minutes of quiet meditation on a provided page followed by a 15-minute discussion of the scripture that was prescribed, to be read every day during the week, meant in their lives. Then 15 minutes of sharing followed by 15 minutes of prayer completed the hour-long activity. Over the first few years at Trietsch, over one hundred members were involved in this activity and an equal number attended Emmaus weekends.

(Later, I was asked to create a Journeymen program for youth and this became the nine-month program of Journeymen Jr. It was used for confirmation training for several years.)

Our outreach involved being in the community as servants and so the congregation became an early support of Christian Community Action, an organization of churches that supported food pantries, clothing thrift shops, and many other ways of helping those in need. Later, the church also was involved in Habitat for Humanity. Every summer, youth groups went on mission trips to assist in various places around the Southwest. This included visiting Native American reservations to help out and going to places both in Texas and across the border to Mexico to assist the elderly by painting houses and cleaning up yards.

The first building included a little over 12,000 square feet of space, including an area for a kitchen. We were almost finished with construction when we discovered a government-sponsored program for diabetic education had been closed down. The building in which it was located was being reconfigured for a different use. If we wanted the stainless steel kitchen (cabinets, counters, etc.) we could have them free but would need to remove them before the following week. Our men organized, and with the use of pickup trucks from many in the church, the kitchen was dismantled and hauled to the church site and with some professional assistance in welding the stainless steel, was fully installed. It was another blessing that fell our way.

Of the early members in the church, the Lee family came from the Houston area. Bob was a pilot with one of the airlines. Linda had training in early childhood development. Under her leadership the first Trietsch Early Learning Center was established. Because of its high quality, it quickly became one of the favored programs in the community. We were limited in space and so it became necessary to have early enrollment for church members before opening it up to those from the community. I believe we gained some members each year because they wanted to be sure they could gain a spot for their child or children in the program! It meant the building was being used throughout the week and not just on Sunday. Linda called the first program Children's Day Out (CDO) rather than Mother's Day Out. She used to say we don't care if the mothers go out or stay home. This is for the children. It was far more than the baby-sitting programs that some churches were offering. It developed into the high quality Trietsch Enrichment Center that is ongoing, recently having celebrated its thirty years of existence.

In the second or third year of the church's existence, the Chair for Evangelism came to see me. He told me, "Preacher, you are taking the wrong people into this church."

I was shook up by his comment. But, he went on to say, "You are taking in all these young couples. They have children that need facilities and they have house payments and lots of family expenses. You need to begin receiving older 'empty nesters' that have the funds to contribute to build the buildings we need to serve these younger families!"

I explored with him how this was possible. In fact, he devised a plan whereby we targeted those members of our church who fit the older concept and worked with them to invite friends and acquaintances similar to them. We continued to receive many young families who had children, but we also began receiving older couples as well. Within two years of moving into that first building, we were on the hunt for the second building. The remaining bonds of the first drive were folded into the second bond issue. Eight years from the first service, the program moved toward a third building. Since then the master plan of the first campus has been completed, more acreage has been added and a seven and a half million dollar family life center constructed. As of this writing, the church is close to 5000 members.

We were back in March of 2013 for the 30th anniversary celebration at the church that included the Bishop as well as Jim Ozier, my successor pastor and John Allen the next pastor. It was a great celebration and an opportunity to see some of the old timers from those days when we first met in the school cafetorium.

By the fall of 1990, Pat and I had built our 'dream' home at Westhaven, a gated development on Canyon Lake, just north of San Antonio, Texas. Our son, Andy had been on the lookout for a place in the general area that we might build. We came down several times and explored the towns from Bastrop to Fredericksburg, hoping to discover just the right spot for our next move in retirement. When he mentioned Westhaven, we came and looked over the prospects, found a lot we liked, made an offer and bought the lot. Then, Pat worked with a builder's wife (a certified home planner) to develop the house we eventually had the builder construct. It was on a sloped lot that allowed us to have 2400 square feet upstairs and 850 square feet downstairs. In the latter, I eventually created a downstairs office as well as a large wood hobby shop. We had a half bath installed downstairs as well.

The situation downstairs lent itself to put a large double doorway to the outside where the wood hobby shop was located. This allowed me to open both doors, roll my Shopsmith out on a concrete pad and let the sawdust fly! Andy and I built a circular staircase from the upstairs study to the downstairs study as well as having access from a deck just outside the dining room and kitchen that had a spiral staircase down to the concrete pad outside the hobby shop below. It was a great arrangement and a very livable house.

After it was completed in September 1989, we often would come down for two or three days at a time and enjoy the quiet times there. Our son, Andy and his wife Judy and their three children (Tucker, Molly and Stuart) lived about twenty minutes away and that added to the enjoyment. During one of these visits in the fall of 1990, we contemplated the time of our retirement from the annual conference. In addition to the very heavy workload of pastoring a growing congregation (up to about 1200 members by then) and serving as secretary of the Annual Conference Board of Ministry and chair of the Committee on Joint Review (the initial committee to consider and attempt to resolve any problems with pastors), I was wanting to spend some time writing the story of my great grandmother and great grandfather. (This resulted in the Dear Lizzie books in the following years.) The church was about to embark on an additional fund raising campaign to start the next building program. In prayer, we determined this was probably the right time to step aside and let someone else take the lead.

I made an appointment to visit with the bishop in October of 1990. When I sat down with him, I began with, "I'm not in trouble. I have no health problems. Our marriage is not in trouble. The church is not in trouble, in fact, perhaps the healthiest it has been. BUT, I've determined with my wife and much prayer that this is the time to retire from the annual conference. I explained my desire to spend more time writing and traveling. He asked if a sabbatical wouldn't work just as well. (Such time for prayer, contemplation and study and travel is well authorized for pastors and can consume six months, or even more if study is involved.) I declined this possibility. The bishop wanted to know when I wanted this to be effective. I suggested 15 January 1991 as the right date. My reasons were, first, it would be after annual reports were due, so that a new pastor wouldn't arrive and immediately be responsible for annual reports. I didn't want to wait till annual conference time, because then the appointment process might put the assignment at Trietsch Memorial in the 'hopper' with many others. I wanted it to be the only one under consideration so that the very best pastoral appointment might take place.

The bishop reminded me that appointments were made at annual conference and retirements took place then as well. I pointed out that I knew that, but thought I could take a five-month leave of absence in January and retire the first of June at annual conference. The bishop told me that would have to be approved by the conference

Board of Ministry and I reminded him that I was secretary of that organization and thought I could get approval! We agreed that my plan was a good one. By the middle of December the announcement had been made and my successor appointed. (Pat and I took four of the couples that had been involved in the initial days of the church's founding to dinner and told them of the plan in advance, so that it would not be a shock to them. We have remained friends with many of those folks.) This led to our moving to our house at Canyon Lake in early January and officially going on 'leave of absence' as of the 15th of January with retirement at Annual Conference in late May 1991.

CHAPTER THIRTY-TWO

Our plans during the months following our departure from Flower Mound to live at Canyon Lake involved travel to as many places as we could find that were mentioned in the 146 letters Edwin Beardsley Campbell (my great grandfather on my mother's side) wrote to his sweetheart and later wife, Susan Elizabeth Lewis (Lizzie). We started by traveling to Des Moines, Iowa where they both were living before the Civil War started. Our first obstacle was in the census data. We were looking for the Campbell family that we thought would include him. We finally found him, not in a Campbell family, but in a Frizzell family. That's when I discovered that his mother had remarried Henry Frizzell! (Ironically, when visiting with an older sister and I mentioned this, she remarked, "Oh, that's who those Frizzell pictures are of. I wondered who they were!")

Our travels over the months and even years after that took us to places in Tennessee, Alabama, Georgia and the Carolinas as we tracked the locations mentioned in his letters or shown on the postmarks of the envelopes. (Alas, as a former stamp collector, I was disturbed that all the stamps had been removed from the envelopes!

My mother always thought one of her brothers might have done that while the letters were still in her mother's possession.) We made our way to Maryland to track his location at the battle of South Mountain where he was wounded. His commander, Rutherford B. Hayes was also wounded that day. This was providential, since three days later the 23rd Ohio Voluntary Infantry was involved in the battle at Antietam and many of Edd's companions were wounded or killed.

From the letters we knew that Edd had been taken to Frederick, Maryland after the battle in which he was wounded. (He took a 'mini-ball' through his left arm, exiting between his shoulder blade and spine.) We visited the historical society there in hopes of gaining some information. The woman told us she thought the wounded had been taken to the Presbyterian Church after the battle of South Mountain. I told her his letters indicated that he was in a private home. In the letter, Edd had indicated that President Lincoln had visited them there, although he didn't stay long because of a storm. A gentleman behind the counter told us that would be the Ramsay House which was about six blocks away. It was the only place in Frederick where Lincoln had visited. We visited that location and saw the plaque that commemorated Lincoln's visit to a General Hartsuff and the troops wounded at South Mountain. We had shivers as we observed the actual place where Edd had recovered from his wounds.

We also visited the presidential library of Rutherford B. Hayes in Fremont, Ohio. When the staff there discovered what I was doing in exploring information concerning my great grandfather's service in the 23rd Ohio, they were most helpful. They brought forth metal bins of Hayes' private papers for me to explore and offered to make copies of anything I found that would be useful to my project. It was most gratifying to find in Hayes' journal his description of a Thanksgiving Dinner he enjoyed with Company A where he listed the menu. Edd had written of this event in his letters with the same menu and the notation that he was the cook that day. Furthermore, he indicated that the 'colonel' had eaten with them that day. (Hayes was a Colonel, promoted later to brevet brigadier general.)

While we were traveling, I was writing. When I got to over 1000 typewritten pages, I decided I had more than one book. Eventually, I wrote and published six books. I made a decision that I wanted to tell the story rather than just publish the letters, because there was so much more than just the printed words on pages. I wrote them as historical novels rather than just history or a replication of the letters. When I began looking for a publisher (after the first couple of books were completed) I discovered that most publishers did not want to talk to a 'neophyte' author, but one had to have a literary agent to present things to publishers. I attended a conference of agents in Austin, Texas in hopes of locating someone who might serve in this capacity for me. The first two I interviewed were not interested in historical novels. The third one suggested I just publish the letters myself. The fourth agent told me that he wouldn't represent me, but suggested that I'd be better off self-publishing the books. I made the decision to do this and established myself as converg publishing. All six of the books were published in this manner. I paid upfront costs to have them printed. I designed the covers myself and 'uploaded' the text to the printer. After I had published and began selling some of the first two volumes, I made enough profit to pay for the printing of the next four as well. As a result, I have not had 'wide' distribution, but have made it financially successful just the same. I never intended to get wealthy from them, but mostly wanted to be sure the story was told and available to children and grandchildren. I often get invitations to speak to various groups about Edd and Lizzie and always sell several hundred dollars worth of books. It took me almost five years to get all six completed. (The last is designed to be the rest of the story of Lizzie's long life in widowhood.)

When we visited the area of the battle of South Mountain (there is no monument there as in other battlegrounds) I found a reddish sandstone rock about the size of a large squash along the roadside. Since we were driving there was no limit on my stashing away such a souvenir in the trunk of my car. It lay in the garden for a long time. One day on a whim, as I was preparing to drive to a program on Edd and Lizzie, I picked up the rock and put it in the car. As I was speaking to the group of about 40 people, I picked up the rock from behind the podium and glibly suggested that I had found this rock at the site of the battle of South Mountain and it was stained with the blood of my great grandfather Edd Campbell. I had been passing around other artifacts from his letters - patriotic envelopes, a small insignia from one of his hats, etc. - so this was just another of those items. When the lecture was over, a gentleman - a professor - took me aside and said he didn't think those were blood stains on the rock, but that it was some kind of iron oxide - rust - that was there. I just grinned. I found it hard to believe that anyone would believe that after 140 years there would be blood stains on a rock I picked up at a battleground that I could identify as belonging to my great grandfather!

CHAPTER THIRTY-THREE

In the late summer of 2001, I was contacted by Chaplain Al Hockaday, Colonel, USAF, retired. I had known Al through the years as a fellow Air Force chaplain, although we never worked directly with one another. During the time I was director of the Department of Social Actions Training at Lackland Air Force Base, San Antonio, Texas, Al was a part of the base chapel team. We lived some distance from the base and my responsibilities did not include chapel functions on the base, although I did fill in a few times at the basic training chapel and the chapel that served the officer training school students. With much travel and a busy schedule all week long, I looked on what weekends I was not travelling as 'free time' with the family. We lived close to Colonial Hills United Methodist Church and became active there. When Al contacted me, it was to invite me to be the speaker at the Air Force Village II Protestant Church annual congregational dinner. I accepted and looked forward to the re-acquaintance with Al and with others that I knew were residing at the village. One of those I really was happy to see at the dinner was Mary Frances Galbreath. She was the choir director at the main chapel at Elmendorf Air

Force Base, Alaska when I was the senior chaplain at that chapel. Her husband, Colonel Sam Galbreath, was our chapel parish council chairperson as well. (Both are since deceased.)

The evening when I spoke at the dinner, I met other members of the staff there at the village, including the senior pastor, Chaplain, Colonel, Jim Thompson (U S Army, retired). Also, I had the opportunity to visit with Mary Frances and discovered that Sam was now in the Alzheimer unit, called Freedom House, at the village. In addition, Hollon Bridges and his wife Jessie whom we'd known first at Stead Air Force Base, Nevada, where he was the survival school commander when I was survival school chaplain, now lived at the village. He also was the commander at Shemya, Alaska when I was there during the great quake. It was an enjoyable evening and, unbeknownst to me, the forerunner of many days at the village!

In January or February of 2002, Al Hockaday contacted me once again. The program at Air Force Village II Protestant Church was actively looking to add a third pastor to their part time staff. Partly this was due to the four worship services then being held each Sunday morning, and partly due to the desire to increase their pastoral visitation to hospitals and rehabilitation centers where residents of the village might be located after health problems. He was contacting me, he said, because at that time I was maintaining a roster of retired Air Force Chaplains and sending out a quarterly newsletter to about 300 retirees (chaplains and enlisted chapel managers). He thought I might know of one of these who might be interested in this pastoral position. I asked him to email me a job description and I would think about those I knew and pass it on. I was actively involved in motivational speaking, president of the Heart of Texas Chapter of the National Association of Speakers, and doing motivational seminars for the Air Force Security Service.

The seminars for the Air Force Security Service came about when the commander of that organization became concerned with a number of issues involving the personnel in his command. One of these issues was the suicide rate among young airmen. (This continues to be a problem in all branches of military service.) It was higher than comparable rates in the civilian world and even in other Air Force organizations. He had heard a motivational speaker and reported at a staff meeting to his senior chaplain that he thought maybe the command should sponsor something like that. As it happens, the senior chaplain was Chaplain, Colonel, Peter Flood, my senior Catholic chaplain at Bitburg, Germany where I spent my last active duty tour. He contacted me and asked what I thought about doing something like that. I proposed a three-hour workshop to assist folks in developing self-motivation, rather than a 'single shot of motivation'. The general liked my idea and was prepared to 'contract' with me for it when his contract folks told him it had to be put out to bid! So I found myself bidding against others to do MY program. Only one other proposal was close to mine, and I was chosen for the contract.

Over the next several months I conducted these seminars at Beale Air Force Base, California and Fort Meade, Maryland. In the latter case, I conducted workshops in 'the black hole', the term that was ascribed to the National Security Agency building, in which there were a number of personnel from the United States Air Force Security Service. The day I was there to conduct these workshops, I was informed that I could not take my laptop computer into the facility because of the high security clearance involved. I have always tried to prepare myself for any eventuality, so I not only had my program on the laptop, but I also carried with me a CD disk that included the program. I even brought along a set of overhead projection slides just in case no computer was available. (I could have done the entire thing with a chalkboard and a piece of chalk!)

It was explained that I could give the disk to the sergeant and he would see that it was taken into the secure area and be ready for me the next morning when I began my workshop. This was done and worked beautifully. I arrived, was identified and given a security badge and allowed to enter. In the space where the workshop was to be conducted, a laptop was set up with my CD in it ready to use.

The workshop went off very well. When it was over, I was to have lunch there and then go 'outside' to conduct an additional workshop in the afternoon for personnel who were assigned to the unit but not working 'inside'. The sergeant gave me my CD and I proceeded after lunch to depart. When I turned in my security badge, the guard asked to see my folder. Of course, in there was my CD that was marked with my name and address on it. The guard asked if I had written authority to remove it from the secure area! I told him the CD was mine and the sergeant had brought it into the area for me to use and now I was on my way to use it in another workshop. He informed me that unless I had written authority that identified it as secure to remove from the area, he would have to confiscate it! I told him I needed it for my program that afternoon. He apologized but said it would have to be 'surveyed' by the security team and then released. He doubted if they could do that immediately, however, the sergeant could pick it up the next morning! I acquiesced to his demands, obviously, and was thankful that I had the whole thing on my laptop that was 'outside'.

The afternoon workshop went off without a hitch. The sergeant went the next morning to the place he had been instructed to go to pick up my CD in order to give it to me before I departed for home. However, then he was told they did not have it and it might take two or three weeks to 'clear it'. They would return it to me by mail when it was cleared! I was thankful that I had lots of back up. Five months later I received a brown government envelope from the Department of Defense. In it was a form letter telling me that the enclosed disk had been cleared and was now returned to me. There was another form within for me to sign and indicate that I had received my returned property. The only problem was that the disk enclosed was not my disk. Furthermore, it was a PC format (and I use MAC format) and I couldn't even open it to find out what it was but it was definitely not mine! I returned it in the enclosed postage paid envelope with the form requested and a notation that it was not my disk, etc. I have never heard from them nor have I ever received my original disk!

I was sent then to Germany to provide the workshops for personnel from the command who were stationed there. I reported to Sembach Air station for these workshops, however, they were conducted at a number of remote locations around Germany. One day, my escort officer told me we had a free day and he had a staff car, was there anything I wanted to do. I suggested a ride to Bitburg, my previous station that had been turned back over to the German government when the U S Air Force moved out. It was a nice ride through memory lane until I arrived at the former base. It was a divided base between the runway/operations/headquarters area and the family housing/school/hospital area. The latter had become annex to the nearby Spangdahlem Air Force Base. When we visited the operations side of the base, I was surprised to see the chapel there (an additional one in the family housing area was still in use) had become a 'disco'. Up the front of the building was an enormous neon sign that said 'Bitte Ein Bit'. This was an advertisement for the local brewery, Bitburger Pils! Also, one of the old aircraft hangars still had the 8 foot letters on the side that identified it as the 36th TFW (36th Tactical Fighter Wing) but enclosed an indoor go-cart track. The Officers Club (located on the side returned to the Germans) still had a sign that said BOOM (Bitburg Officers Open Mess) but was a honky tonk of some variety! On this same trip, we journeyed up to Prum where the Air Force used to have a small communication site. Our reason for making this side trip was to survey the old 'Tiger Traps' that Hitler's army had built to frustrate the advance of American tanks when invaded. My escort officer's father had been in the Battle of the Bulge that included this area and he remembered his Dad talking about the area. So it was interesting to him to view some of the remaining pillboxes and tiger trap concrete barriers. Sadly, the Prum Air Station was totally abandoned with a padlock on a chain at the gate and the ground cover all overgrown and uncared for.

One other eventful occurrence was included in this journey. One of the small detachments was absent its commander who was TDY (temporary duty) in Italy. The young Captain in charge in his absence announced that prior to the workshop, he wanted to provide me a briefing on the mission of the unit. I was pleased at this possibility, until he put his first slide on the screen. I stopped him gently. The slide announced it was Top Secret, No Foreign Dissemination. I told him that I had carried a Top Secret clearance for most of my Air Force career, but that I was pretty sure that was gone after my retirement and I would prefer he gave me the unclassified briefing. He was embarrassed (and I think worried I might tell someone of the situation - which I never did until now and I've forgotten his location and his name!). He proceeded to give me a fine briefing designed for an unclassified audience.

After my return from Germany, they spoke to me about continuing the contract. The schedule called for some workshops in three other places in the United States and then an extended tour to Japan and Korea. As I often insisted, we did some post-workshop questionaires to determine the response of those participating. All the responses had been very positive to the workshops. This was early September 2001. The attacks on September 11, 2001 was a watershed in most of the national security of the United States. Suddenly, the Security Service command found they had a shortage of funding and good motivation for whatever they were doing. Although my contract remained in effect for over another year, it was never activated after the trip to Germany.

CHAPTER THIRTY-FOUR

Without the requirement to block out time for Korea and other places for the Security Service contract, I turned my attention to other speaking opportunities. On my return from one of these trips with Pat traveling with me, she asked what I had done with the job description that Al Hockaday had sent me by email concerning the pastoral position at Air Force Village II Protestant Church. I told her it was in one of the pockets of my briefcase and so while I was driving, she dug through my paperwork until she found it. She read it aloud and then asked, "Have you thought about doing this? The job description pretty much describes you."

"No, I hadn't really thought about it," I replied.

We talked about this possibility and when we returned to San Antonio, I called Al to see if the position had been filled. No, he told me. Well, I might throw my hat in the ring. Al replied, "That's what I was hoping for when I got in touch with you in the first place. You'd be ideal for this job." From this, I found myself sending a resume to the pastoral search committee and then meeting with the committee for an interview. I explained to them about my contract with the Air Force and that I would like the privilege of responding to requests for workshops in that regard, if offered. I was invited to preach in the two main worship services and the congregation was given the opportunity to vote to 'call' me as the third pastor on the staff. (Chaplain Jim Thompson told me later that only one vote was cast against me and it was a woman who told him she had done it because she didn't think they needed a third pastor!) As a result, I began serving as one of the Protestant pastors at Air Force Village II on 1 July 2002. (The need to take time for workshops with the Security Service never came after 9-11!)

The program at the village included four worship services each Sunday morning. Two were held in the 'High Flight" Chapel, which is the main place of worship, used by all denominations. Catholics have mass there on Saturday morning when a priest from nearby Castroville is available. Episcopal services are held on Thursday afternoon. Protestants hold two services there, one at 0930 and one at 1100 on Sunday. The attendance at the two services is greater than would be accommodated in a single service. In addition, a Protestant service is held in the Willow chapel, located in the Health Care Center (now known as the Vista.) Another service is held in the open lounge area of Freedom House, the facility designed to handle Alzheimer or other dementia cases.

In addition to the worship services on Sundays, services are held for the various high season events, such as Maundy Thursday, Good Friday, and Christmas Eve. Many of the memorial services for those who have died while living in one of the areas of the village are held in the High Flight Chapel as well. During my tenure, there was an average of 45 to 50 deaths per year among the residents. Not all resulted in memorial services. Some had only graveside services, usually at Fort Sam Houston National Cemetery across town. Some had services elsewhere and for a very small few, no services were held at all. Most of the services held were Protestant and the pastors held them either alone, or in concert with one of the other pastors, depending upon the request of the family.

Pastoral visits to all those from the village who are hospitalized was a part of the responsibility as well. The Protestant pastors visited everyone whether they were Protestant, Catholic, Jewish, or not religious at all. Most days there would be from 3 to 5 in some hospital nearby. When I first began my ministry at the village, most of our patients were in nearby Wilford Hall Medical Center at Lackland Air Force Base, however, increasingly this shifted until the inpatient work at Wilford Hall ended completely. Then residents were in civilian hospitals all across town or at the Brooke Army Medical Center at Fort Sam Houston. (Now this is known as SAMMC - San Antonio Military Medical Center.) It was not unusual to have four or more patients to visit in as many hospitals, including those on the North side of town in the area known as medical center. The most I ever had to visit was on one Sunday when I had eleven different patients to visit in five different hospitals. This ministry was and is perhaps the most important duty of the pastors, much appreciated by all, even the non-religious.

The pastors are contracted for service by the Protestant Church board for a year at a time. The contracts called for each pastor to be available for duty two days each week plus Sundays. Jim Thompson was already working on Tuesday and Thursday and his wife Kay was employed as the part-time church secretary on those same days. Al Hockaday decided he would like to work Thursday and Fridays, so I was allocated Mondays and Tuesdays. This worked out very well. I overlapped in duty with Jim on Tuesdays and Al overlapped with him on Thursdays. After the first year, at my suggestion, the board began paying $25 per month toward the pastors' cell phones. This provided the basis for publishing the phone numbers so that we were available on call if needed. After Jim Thompson decided to retire and move to the Pacific Northwest to be near grandchildren, Al suggested that he did not want to be the senior pastor, and could he and I be co-pastors. This worked well. He and I decided it would be good to publish a regular calendar for folks in the congregation to know who was on duty and who was on call. Also, I began a monthly on-call letter that was sent to all the various staff agencies of the village so that personnel would know whom to call in case of emergencies where a pastor was needed. This worked very well. Another innovation was to print all the bulletins for the various services in large print format. We also began printing a copy of the hymns for the services in an enlarged format for those who had difficulty reading. We arranged for a wireless microphone system so that the preacher was not 'tied' to the pulpit/lectern during the sermon. In addition, we installed amplified headphones for those who had difficulty hearing.

The board decided to add a third pastor again when Jim Thompson retired. Gary Higgs was added to the staff. Al, Gary and I worked very well together. The first Christmas the three of us put together a CD of Christmas Carols. Geri Grady accompanied us on the organ and Bill Agre ran the recording process. I took the several CDs on which we sang (some of the numbers several times) and on the computer tweeked them into a single CD, entitled the Three Pastors. We made multiple copies, and we three pastors delivered a copy to every church member's door clip as a Christmas greeting and gift. The response was one of great appreciation. Unfortunately, Gary resigned later due to health problems. Later yet, a fourth pastor was added to pick up the extra pastoral work involved with supporting the 'in-house' hospice program. Ren Vandesteeg and Steve Sill were added to the staff in this manner. When Al retired and Gary left, we also looked to keeping four pastors on staff and Will Peacock, a retired Army chaplain was added to the staff. After a few months, Will decided this was not fitting his sense of ministry and he resigned. Then another retired Army chaplain, Gilley Richardson was added to the staff. Later, when the hospice program employed their own chaplain, it was difficult to justify four pastors on the staff, however, the board decided to retain all four.

At this point, I was on duty on Monday and Tuesdays, Steve was on Tuesdays and Thursdays, Ren was on Wednesday and Thursday and Gil was on Wednesday and Fridays. Gil and I were the only ones that were on duty alone - myself on Monday and Gil on Friday. Steve overlapped with me on Tuesday and with Ren on Thursday. Ren overlapped with Gil on Wednesday and with Steve on Thursday.

Early in my ministry at the village, I began a class following the Journeymen program I had developed and used successfully several places. After we spent a year with one group and started another, several of the first group came to me and asked if we could continue with Bible study. This was established and I began teaching a class each Tuesday morning. While Gary Higgs was still on staff, we began a midweek program at the Assisted Living (Liberty House) area. However, those who were most faithful to that group moved to the Health Care Center (Vista) because of their decline in health, and so Gary moved the group to the Willow Chapel in the Health Care Center and it became a short (20 to 30 minute) midweek worship service. After Gary departed the staff, Steve picked up this responsibility and moved it to Tuesday to fit his schedule. (Currently, as of this writing, this program has moved to Wednesday to fit the schedule of Gil Richardson who is conducting it.)

Later, women's Bible study programs were instituted with lay leadership and a study was begun during the week to serve the folks in Liberty house since the move of the other program to the Willow Chapel left them without a program midweek. This was taught at various times by a layman, Jim Peck. There had been a regular Sunday morning Bible class for eighteen years taught by Ken Crawford, a retired Army judge advocate and fine Bible scholar. After his health declined and his death, this class stopped meeting.

While Will Peacock was on staff, I challenged him to see what we needed to do to serve the Liberty House folks better. Several of them had come to me and asked for worship services in their area, because it took them so long on their walkers or scooters to get to the High Flight Chapel and their meals were served in their own dining facility so that after worship they returned to Liberty House. Over a period of weeks, Will told me several times he had not had an opportunity to speak to anyone about doing something. Finally,

I announced we would begin services there on Sunday morning on a particular date. (Later, when I announced that I had made the arrangements and we would hold services in the lounge, Will decided this was not the place for him and he resigned.) I worked with the carpentry shop to design and build for us a cabinet that worked as a large lamp table during the week, but was moved to the center as an altar on Sundays. It included storage space for all the necessary paraments and altar equipment. Colonel Tom White volunteered to pay for altar hangings and equipment (cross and candles, communion ware and offering plate) for the use of that service. It meant we had five services to cover on Sundays, however this was not a problem with three or four on duty each Sunday. Only on those rare occasions when two pastors wanted to be away on the same weekend, was it necessary to make adjustments. Usually this meant calling on one of the other retired chaplains who were residents in the village to fill in at one of the services. Chaplain Roger Spencer (Navy retired), Chaplain Jack Duncan (Air Force retired) and Chaplain Frank Sherman (Air Force retired) were available and frequently helped out. (As of this writing, this service in the assisted living area has been discontinued.)

In 2005, Al Hockaday and I had a discussion about the need for better chapel facilities, to include more office space. I composed a letter from us to the CEO of the AF Villages, Inc at the time (Harry McMillin) indicating our need. During this period I worked with the executive director, Fred Ryder, to provide better interim office space for the Protestant program. When this was identified, plans went forward to modify it for our use. Although down the hallway from the chapel, it provided a large office/workroom space for the secretary and a small office for the senior pastor. The other three pastors continued to use the office adjacent to the chapel. This was not a problem since for the most part only one or two of them were on duty on the same day. Also, we purchased electric altar candles for the program in the Willow Chapel, the Freedom House Chapel and the Liberty House/lounge chapel. I had been concerned from the time I arrived at the village with the open flame candles being used in the Willow Chapel when we had a number of residents attending worship with oxygen support.

Subsequent to solving the office problem for the chapel, we began to look at the need for new worship space as well. Although the Protestant services could handle the attendance by holding two services on each Sunday morning in addition to the services at the Willow chapel (in the Vista nursing care wing) and one at Freedom House (the memory unit). When memorial services were held, it was not unusual to be overly crowded. At one time audio for these special services could be remotely transmitted to either the Willow Chapel or to the sunroom. The latter, however, was converted to a dining facility for the Vista and no longer available for an overflow attendance. In addition, the community rooms near the main dining room were not large enough for other community activities such as concerts and community briefings. As a result, steps were taken toward raising funds for a new chapel/worship space facility. This morphed into a Community center designed for worship and other cultural events. That is underway even now as this is written, with intentions for construction to begin in no more than three years away. It will provide worship seating for at least 275 to 300 and be designed for other cultural events such as concerts.

In the winter of 2012, I began to think about the possibility that I should retire from the pastoral position so that I would be free to do more travel and to write more (this included.) In late December, I discussed this first with Pat, my wife, and then with two of the board members in whom I had great confidence, Bill Miller the chairman and Bill Agre who had been the Treasurer. While Pat and I were on a week's vacation in Galveston, after considerable prayer, we made the decision to do this. I gave a letter to the Board Chairman, Bill Miller, to be read at the January Board meeting announcing my plan to retire as of the 1st of April 2013, which meant the day after Easter. I deliberately encouraged this to be read while I was out of town since I felt this would be better than having people ask me a myriad of questions concerning my decision. If I were not present this would not be possible.

The Board requested subsequently that I serve as a consultant to the process of choosing a fourth pastor upon my retirement. The board organized a committee for pastoral search to select the fourth man. I was not present when they determined that they would interview the remaining three pastors before they made a decision about the role of senior pastor, which I had been fulfilling after Al Hockaday retired. After these interviews they informed me that they had agreed upon finding the fourth pastor and then choosing a senior pastor, since, as a result of the personal interviews with each of the current pastors, they did not feel comfortable naming any of the three to that task. Several possible pastoral candidates were interviewed and eventually two of them were invited to preach. The names of these two were subsequently put to a written ballot by the congregation and another retired Air Force Chaplain, Wayne Knudson, was chosen. After further interviews, the committee recommended and the board approved his role as senior pastor.

The board requested that I continue to serve until the new senior pastor was on board on the 1st of July. I agreed to do this on a 'part time part pay basis' - essentially only being paid half of what I had been paid and being free to work only one day plus Sundays. I have continued the monthly Care and Share responsibility, in which the resident counselor and I provide a sounding board session for those who are or have been caregivers.

Since this retirement on 1 July 2013 - eleven years from my beginning ministry at the village Pat and I have embarked on several 'vacation' trips. We've enjoyed these, especially the long grand voyage from Seattle to San Diego by way of every place in the Far East and South Pacific. And we have enjoyed visiting Methodist churches in the greater San Antonio area where we sit together in worship (something preachers and their wives do not get to do very often!) We attended the annual Air Force Chapel Staff retiree weekend in

Santa Fe, New Mexico, where we renewed old friendships and made some new ones.

When I began this narrative, I thought it appropriate to call it 'a larger circuit' in echo of the words of several early mentors who encouraged me in my ministry. Indeed, the Lord has made it possible for me to serve in many places and in many ways, most of which I would not have guessed and some of which I would not have chosen! Before my call to ministry as a fifteen-year old youngster, I would not have expected to spend as many years in academia as I have. I thought a four-year college career might lead to a life of engineering, maybe architecture. Even with my sense that God was moving me toward military chaplaincy, I did not know how many places around the world this would lead to. I would not have guessed my early involvement in the inner city with those whose addictions were controlling their lives would lead many years later to establishing a program that had Air Force wide impact. And from the friendship with a couple of chaplains, I would be involved in workshops around the world and later one of these friends would lead me back to ministry with retirees in San Antonio. Indeed, God has led me to larger circuits in many wonderful and humbling positions of ministry.

Throughout these perambulations, I have been supported, encouraged and aided by my wife, Pat. She has lifted me up when I've been down and sometimes, brought me down when I was sailing too high! We were brought together over sixty years ago in what could be described as a coincidence, or more correctly a divine moment of blessing! She endured separations, short and long, in which she was responsible for caring for the children and the family structure. She bought and sold houses while I was somewhere on assignment. She quickly adapted to every community in which we found ourselves and readily took up whatever cause of ministry available to her. Her service has magnified what I might have attempted in many ways and in many places. In some ways, her circuit has been larger than my own and yet always compatible and supportive. Our decisions have been made prayerfully together throughout these many years. I can only echo Proverbs 31 with "A good wife, who can find? She is more precious than jewels."

I find myself contemplating the years of ministry in the larger circuit and am reminded that it is not over. The poet Robert Browning, in his poem "Rabbi Ben Ezra" has said it well: "Grow old along with me! The best is yet to be, the last of life, for which the first was made. Our times are in his hand who saith, 'A whole I planned, youth shows but half; Trust God: See all, nor be afraid!'" The larger circuit awaits our calling and each day we seek to follow His lead in this regard. Whether it ends in our present circumstance or in some far beyond our imagination is not ours to choose. It is only ours to follow His lead. Wesley's hymn still rings true, "A Charge to Keep I have, A God to glorify."

Printed in the United States
By Bookmasters